IMAGES
of America

AROUND HORRY COUNTY

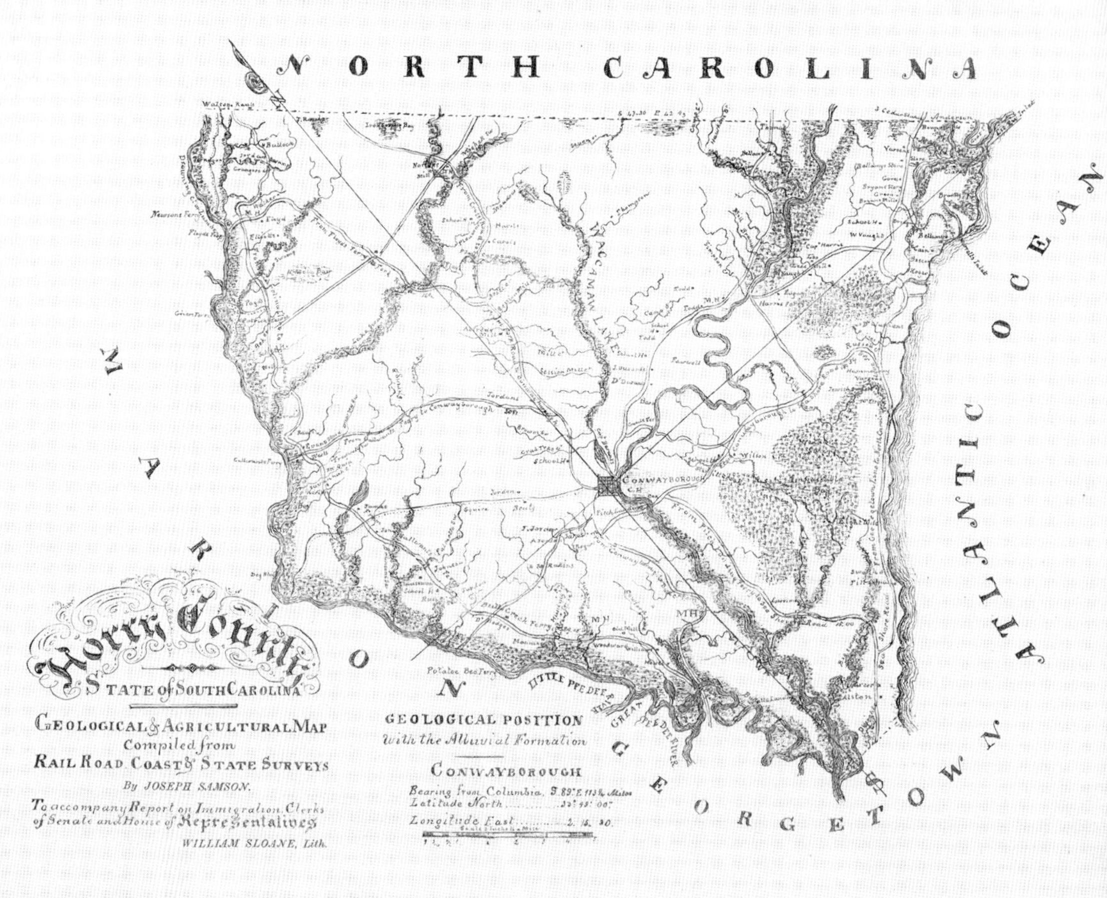

Horry County gained its current moniker in 1868, and its modern-day boundaries were drawn in 1785 with land carved from the Georgetown District. In this image dating from the mid-19th century, Horry County's rivers, early townships, and communities are shown at a time when turpentine, naval stores, and lumber served as the economic driving forces behind the region. (Courtesy of the University of South Carolina).

ON THE COVER: Myrtle Beach's prime oceanside location resulted in a state park being established there in 1936. Though not South Carolina's first planned state park, Myrtle Beach State Park, established on land donated by the Myrtle Beach Farms Company for its construction, was the first state park in South Carolina to open. Seen here are groups of visitors fishing on a pier at the state park in June 1957. (Courtesy of Clemson University.)

IMAGES
of America

AROUND HORRY COUNTY

Ryan A. McRae

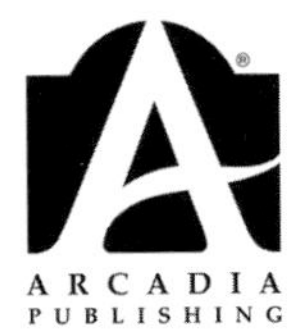
ARCADIA
PUBLISHING

ISBN 978-1-4671-6227-2

Published by Arcadia Publishing
Charleston, South Carolina

Printed in the United States of America

Library of Congress Control Number: 2024952311

For all general information, please contact Arcadia Publishing:
Telephone 843-853-2070
Fax 843-853-0044
E-mail sales@arcadiapublishing.com

Visit us on the Internet at www.arcadiapublishing.com

I dedicate this book to all who have faced adversity in their efforts to preserve history . . . keep the faith and hold strong, even when difficult.

Contents

ACKNOWLEDGMENTS

I would like to acknowledge my trusted, respected, and cherished parents, David McRae and Angela Heaton McRae, who have stood with me through and through; my loving grandmother Sharon Ilges McRae, who hears and listens to my life stories during our daily talks; and all of my close family members for their support during the process of writing this book, including several of my dear aunts and uncles.

During this process, many obstacles and challenges have arisen, several of which were stressful and burdensome. However, this book is finished, is special, and bears the stories of people and communities from all walks of life in Horry County.

As I am a member of the Horry County Historic Preservation Commission; a contributor to and researcher behind historic markers for Horry-Georgetown Technical College and the Hickory Grove community in Conway; a graduate of local schools (and former president of the history honor society at Coastal Carolina University); and a professional writer and someone who cares deeply about this region, I hope this book may be something loved by the community and will be something appreciated for its efforts to preserve Horry County's unique history.

With that being said, stories heard about my matrilineal family inspired my interest in Horry County's history, as stories from my parents, cousins, uncles, and aunts always provided comfort and humor to me. Particularly, I find myself reminiscing often about countless tales told to me by my late dear aunt Belinda Heaton Blair, to whom I was very close, talked to almost daily, and whose stories and love were a vital part of my younger life. She often talked about her and my mother's childhoods in Myrtle Beach, as well as stories about their oldest two siblings and my maternal grandparents and great-grandparents. Without all of these collective stories, my interest in Horry County's past may have never blossomed, and without Horry County, I would not exist, as my parents met in Myrtle Beach. So I thank my family for starting my interest in a place that eventually led to my being. I could not fit every name on this paragraph, but I love you all.

Additionally, I would like to thank the staff of the Horry County Museum for their insight regarding the context of images included in this publication, as well as my fellow local historical enthusiasts for their assistance in identifying sites seen in photographs and discussing their knowledge of these historic places. In addition to my use of primary sources, local publications also played a strong role in my research, and those works are cited in my bibliography; I recognize the authors of those secondary sources and now consider them my peers. Lastly, I would like to thank all who generously shared their images with me and recognize the companies and people who captured photographs now in the public domain, such as the photographers for local institutions, the Plyler-Brandon Sales Co., Dexter Press, and other similar businesses and organizations. I would also like to thank the staff of Arcadia Publishing, including Erin Vosgien, Amy Jarvis, and Mike Litchfield for helping make this book possible. Unless otherwise noted, all photographs are courtesy

Introduction

Located along South Carolina's Coastal Plain, as of 2025, Horry County holds 4 cities, 4 towns, and 49 unincorporated communities (including census-designated places) and boasts a unique history and distinctive heritage that can be traced back to the prehistoric era.

According to state resources, northeastern South Carolina was historically inhabited by several Native tribes, including the Chicora, Waccamaw, Winyah, and Pee Dee peoples, among others. Native Americans had a significant impact on Horry County's heritage, and efforts to recognize their history is paramount to locals and preservationists today.

Though a Spanish settlement temporarily occurred in present-day South Carolina in the 1500s, no permanent inhabitants remained in this area. This region fell under British authority in the 17th century and was carved into colonial jurisdictions. Horry County was once part of old Craven County, founded in 1682. Craven County was one of three counties formed by the Lords Proprietors of the Carolina Colony.

Most European settlers arrived in present-day Horry County after 1700. Following the area's consistent influx of European colonists in the 18th century, many of Horry County's Indigenous forebears were killed or enslaved, subsequently leaving only a miniscule number of Native Americans in the vicinity. As many places along coastal Horry County long served as coastal retreats for Natives, signs of Indigenous habituation can still be found across Horry County today, including on Waties Island, which has been known to hold tribal mounds.

A new community, Kingston, was established in 1732 and was born from the Township Scheme promoted by Royal Governor Robert Johnson. Though its population was minuscule, the community was the first official township in present-day Horry County. According to local historic markers, the region was part of the Prince George Winyah, Prince Frederick, and All Saints Parishes throughout the 18th century. Though lacking true administrative structure and authority, these religious parishes acted as governmental jurisdictions.

Upon further governmental restructuring, the region became part of the Georgetown District. This would not remain permanent, and in 1785, lands from the Georgetown District were carved to form the boundaries for present-day Horry County. The newly drawn jurisdiction was first called Kingston County. In 1801, Kingston County was renamed Horry District. Its name was derived from Peter Horry, a general in the American Revolution. In 1868, Horry District was renamed Horry County, and it holds this moniker today.

A rural, forested, and sparsely populated place in the 18th and 19th centuries, Horry County did not have the success in plantation agriculture that neighboring jurisdictions held. Though Horry County did hold several large plantations, the region's sandy and swampy terrain made it difficult to sustain many of them. Even so, cash crops such as indigo, rice, and cotton were still grown in the vicinity. Toward the 20th century, Horry County's agricultural pursuits would ultimately triumph as tobacco became an invaluable commodity that allowed other Horry County communities, especially Galivants Ferry and Aynor, to become nationally known for their tobacco production and output.

Though Horry County's early years were not necessarily defined by agricultural success, the bountiful pines that grew across the region led to the naval store, turpentine, and lumber industries becoming the backbone of the young county's economy. These industries also led to the creation of several historic communities such as Bucksville and Bucksport (both established by Henry Buck), which both made immense contributions to the American timber trade. The town of Kingston, which was renamed Conwayborough after the Revolutionary War and Conway in 1883 (for Robert Conway, a South Carolinian military hero), also made vast contributions to these trades, as did

Loris, another nearby community. Conway gained further attention for its history with steamships and other timber enterprises due to its location along the Waccamaw River, one of three rivers that surround Horry County. Many claim the county's nickname of the "Independent Republic" comes from these rivers isolating early Horryites. However, this allegation is challenged by contemporary historians, who feel Horry County's multiple waterways allowed for greater transportation and cultural exchange, negating exaggerated claims of isolation.

In the wake of the lumber industry's popularity in Horry County, Conway entrepreneurs from the Burroughs and Collins Company began sourcing timber in the Withers Beach area, a site named after a family who once owned much of the land in its vicinity. The Withers family largely abandoned Withers Beach due to a deadly 1822 hurricane that devastated the area. In 1881, the Burroughs and Collins Company bought much of this property, and a post office for the sparsely populated Withers community was established by 1888. By doing this, Conway businessman F.G. Burroughs planted the initial seed of tourism on the coastline of Long Bay, a 60-mile-long stretch of coastline that has been known as the "Grand Strand" since the 1940s.

In 1900, the Conway Seashore Railroad (eventually renamed the Conway Coast & Western Railroad) opened to bring timber from the coast into Conway. The railroad first came to Pine Island, a lumber camp a short distance inland from the coast. Narratives argue that early railroads allowed greater travel to the coastline, thus exposing its beauty to inland residents and inspiring more people to visit this area. At the time, present-day Myrtle Beach was called "New Town" by visitors. The name was inspired by the community's contrast to Conway, which was referred to as "Old Town." A contest to give the community a formal name was held; Adeline Burroughs suggested naming the community Myrtle Beach for the wax myrtles in the vicinity, and the name was chosen.

Though many early visitors were known to camp on the beach, Myrtle Beach's first hotel, the Seaside Inn, was opened in 1901 by the Burroughs and Collins Company. This hotel helped spur tourism in the area, but Myrtle Beach remained relatively quaint at the time it was incorporated as a town on March 12, 1938. At this point, the tourism industry, consisting of many small, family-run inns, continued to remain successful, and Horry County's beach communities steadily gained momentum. Atlantic Beach (a segregated beach resort for African Americans) also gained a reputation for its popularity and quickly became a sought-after vacation destination for Black Americans.

Even as a rural region, in the 1940s, Horry County became the site of a military post (later the site of Myrtle Beach Air Force Base), and more beachside attractions, such as the third Myrtle Beach Pavilion, were constructed. During that period, Myrtle Beach's population peaked in the summer, and most of the tourist economy was dominated by small establishments. Sadly, many of these businesses (and 80 percent of Myrtle Beach's structures) were destroyed in 1954 following Hurricane Hazel. Hurricane Hazel marked a turning point in Myrtle Beach's history, as it cleared much land and forced many to abandon the area. Developers especially took advantage of this situation and bought much-cleared parcels, placing more hotels, businesses, and other commercial enterprises in Myrtle Beach. As a result, the ensuing years created the atmosphere in Myrtle Beach many recognize, as the community was incorporated as a city in 1957 and continued to expand in these postwar years.

Horry County's other communities also expanded in the later 20th century. Throughout the 1960s and 1970s, communities in the "South Strand" such as Garden City Beach and Surfside Beach expanded, with the latter incorporating in 1964. The incorporation of North Myrtle Beach, formed from the townships of Ocean Drive Beach, Windy Hill Beach, Crescent Beach, and Cherry Grove Beach, occurred in 1968. The latter 20th century especially brought continued development to Myrtle Beach and Horry County, with new communities and subdivisions being established to make way for thousands of new residents.

Overall, though missing many nostalgic landmarks, with a bustling year-round population, Myrtle Beach remains one growing element of this region, now one of the fastest-growing metropolitan areas in the United States.

It is this writer's goal to give insight to histories likely forgotten, and he hopes readers will enjoy a journey *Around Horry County*.

One

America's Vacation Destination

Myrtle Beach and Its Vicinity

Now largely defined by tourism, Myrtle Beach holds a history remembered for its rustic and quaint nature. The Withers family owned thousands of acres of coastal land in the 1800s that are now the site of present-day Myrtle Beach. They operated an indigo plantation that overlooked a local body of water named Withers Swash, previously known as Eight Mile Swash on earlier maps. "Swash" refers to coastal creeks that empty into the ocean, and the Myrtle Beach area holds several of them.

The Withers family maintained a presence on Long Bay for several decades, but many members were killed in the Great Storm of 1822, a deadly hurricane that devastated the area. Afterward, much of their property lay abandoned, and the region remained undeveloped for the next half-century, but salt works existed in the region by the Civil War. By 1881, the Burroughs and Collins Company, located in Conway, purchased much of the coastal property once belonging to the Withers family, and a post office for the Withers community was established by 1888. Contemporary historians believe this post office existed near Pine Island.

By 1900, the Conway Seashore Railroad opened to bring timber from this vicinity into Conway. Later renamed the Conway Coast & Western Railroad, it exposed the vicinity's beauty to inland residents and spurred entrepreneurs' interests in capitalizing on the area's beauty through tourism. Myrtle Beach's first hotel, the Seaside Inn, was opened in 1901 by the Burroughs and Collins Company, and Myrtle Beach remained a small community at the time it was incorporated in 1938.

Hurricane Hazel would change this image of Myrtle Beach and would clear much of the community's land, spurring developers to take advantage of this circumstance by establishing more commercial enterprises on abandoned or cleared parcels. This increased development created the atmosphere in Myrtle Beach many now recognize, as the community expanded, became a city in 1957, and continued to grow its tourism-based ambience.

Today, it missing many landmarks that are nostalgic to residents and is certainly not a small city. With a bustling year-round population, Myrtle Beach maintains an expanding population as one of the fastest-growing metropolitan areas in the United States.

OF SOUTH CAROLINA. 227

A. D. 1899.

No. 147.

AN ACT TO INCORPORATE CONWAY SEASHORE RAILROAD COMPANY.

[A Concurrent Resolution allowing this Bill for a special charter to be introduced, having been passed by a two-thirds vote of each House, as required by the State Constitution.]

Conway Seashore R. R. Company, Incorporated.

SECTION 1. *Be it enacted* by the General Assembly of the State of South Carolina, That Frank A. Burroughs, Benjamin G. Collins, Donald T. McNeill, M. W. Collins, H. L. Buck, D. A. Spivey, and their associates, be, and they are hereby, created a body politic and corporate, by the name and style of Conway Seashore Railroad Company, and by that name shall have perpetual successions; may sue and be sued; may adopt a common seal and alter the same at will; may make all necessary by-laws for the government of said company not inconsistent with the laws and Constitution of this State and the United States; may make, control and acquire, purchase, hold, enjoy and transfer property, both real and personal, including shares of stock in other corporations, possessing the same powers in reference thereto as individuals now enjoy; and shall be vested generally with all the rights, powers and privileges conferred by law on railroad corporations in this State, pursuant to chapter LI., sections 1542 to 1551, inclusive, Revised Statutes of South Carolina, 1893, volume I., and the general railroad law of this State.

Power to construct railroad, &c.

SEC. 2. That said company shall have power and authority to construct and maintain a railroad by the most practicable route, to be selected by said company, from Conway, on the Waccamaw River, to the Atlantic Ocean, at or near Withers Swash, in Horry County, with the privilege of extending the same to Pawley's Island, in Georgetown County; and to operate thereon cars for the carriage of passengers and freight to be run in whole or in part by steam or electricity, or by any other motive power, upon such reasonable rates as may be fixed by said company; and shall be further authorized to connect the Conway terminus of said road with the town of Conway by bridge across said river, or by a ferry, if deemed advisable, with full authority to operate such ferry in the manner deemed most practicable by it. That said company shall have the right to connect at Conway with existing lines, and make such joint rates as may be lawful and mutually satisfactory, for the trans-

The Conway Seashore Railroad Company was incorporated by the South Carolina General Assembly on February 28, 1899, in Legislative Act 147, shown at left. The railroad, operated by the owners and associates of the Burroughs and Collins Company, opened in 1900. In 1904, the name of this railroad changed to the Conway Coast & Western Railroad, and a line to Aynor was eventually established. When the railroad first opened, its main purpose was to transport lumber to Conway from the coast, but twice-daily train services between Conway and Myrtle Beach began in May 1900. The steam engine that powered this train, known as the *Black Maria*, is shown below along with the first railroad depot in Myrtle Beach. This wooden depot is believed to have been built in 1901 but was replaced in 1937. (Left, courtesy of the South Carolina Department of Archives and History; below, courtesy of the Horry County Museum.)

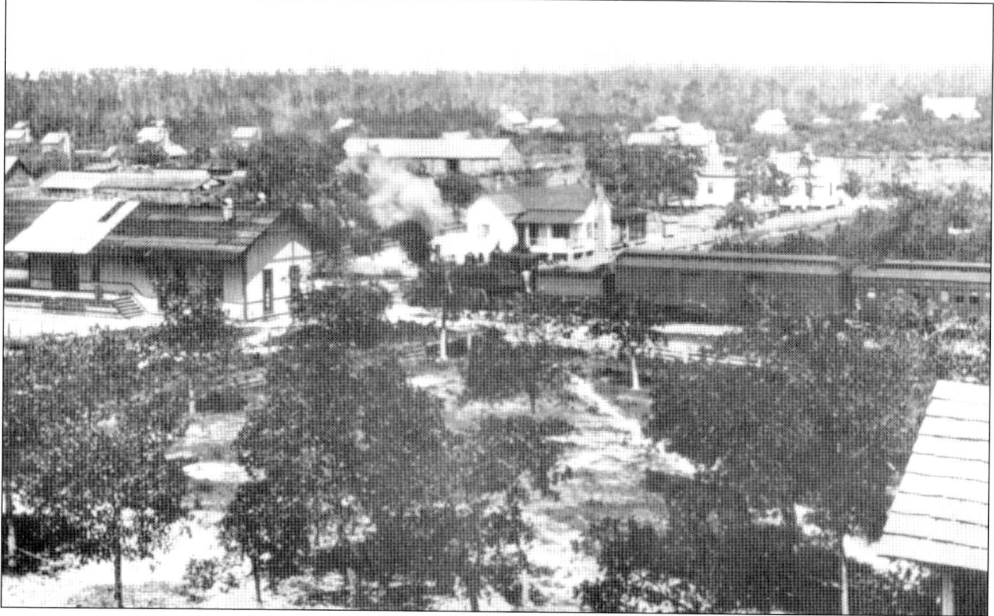

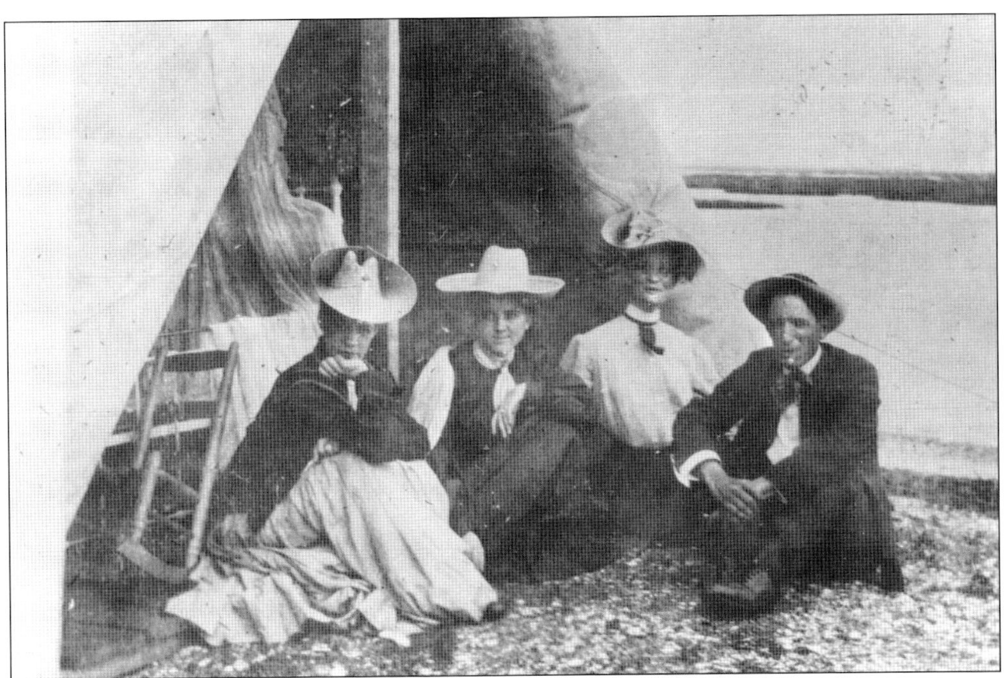

Franklin G. Burroughs, an owner of the Burroughs and Collins Company, envisioned the present-day Myrtle Beach area becoming a tourist destination. Though he died in 1897, Burroughs's vision would be realized when railroads opened and spurred interest in Myrtle Beach's natural beauty. Myrtle Beach's value as a resort site was quickly seen by subsequent leaders of the Burroughs and Collins Company, who constructed the Seaside Inn, Myrtle Beach's first hotel, in 1901. Seen below, the Seaside Inn operated until the 1920s. It held buildings viewed as predecessors to the Myrtle Beach Pavilion before the first recognized pavilion was built in 1908. Prior to the construction of these hotels, it was common for early visitors to Myrtle Beach to camp on the shore, as shown above. (Above, courtesy of Horry County Museum.)

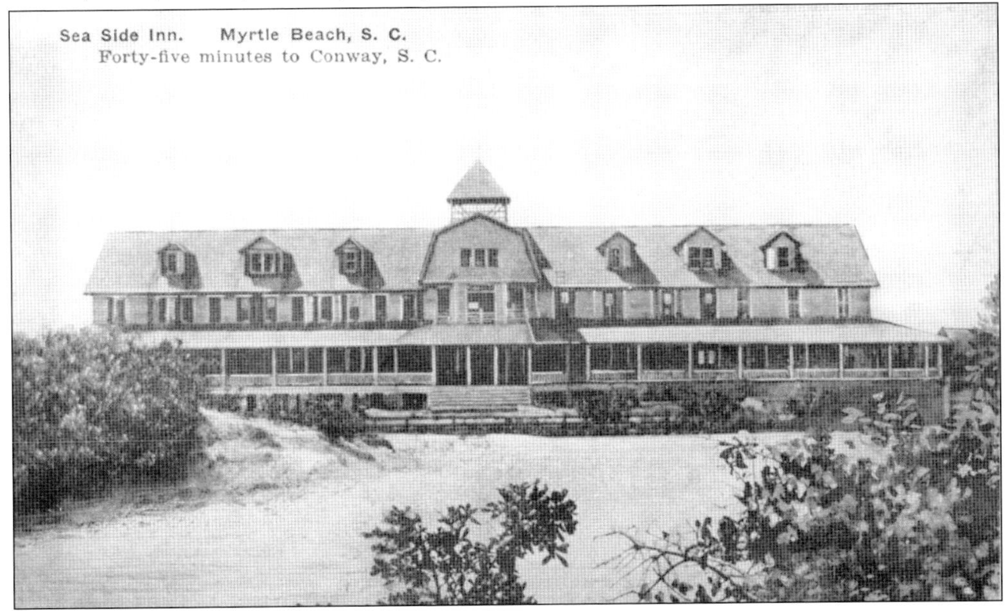

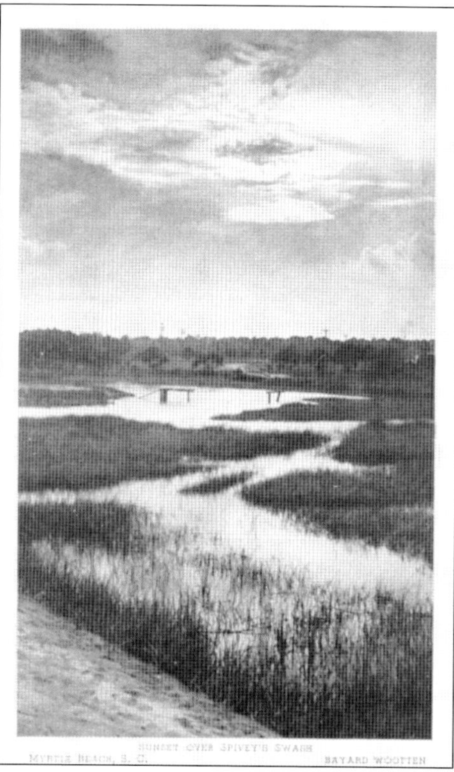

Coastal Horry County is home to several natural creeks that flow into the Atlantic Ocean, otherwise known as swashes. Withers Swash, once a popular fishing and swimming site for early residents, is a particularly well-known example. Fishing camps near swashes were once popular, as these creeks often held large quantities of fish available for catch, especially flounder. Here, Spivey's Swash is seen in a postcard view.

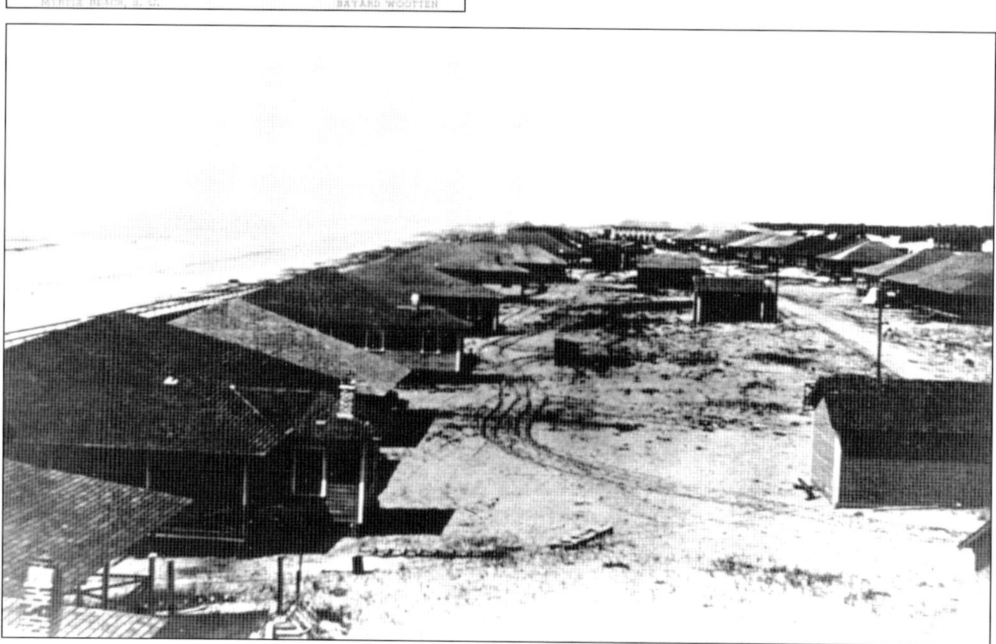

In the wake of Myrtle Beach's once-rural setting, this early scene of Ocean Boulevard gives a glimpse of the summer cottages and bungalows that lined Myrtle Beach's first oceanfront street before it became filled with attractions within the next several decades. These bungalows were mostly built by summer residents, who could purchase oceanside lots for $25 in the early 1900s. (Courtesy of the Horry County Museum.)

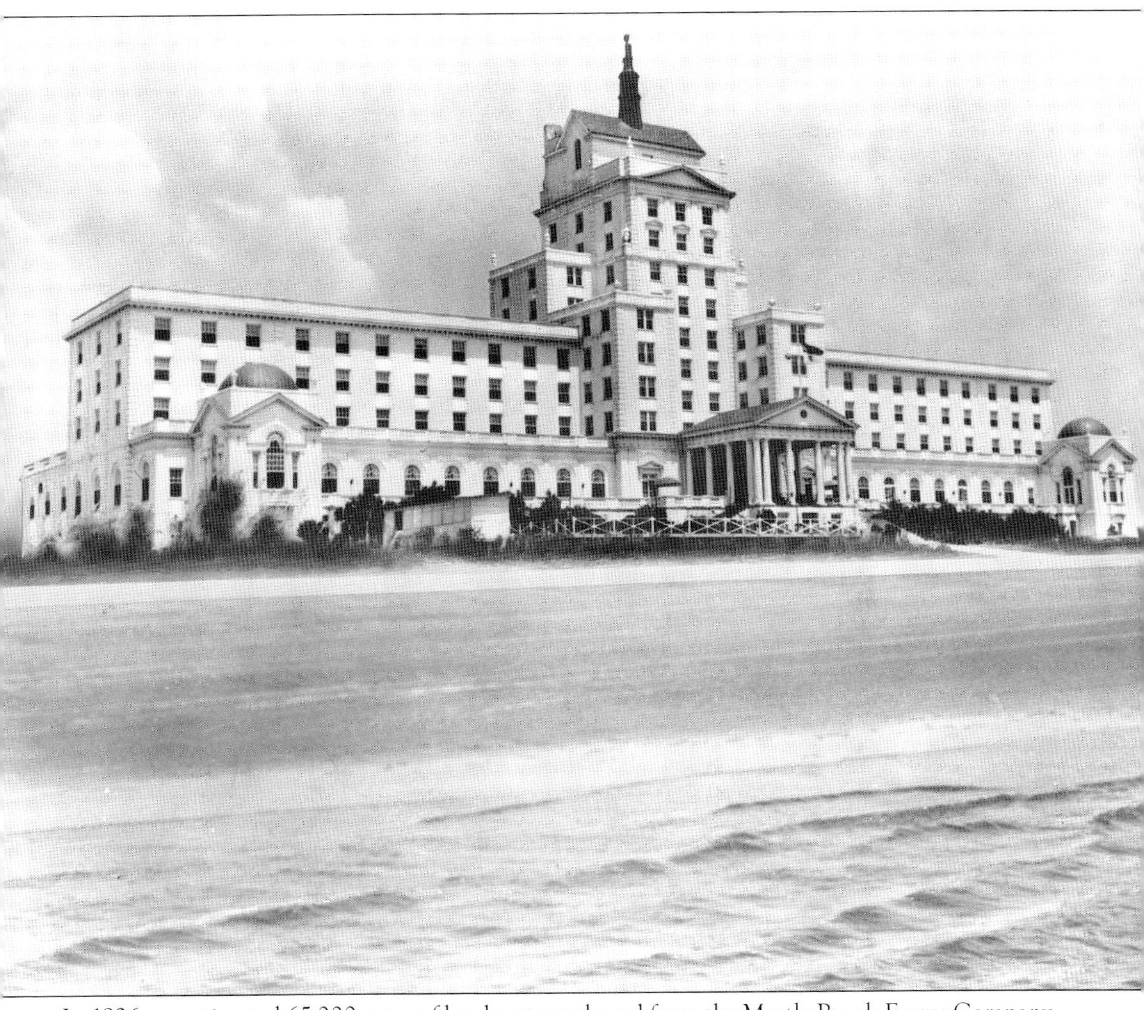

In 1926, an estimated 65,000 acres of land was purchased from the Myrtle Beach Farms Company by John T. Woodside, a Greenville, South Carolina, entrepreneur, and his associates. Most if not all the land encompassing Myrtle Beach was thus sold to Woodside. Here, a major development project titled Arcady was planned, and its intentions were to make this area an exclusive resort for upscale patrons. However, upon the 1929 Stock Market Crash, Woodside lost his fortune, and Arcady did not come to fruition; remaining parcels were sold or repossessed. The only parts of the project that blossomed were the construction of the Ocean Forest Hotel, seen in this image, and the creation of the Ocean Forest Country Club. The Ocean Forest Hotel was owned by several entities and was a pillar in the Myrtle Beach community. Construction on the elegant 10-story hotel began in 1929, and it officially opened on February 21, 1930. Though the much-loved hotel operated for over 40 years and was even known to serve celebrity clientele, it eventually fell into disrepair, was sold to developers, and was demolished in 1974.

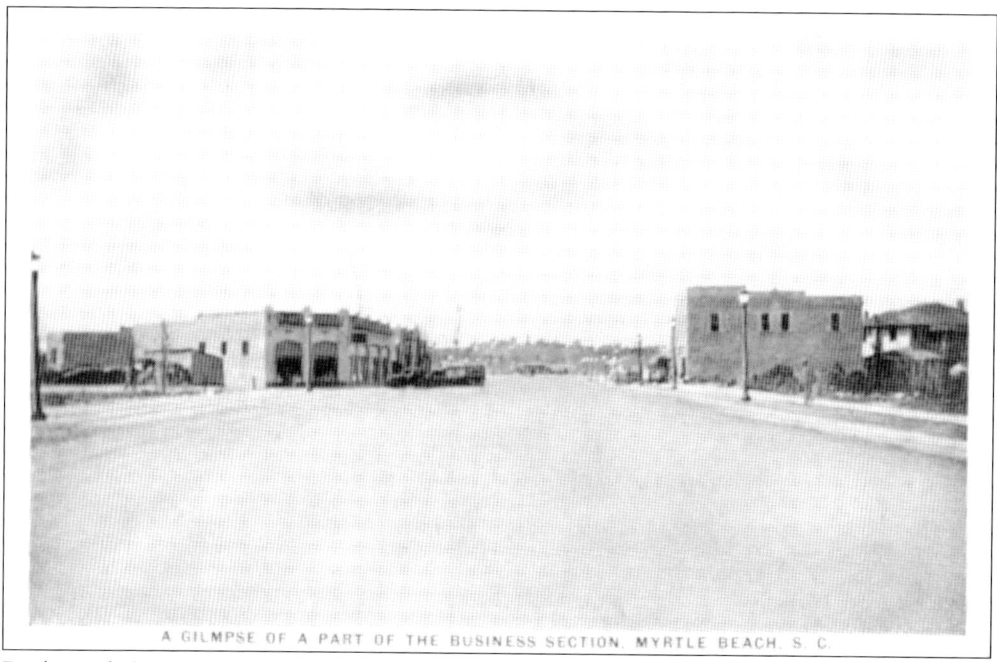

By the mid-1920s, more residences were constructed in Myrtle Beach, and the community held a permanent population of roughly 200 residents. At this time, Myrtle Beach's population mainly consisted of summertime residents, and most stores operated seasonally, leaving residents only a handful of places to purchase goods and other commodities when the tourism industry was dormant. This 1920s postcard view of Myrtle Beach's "Business Block" displays the community's atmosphere at that time.

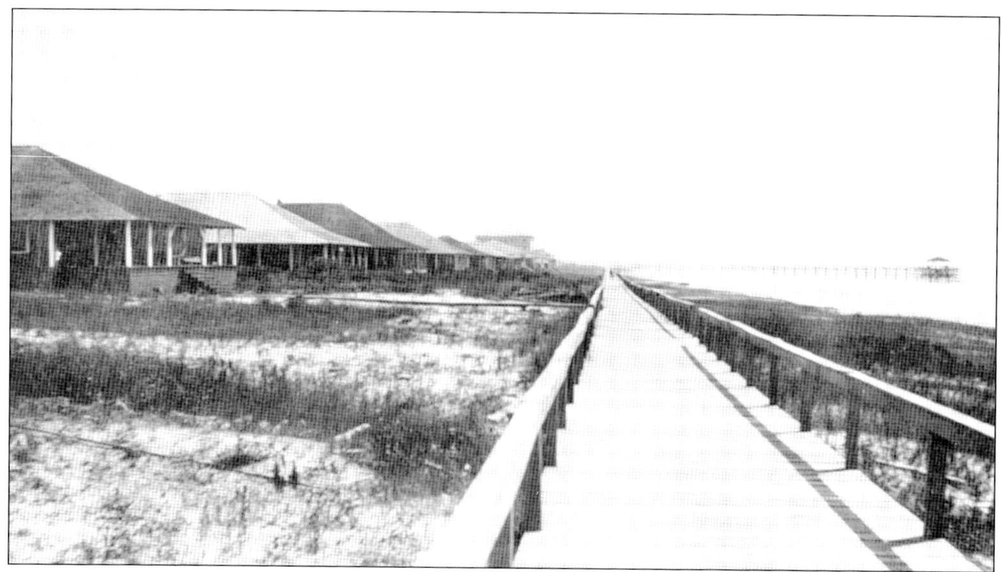

The Myrtle Beach Boardwalk has been rebuilt several times. The first wooden boardwalk, seen here, was established by the early 1930s and was replaced by a concrete boardwalk in 1940. After being destroyed by Hurricane Hazel, all that remained of the boardwalk was a small strip between Ninth and Eleventh Avenues North. Myrtle Beach's present-day boardwalk was built along Ocean Boulevard in the 2000s. (Courtesy of the Horry County Museum.)

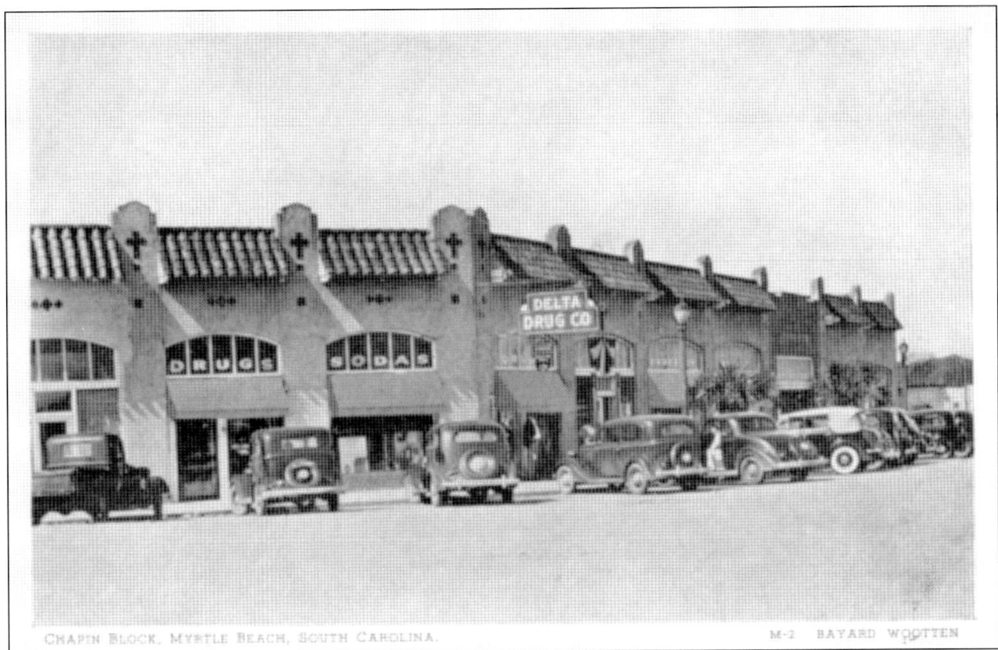

Due to Myrtle Beach's minuscule population in the early 20th century, only a few stores served the community. In its early years, Myrtle Beach citizens shopped at the Chapin Company Department Store, an essential store for residents that was also once the largest department store in northeastern South Carolina. An early-1930s view of the store can be seen above. Though many locals frequented the store, it served great importance to residents across Horry County as well. For example, the receipt at right, from 1935, shows the purchase of building materials for customers in Conway, representing the vital services the store provided to locals of yesteryear from both Myrtle Beach and the surrounding area.

CHAPIN CO.

Myrtle Beach, S. C. .... 193....

M ....

Address ....

SAVE YOUR TICKET WE DON'T ITEMIZE BILLS AT END OF MONTH

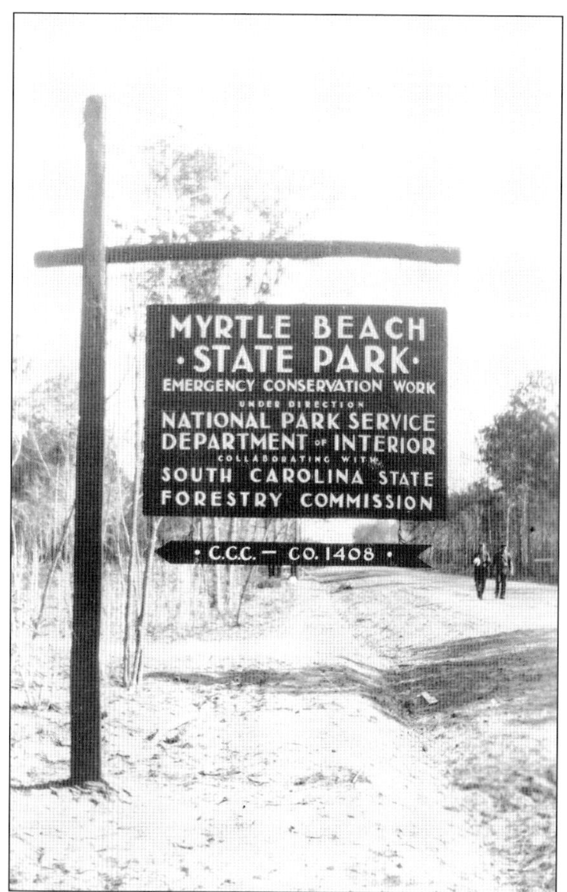

As a result of the community's prime oceanside location, Myrtle Beach State Park opened on July 1, 1936, after 320 acres of land were donated by the Myrtle Beach Farms Company in 1934 for its construction. It was the first state park to open in South Carolina. This park was one of 16 South Carolina state parks constructed by the Civilian Conservation Corps, and a 1930s sign for the state park, showing its CCC association, is seen at left. Myrtle Beach holds natural phenomena that inspired outdoorsmen long before the establishment of the state park system. For instance, the Hurl Rocks, seen in the postcard below, were documented in the notes of colonial naturalist William Bartram in the 1770s. Since covered by beach renourishment programs, they were some of the only rock formations in northeastern South Carolina. (Left, courtesy of the South Carolina Department of Archives and History.)

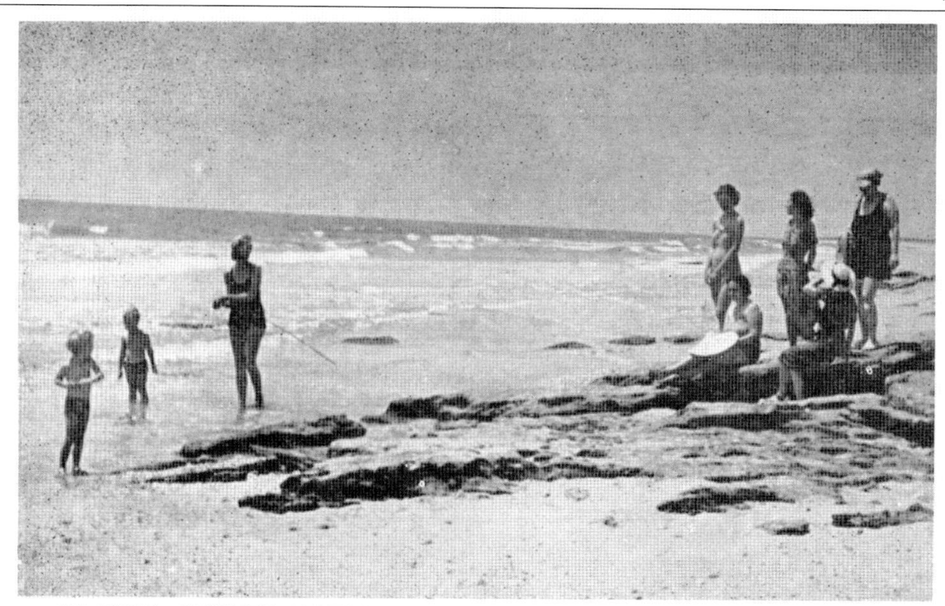

Built in 1901, the wooden rail depot operated by the Burroughs and Collins Company closed in 1928, leading to the present-day Myrtle Beach Rail Depot's construction. The depot seen below was opened in 1937 by the Atlantic Coast Line Railroad, which began operations in Myrtle Beach during the 1910s. Though it eventually closed and was almost demolished, preservation efforts in the 1990s saved the depot. The Pine Island Drawbridge, also built in 1937, was vital to local railroads and was once the only route into Myrtle Beach. Though still standing, as of 2025, the bridge remains unused. (Both, courtesy of the South Caroliniana Library.)

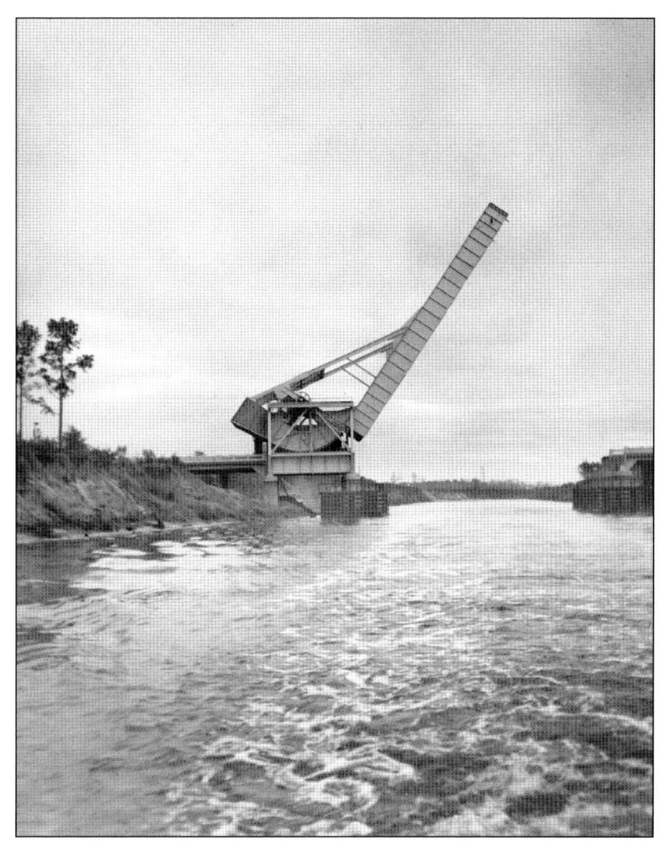

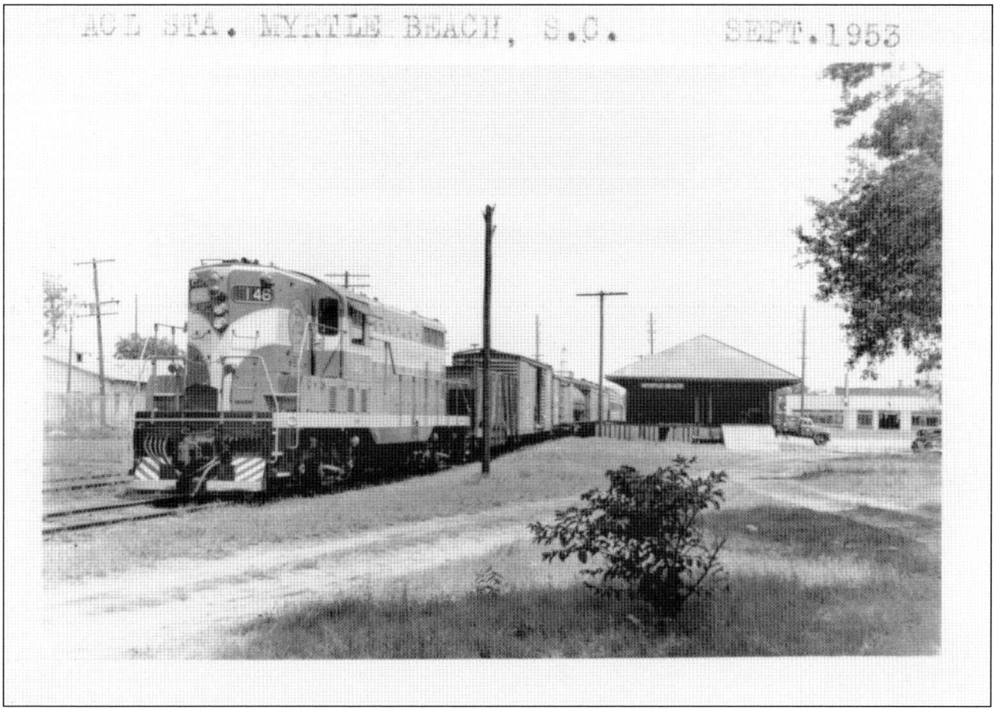

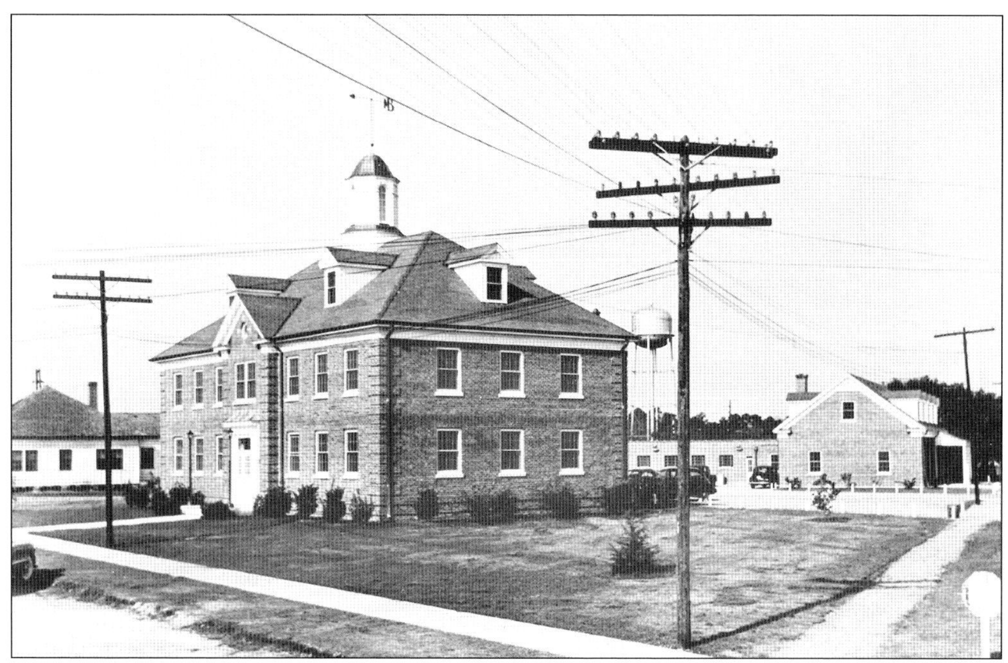

After continued growth, Myrtle Beach was finally incorporated as a town on March 12, 1938; its town hall was built in 1949, and funds for its construction had been secured in 1941 through the Works Progress Administration. In the decades since, the town hall building has undergone expansions and renovations. Myrtle Beach's spiritual roots date as far back to the community's origins: the First United Methodist Church, which holds an over-century-old congregation, is one of Myrtle Beach's most recognizable churches. This church's congregation dates to 1900, and its first sanctuary, built in 1921, was once Myrtle Beach's sole church. Its current sanctuary, seen here, was constructed in 1939. (Above, courtesy of the City of Myrtle Beach.)

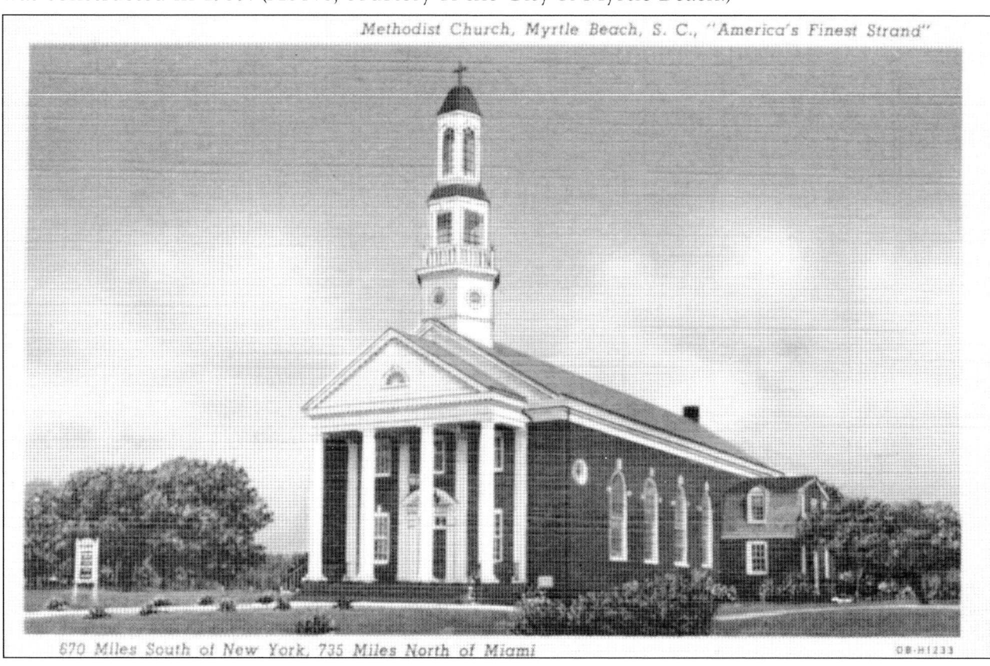

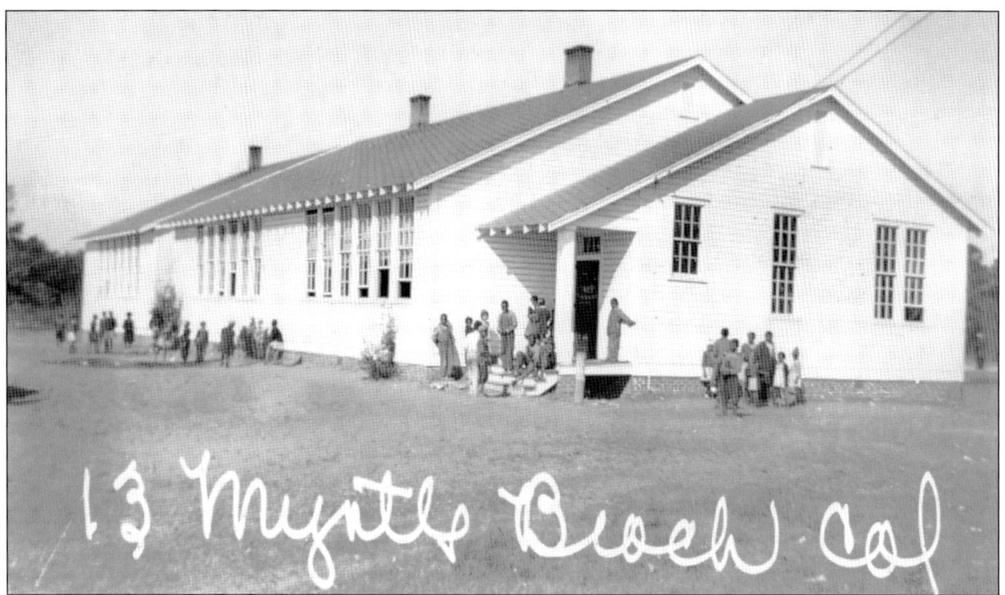

Religion in Myrtle Beach's African American community is also historically strong, and before the 1930s, Black children were mostly educated through churches. The Myrtle Beach Colored School, seen here, was built in 1932 as Myrtle Beach's first public school for African Americans. It operated until 1953. Though the schoolhouse was unable to be preserved, the Historic Myrtle Beach Colored School Museum and Education Center promotes its history. (Courtesy of the Horry County Museum.)

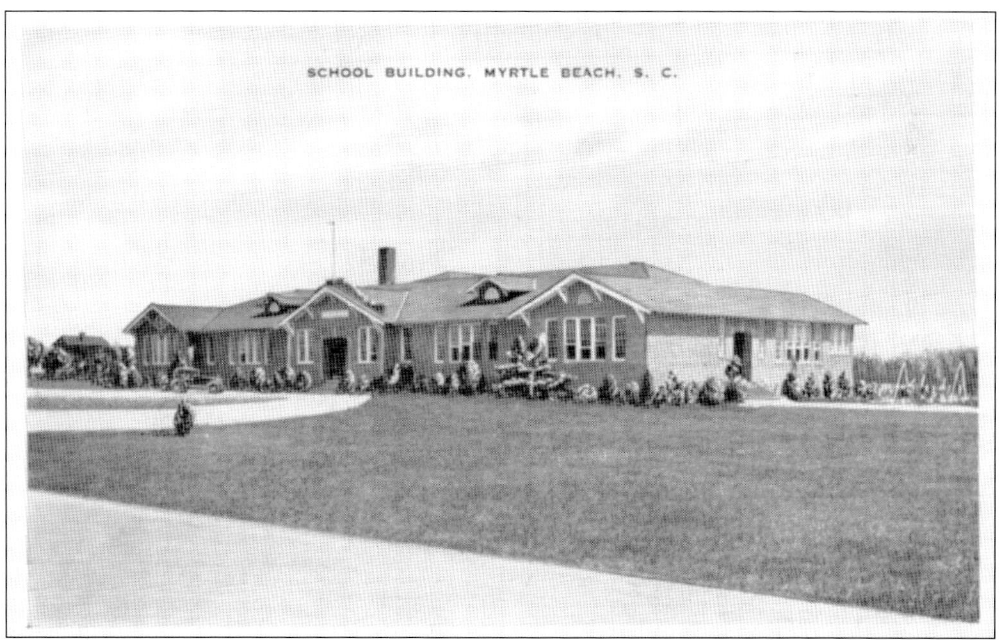

During segregation and in the community's early years, Myrtle Beach's White students of all ages were once educated in the same building (seen here). This building burned down in 1947, and by 1948, the first official Myrtle Beach High School was constructed. Integrated in 1965, the first high school was demolished by 1990, and a new high school was built thereafter.

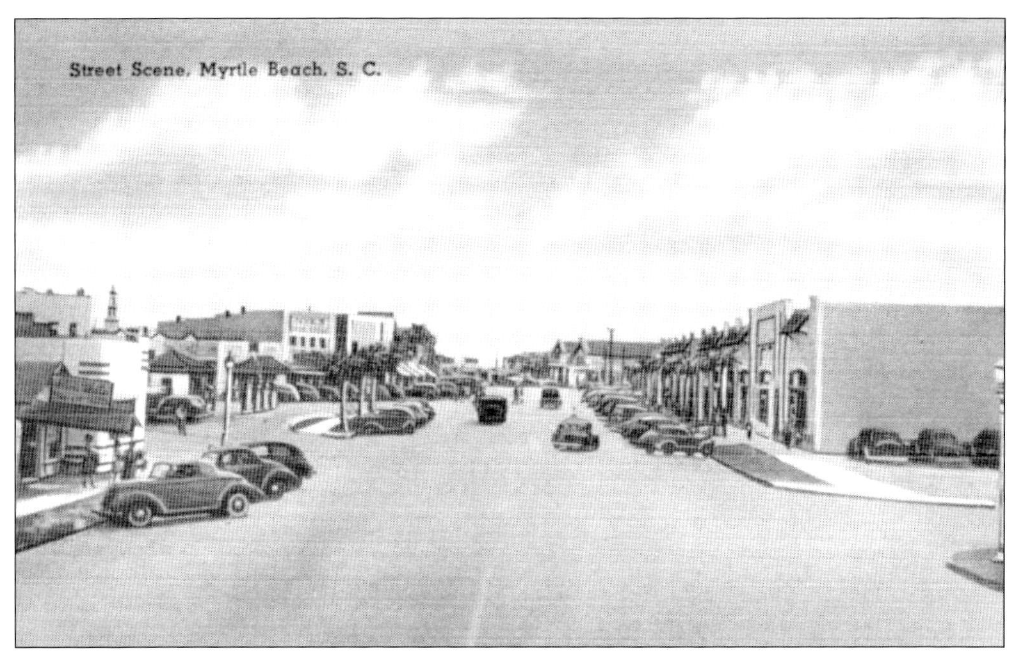

By the 1940s, the Myrtle Beach area's nickname of the "Grand Strand" was coined, and it came with validation as the region now had a paved highway, growing infrastructure, and an expanding tourism industry. For example, Myrtle Beach Bike Week began at this time, the Myrtle Beach General Bombing and Gunnery Range (a prelude to Myrtle Beach Air Force Base) started operations, and numerous famed attractions, such as the third Myrtle Beach Pavilion, also opened. Here, a bustling scene of Main Street in Myrtle Beach is shown in the late 1940s, displaying the town's Esso station and storefronts. In the 1944 image below, Ninth Avenue North is seen, showing glimpses of Peaches Corner, various stores, and the side of a building that housed the Gloria Theatre.

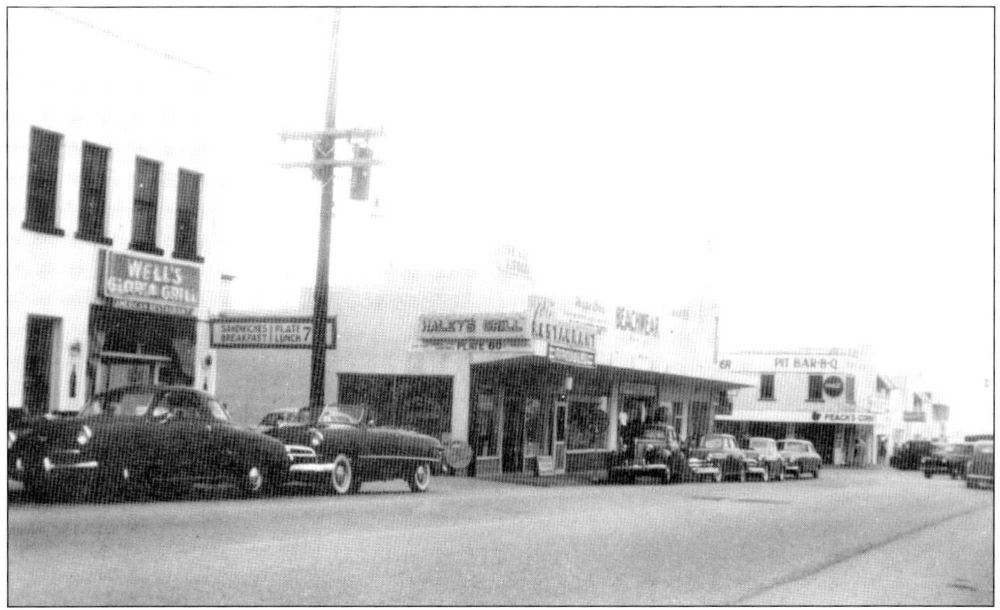

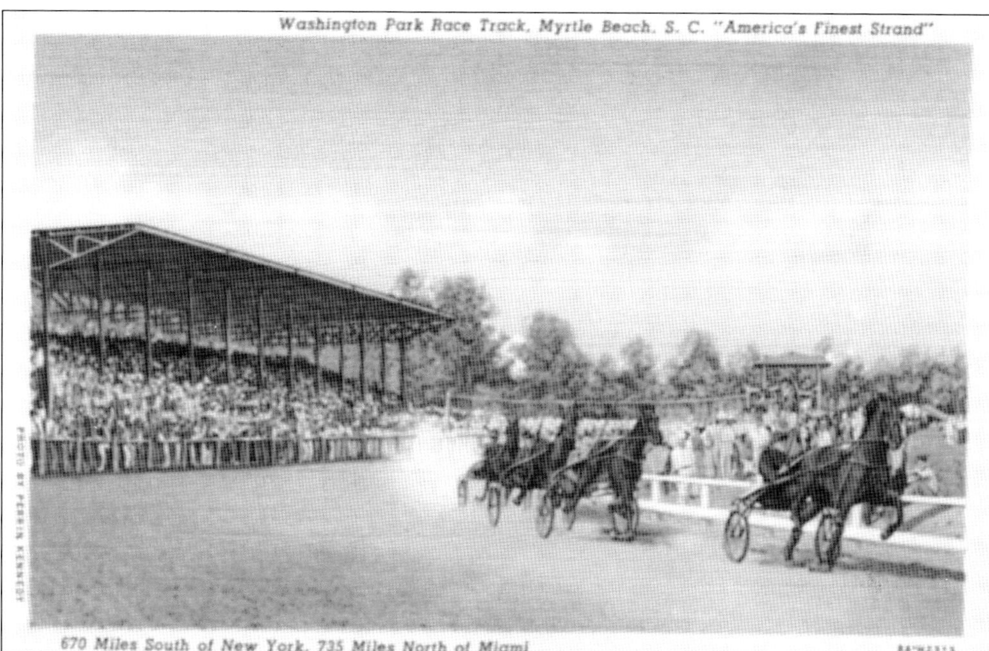

The Washington Park Horse Track opened in 1938 and attracted a myriad of visitors before closing in 1947. Above, a postcard scene from 1943 shows the track and crowds in grandstand seating. After the track's closure, automobile racing took precedence as a popular spectator sport, and several raceways opened in Myrtle Beach in the ensuing decades. However, during the segregation era, White and Black residents legally had to maintain separate entertainment venues. Shown at right is an excerpt of *The Negro Motorist Green Book*, which listed venues safe for Black travelers to visit. Charlie's Place was one of the only attractions African Americans could frequent in Myrtle Beach during the Jim Crow era and held the Fitzgerald Motel (shown in this excerpt), a restaurant and famed nightclub that was frequented by several notable Black entertainers of the era, including Ray Charles, Billie Holiday, and Little Richard. (Right, courtesy of the South Caroliniana Library.)

Cheraw

Mrs. M. B. Robinson Tourist Home	211 Church St.
Mrs. Maggie Green Tourist Home	Church Street
Liveoak Tourist Home	328 2nd St.
College Inn Restaurant	324 2nd St.
Gate Grill	Second St.

Columbia

★**MOTEL SIMBETH** .... **U. S. 1 8 miles North of Columbia**
Write to: Rt. 3 Box 988 — Phone: 4-9189

Y.W.C.A.	1429 Park St.
Nylon Hotel	918 Senate St.
Mrs. Irene B. Evans Tourist Home	1106 Pine St.
College Inn Tourist Home	1609 Harden St.
Mrs. S. H. Smith Tourist Home	929 Pine St.
Mrs. H. Cornwell Tourist Home	1713 Wayne
Mrs. W. D. Chappelle Tourist Home	1301 Pine St.
Beachum Tourist Home	2212 Gervais St.
Mrs. J. P. Wakefield Tourist Home	816 Oak St.
Green Leaf Restaurant	1117 Wash. St.
Savoy Restaurant	Old Winnsboro St.
Cozy Inn Restaurant	1509 Harden St.

Darlington

Mable's Motel	U. S. 52

Florence

★**EBONY GUEST HOUSE** .... **712 North Wilson St.**

Richmond Tourist Home	108 S. Griffin St.
John McDonald Tourist Home	501 S. Irby St.
Mrs. B. Wright Tourist Home	1004 E. Cheeve St.
Ace's Grill	1109 E. Chenes St.

Georgetown

Mrs. R. Anderson Tourist Home	424 Broad
Mrs. D. Atkinson Tourist Home	811 Duke
Jas. Becote Tourist Home	118 Orange
Mrs. A. A. Smith Tourist Home	317 Emanuel

Greenville

Dr. Gibbs Tourist Home	914 Anderson Rd.
Miss M. J. Grimes Tourist Home	210 Mean St.
Fowlers Restaurant	16 Spring St.

Mullins

E. Calhoun's Tourist Homes	535 N. Smith St.

Myrtle Beach

Fitzgerald's Motel	Carver St.
Charles Motel	Myrtle Beach

Orangeburg, S. C.

★**JOHNSON'S TOURIST HOME** .... **1220 Lancaster St.**
Rates: Single—$2.00; Double—$3.00 **"A Home Away from Home"**

58

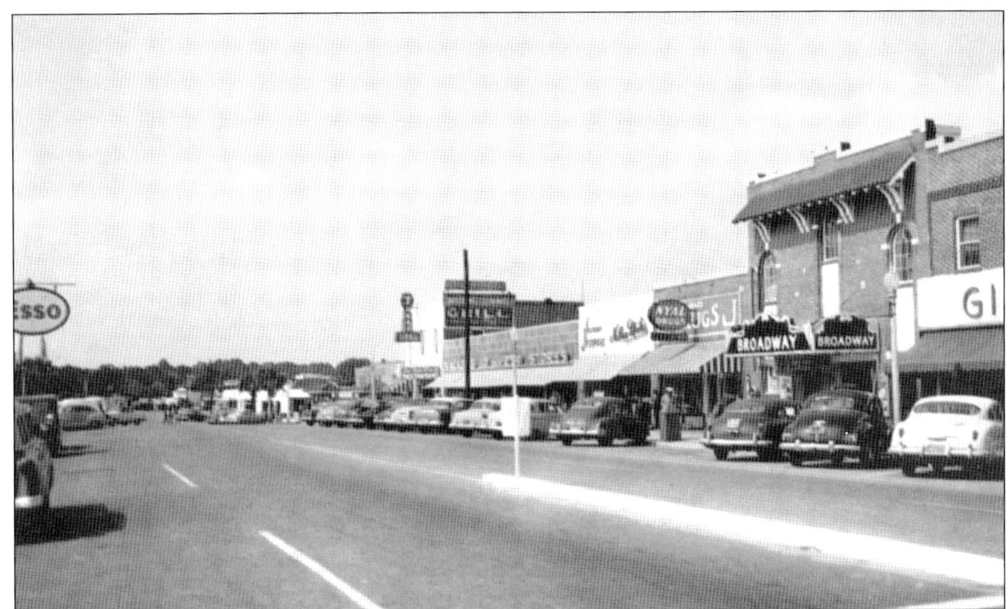

This postcard, produced by Mack's Five and Dime stores, shows businesses on Main Street in Myrtle Beach in the early 1950s. Seen in this image is the Broadway Theater, which was first opened as Ben's Broadway Theater in approximately the late 1930s. It was Myrtle Beach's first theater to open and has changed names and ownership several times. Though no longer known as the Broadway Theater, the building is standing as of 2025.

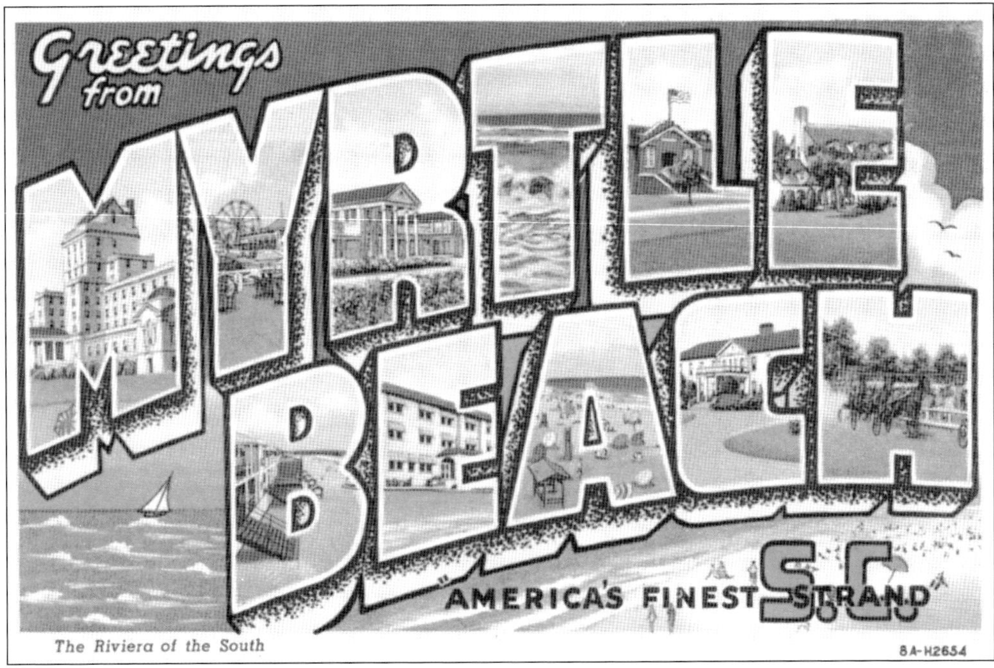

Representative of Myrtle Beach's popularity at the time, this 1940s postcard advertises snapshots of the city, including the former Ocean Forest Hotel and several entertainment venues. Though these postcards helped showcase the area's beauty, they also served as popular souvenirs and keepsakes during this era.

As Myrtle Beach's quintessential atmosphere continued to blossom in the 1940s, photographs such as this particular example became popular keepsakes for visitors. In this image, a couple is seen in a classic prop in 1949, taken most likely at the Myrtle Beach Pavilion. Other communities, such as Conway and Atlantic Beach, also had moon photography props available for visitors.

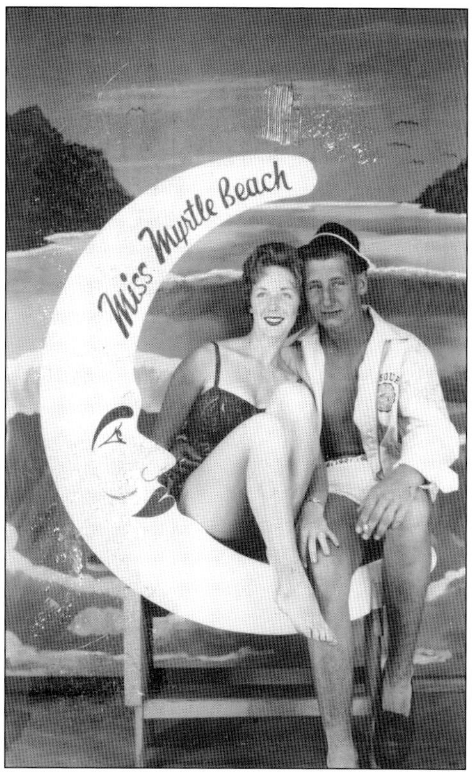

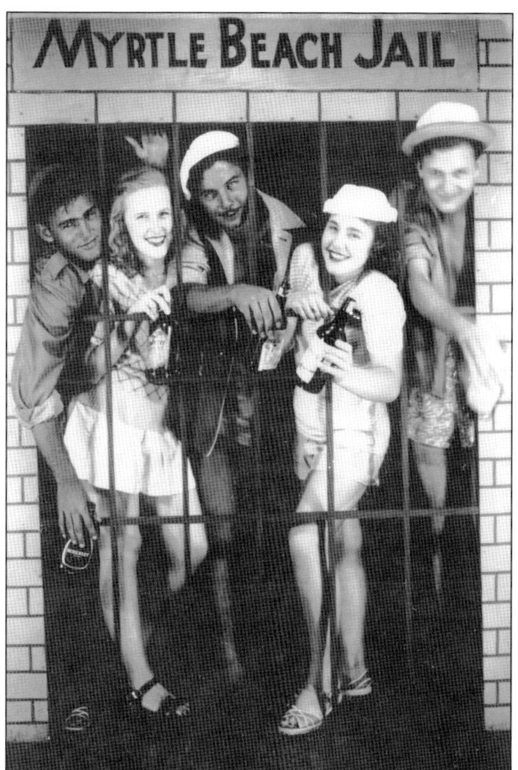

The Myrtle Beach Pavilion held several different picture props, including this "jail," where six youthful yet unidentified tourists are seen in the 1940s. Similar props were also used during the Sun Fun Festivals in the 1950s, where visitors not in beach attire or shorts would humorously be sent to "jail" and would have to post "bail." Funds from the "bail" were used to help build Ocean View Memorial Hospital, Myrtle Beach's first medical center.

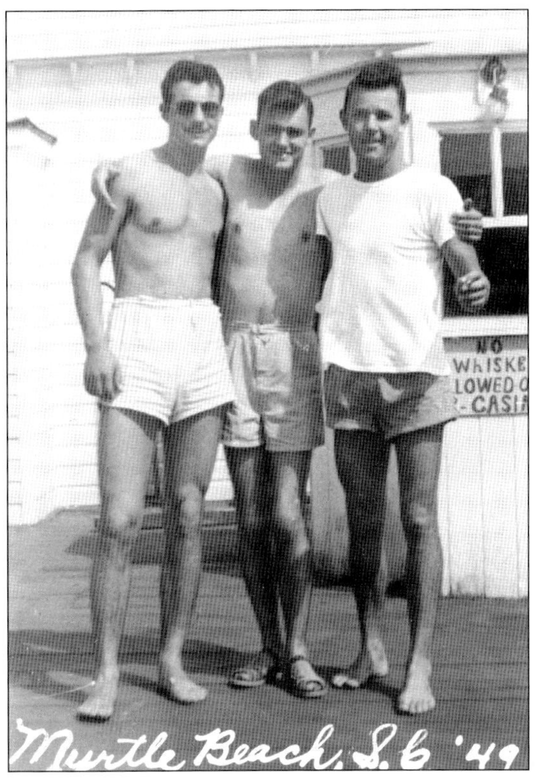

Representative of Myrtle Beach's tourism industry in the mid-20th century are these two images from the Ocean Plaza Hotel, which first existed as the Myrtle Beach Yacht Club. It became the Ocean Plaza Hotel by 1937, was home to a pier (now Pier 14), and at one point briefly held a casino. At left, three unidentified tourists are seen on the Ocean Plaza Pier in 1949. Though the pier prohibited alcohol, the casino permitted gambling, as the activities technically occurred off land. The pier and casino were destroyed by Hurricane Hazel, though the pier was rebuilt. Additionally showing the Ocean Plaza's popularity, below, Betty Leonard and Donald Huff pose on a vehicle owned by the hotel. The Ocean Plaza was demolished in 1973, and the Yachtsman Hotel was built on its site.

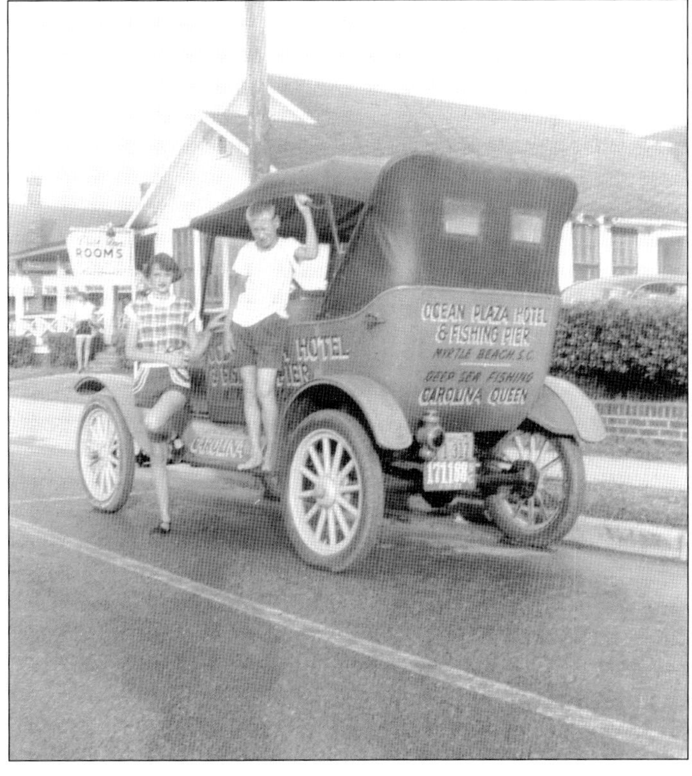

The Second Avenue Pier, opened in 1936, was built by Julian Scarborough and St. Julian Springs. Measuring 906 feet long, the pier has been rebuilt twice in the aftermaths of Hurricane Hazel in 1954 and Hurricane Hugo in 1989, but it is still one of the city's most beloved landmarks. This 1942 image shows the original Second Avenue Pier behind an unidentified tourist.

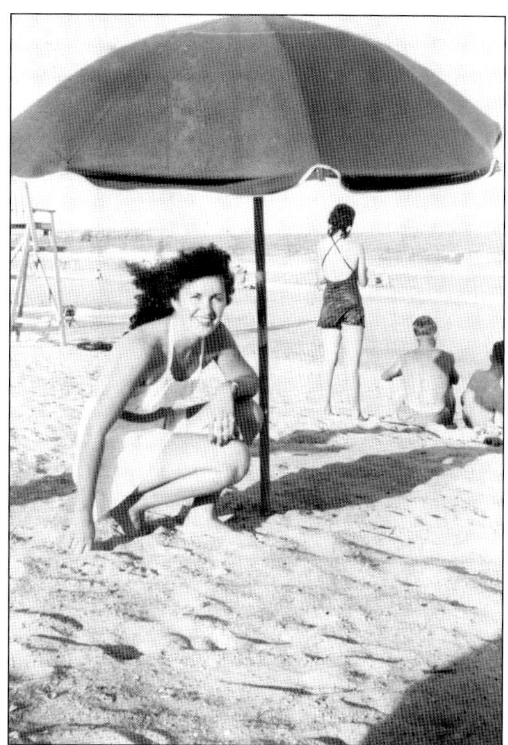

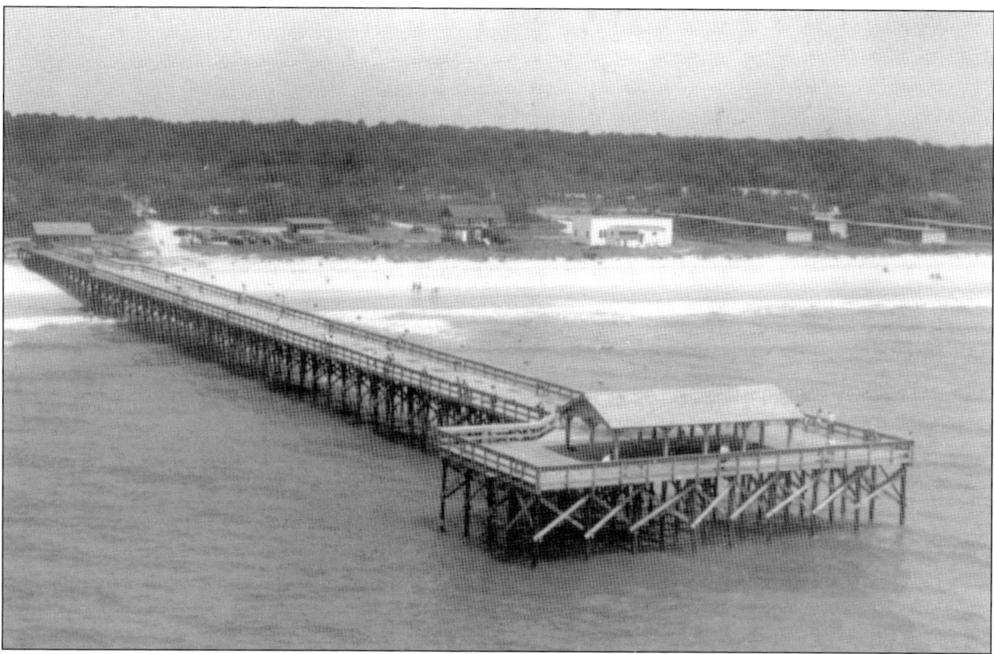

The Springmaid Beach Resort was founded by Springs Industries, a textile company, on 27 acres of oceanfront land in 1948. Access was initially restricted to only Springs Industries employees and their families, but the Springmaid Resort opened publicly in 1953. The Springmaid Pier, seen in this image, has become a Myrtle Beach landmark but has been rebuilt several times due to hurricane damage.

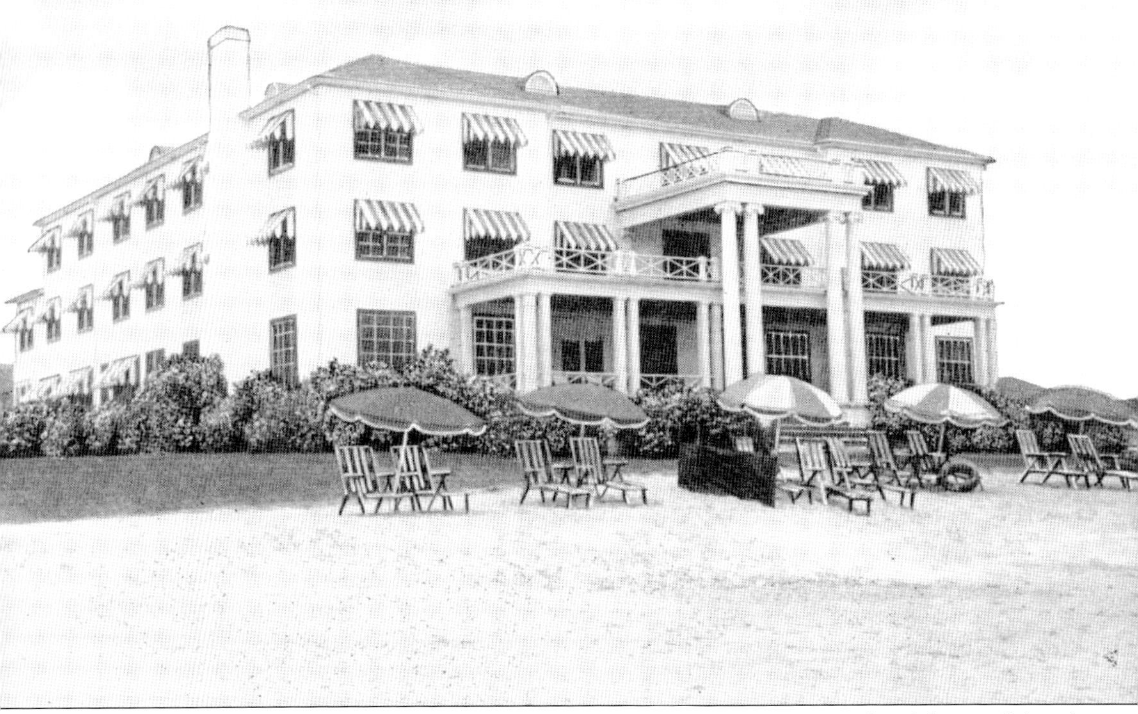

The Patricia Court, built in 1936 and destroyed in 1985, is a great example of the small hotels that were built in Myrtle Beach in the early to mid-20th century. At this time, Myrtle Beach was becoming an increasingly popular vacation destination but still maintained a small-town setting. Hotels similar to this one were often family-owned, operated seasonally, and, in the fashion of the hospitality industry in past eras, often provided homemade meals and other personable accommodations to guests. Notably, many of these hotels were built from wood, causing them to be destroyed by hurricanes. Hurricane Hazel particularly cleared many in the storm's wake in 1954, leading to a reconstruction of Myrtle Beach's tourism industry that gave way to the era of high-rise hotels and condominiums along the coastline. Though many early hotels were rebuilt, eventual disrepair from age led them to face later demolition or sale to developers, contributing to further changes in Myrtle Beach's hospitality industry and skyline.

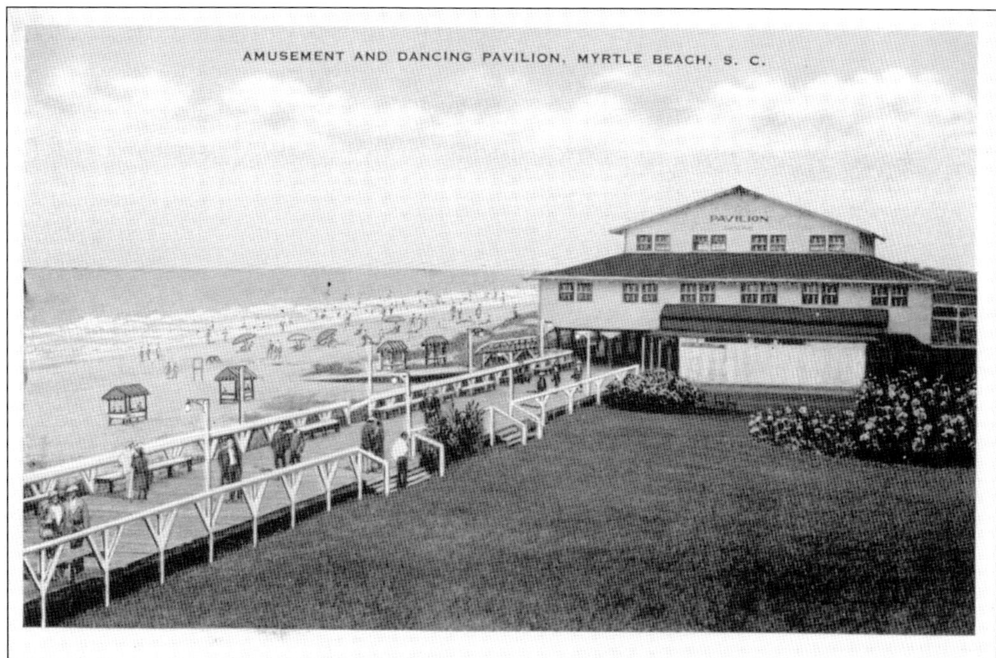

Myrtle Beach's second pavilion, seen in the above image, was built in 1923. Though very popular among tourists and residents, it burned down in 1944. The pavilion was rebuilt a third time in 1948 out of concrete. Seen in the image below, the third pavilion operated seasonally from March to September and held three stories of attractions. Soon after its construction, the property was expanded and featured a large, separate amusement park that only boosted its popularity with patrons. A dancing room on the top floor of the pavilion was opened in 1960 and was known as the Magic Attic. The Myrtle Beach Pavilion, which also survived Hurricanes Hazel and Hugo in 1954 and 1989, sadly faced financial decline in the early 2000s and was closed in 2006.

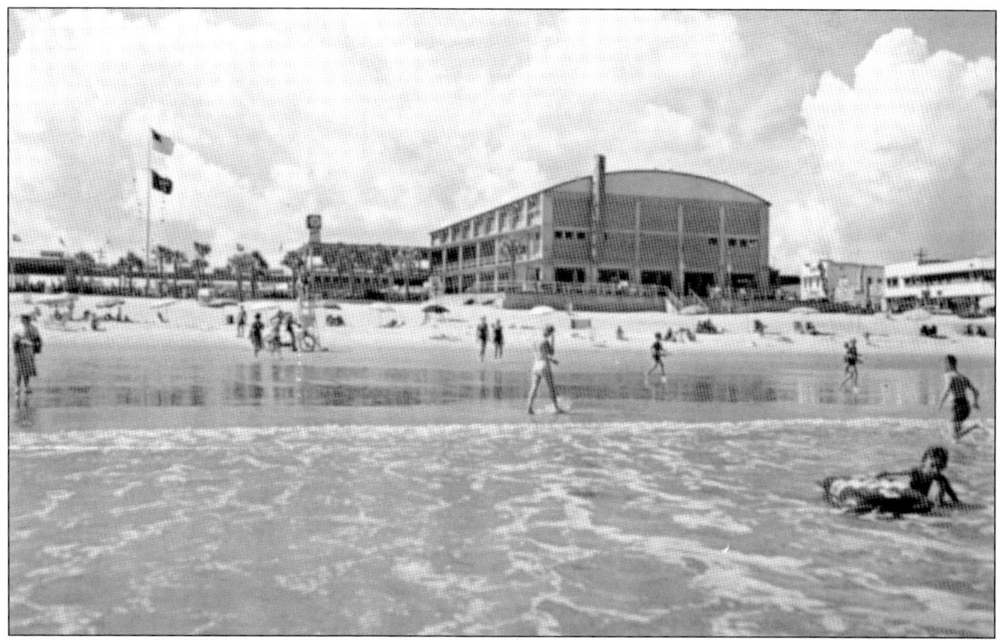

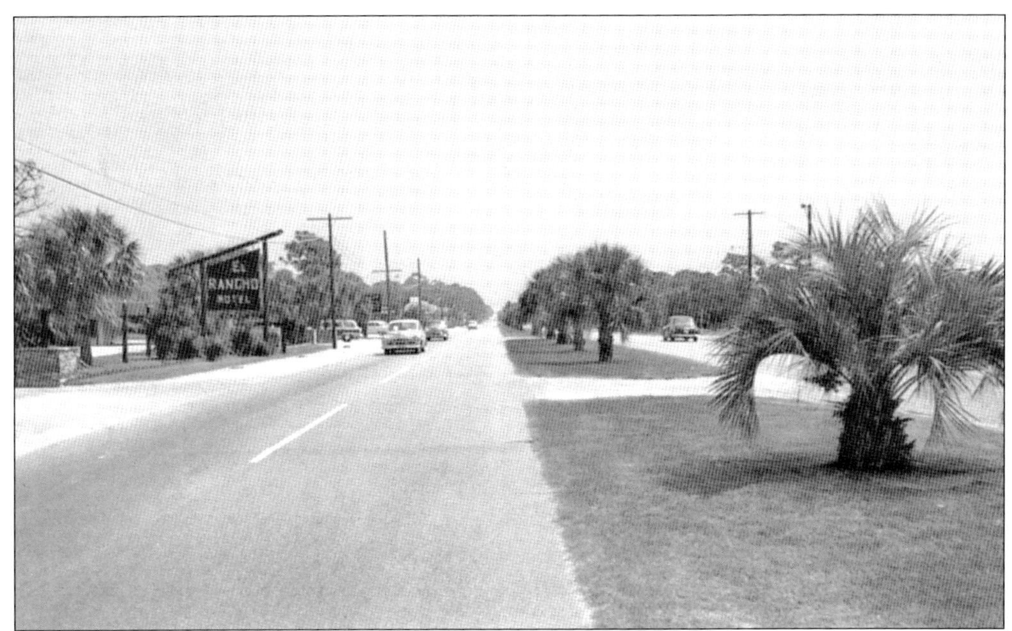

Though many were built prior, by the 1950s, motor courts and motels became staples of America's hospitality industry. After World War II, when America saw an economic upturn and highway infrastructure was expanded, traveling became an accessible luxury. Numerous Americans traveled by road, leading to the popularity of motor courts and motels for easy lodging as most were located near major roadways. Seen in the above image, Horry County's stretch of US Highway 17, known as Kings Highway (named for the old King's Highway established by Charles II of England to connect Charleston, South Carolina, with Boston, Massachusetts), was a major transportation corridor for the region that allowed tourists to travel through the area. Numerous motor lodges and motels were built along its roadway, such as the El Rancho Motel, which is seen in both images.

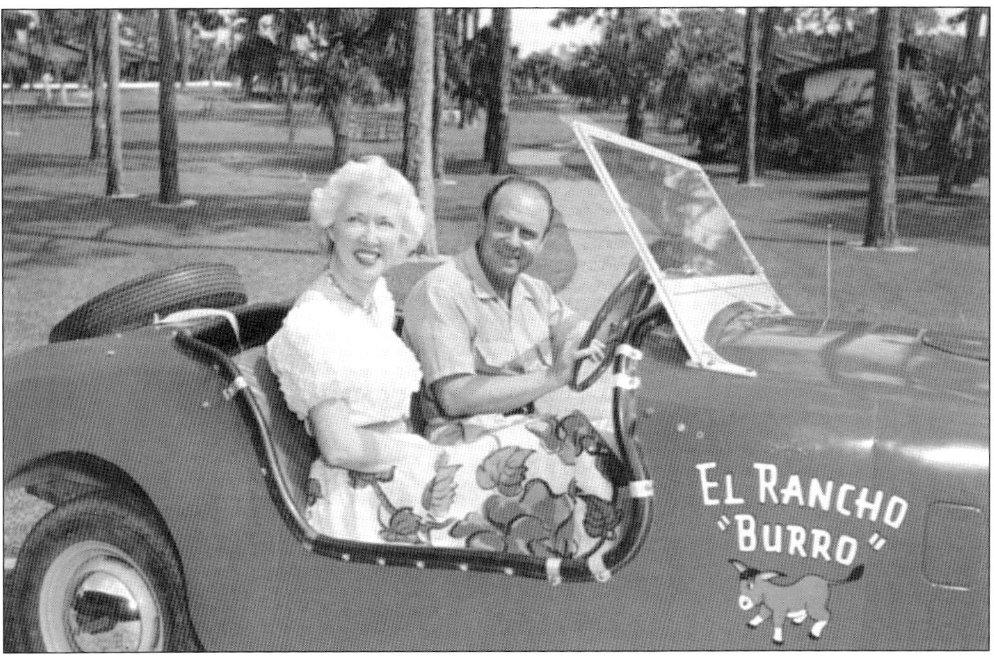

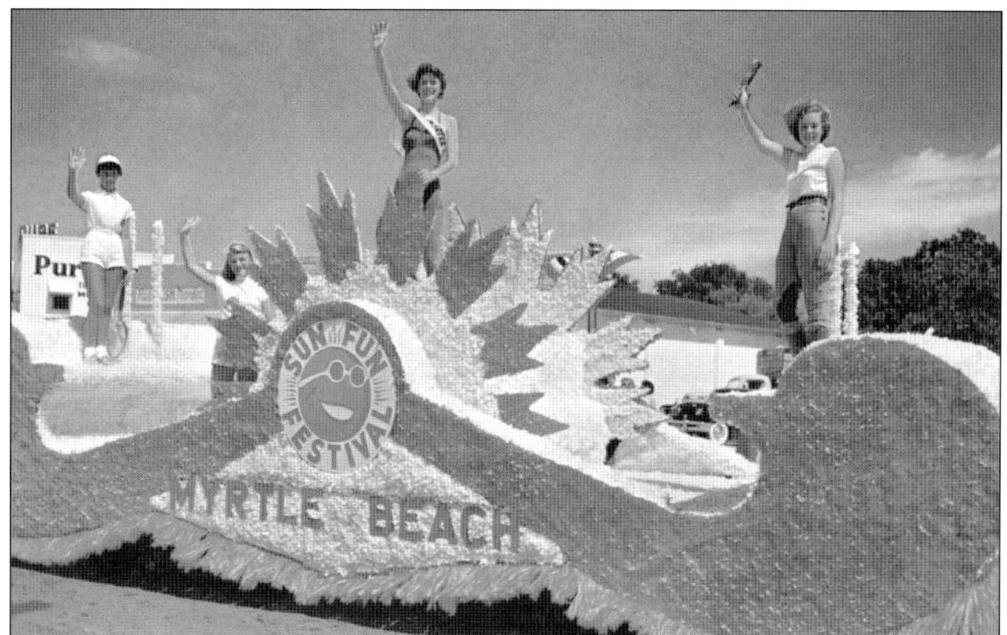

The Sun Fun Festival, established in 1951, is an annual festival held in Myrtle Beach during the beginning of the summer season and was once mainly held in the former Pavilion. Though briefly discontinued after the 60th festival in 2011, it was renewed by the Plyler family, whose patriarch, Justin Plyler, helped found the original festival. The Sun Fun Festival has been historically known in Myrtle Beach for its parade and beauty contests, including the Miss Sun Fun pageant and the Miss Bikini Wahine pageant. Above, women in swimwear are seen riding on a parade float in 1954. Winners of both pageants also participated in larger pageants and served as ambassadors of Myrtle Beach for one year. An image from the 1966 Miss Sun Fun pageant is shown below. (Below, courtesy of the Horry County Museum.)

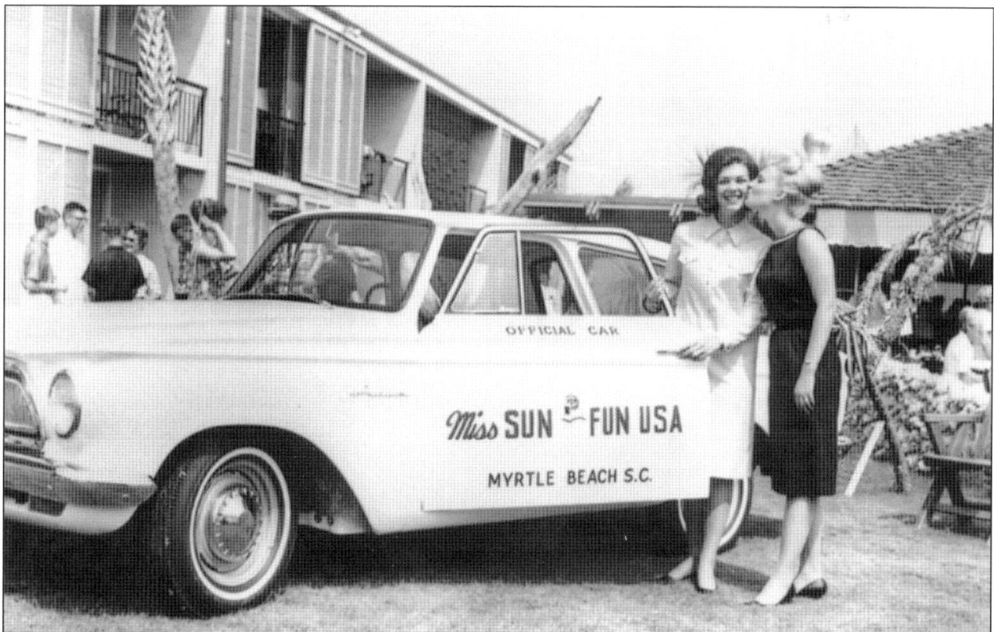

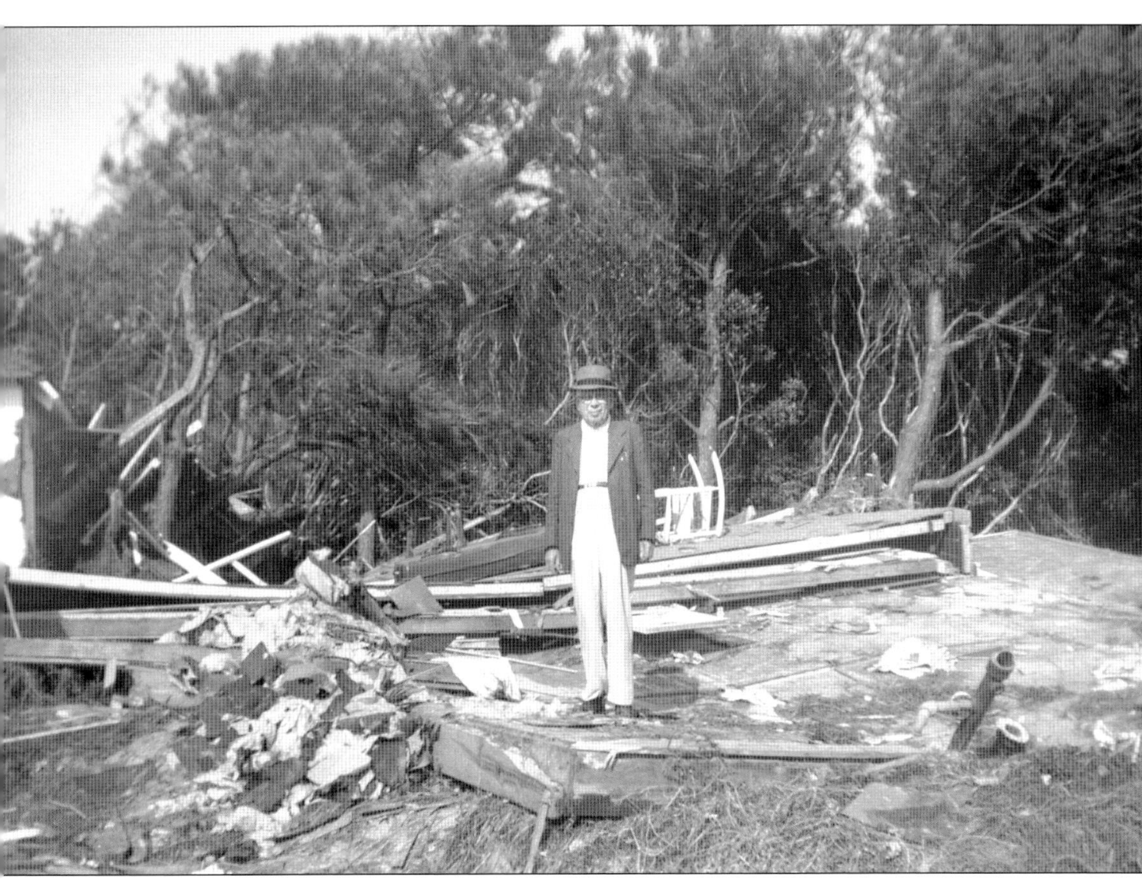

Hurricane Hazel was a category four hurricane that made landfall near the North and South Carolina state line (in approximately Calabash, North Carolina) on October 15, 1954. The hurricane, which had maximum winds of 130 miles per hour, utterly devastated and permanently changed Myrtle Beach, destroying 80 percent of the buildings in the community and flattening numerous hotels, restaurants, homes, piers, and storefronts. Myrtle Beach as it was then known was decimated; a resident standing on rubble in the above image portrays this concept. Lands where many enterprises had once sat were cleared, and numerous longtime residents either had to start over or decided to leave the area. This led developers to seize an opportunity and purchase cleared land, which led to the development of further attractions and hotels. This marked the beginning of a shift in Myrtle Beach as post–Hurricane Hazel development led to increased tourism, population growth, and a general shift in the area's atmosphere. (Courtesy of the Horry County Museum.)

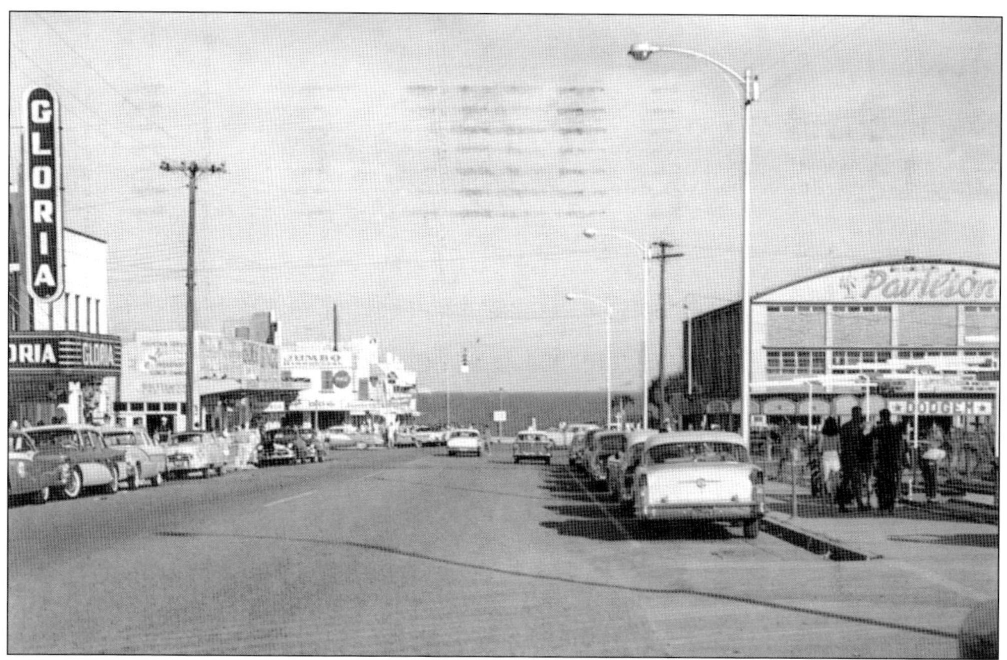

Though Hurricane Hazel destroyed most of Myrtle Beach's small lodges, hotels, restaurants, and houses in 1954, this led to opportunities to further develop commercially, which is conveyed in the above image that shows a busy downtown in 1959. Noted attractions include the Pavilion, the Gloria Theatre, and Peaches Corner, while the image below shows Second Avenue Pier in a postcard mailed in 1956. This period also saw the development of numerous motels, popular amongst tourists traveling Kings Highway, as well as more resorts that further expanded Myrtle Beach's growth in the mid-20th century and provided the city with a more developed, defined tourist industry.

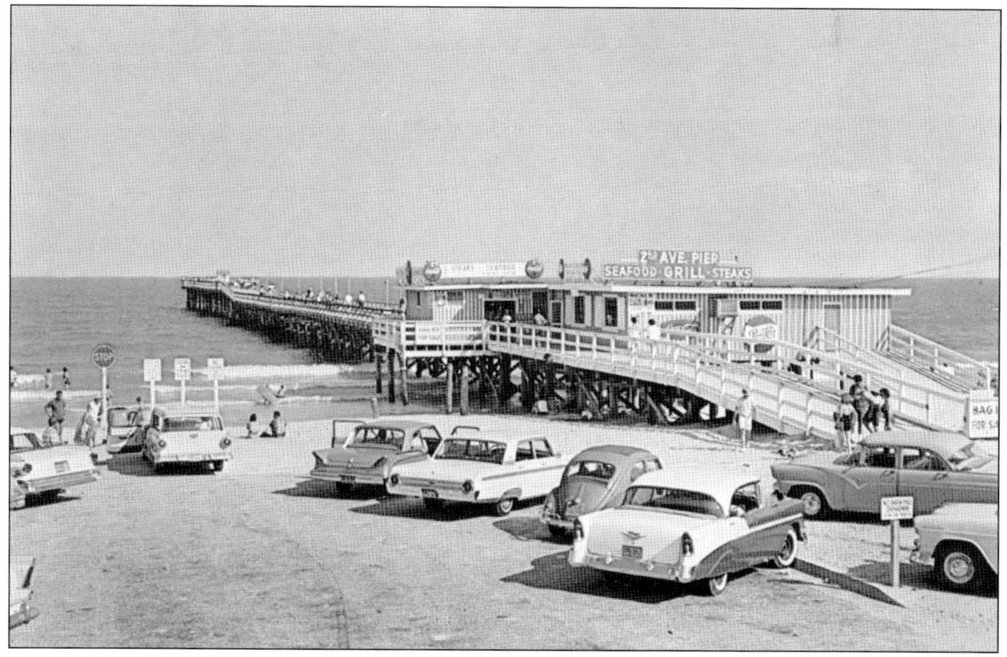

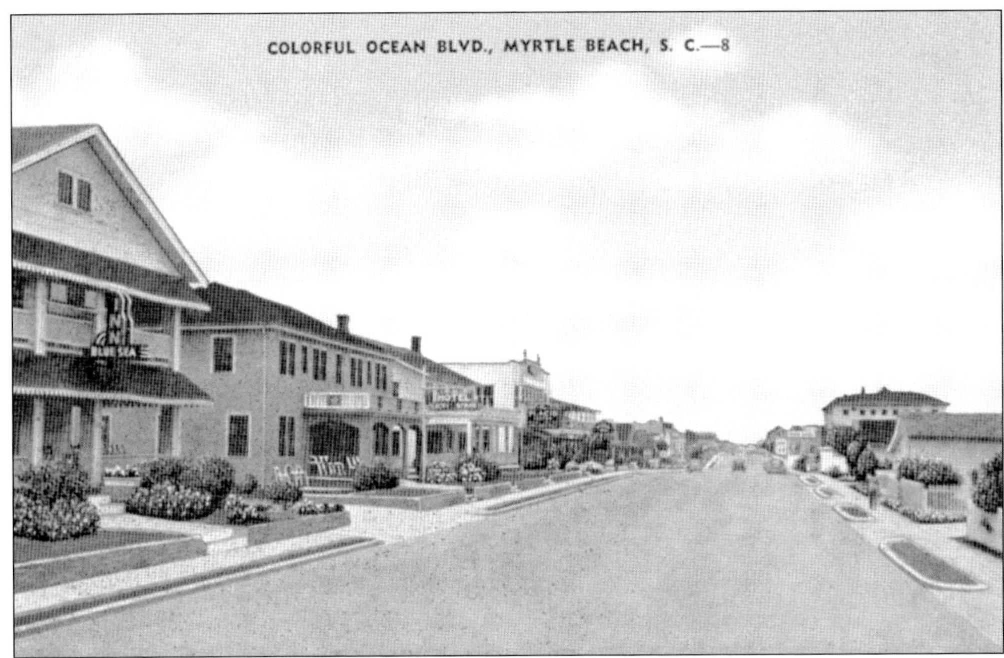

Along with Myrtle Beach's smaller, wood-built inns reminiscent of its early tourism days, like those shown above, motor courts were a major aspect of the area's tourist environment as well, dotting highways in the Myrtle Beach region beginning around 1940. These motor courts were especially popular by the time automobile travel became more accessible after World War II. Motels were a popular lodging option for their affordability, economic practicality, and closeness to major roadways and were a feature of downtown Myrtle Beach by the mid-20th century. Many of Myrtle Beach's motels from 1955 until the late 1960s were designed in the "populuxe" style, an iconic element of Mid-Century Modern architecture known for its colorful, modern design. An example of a Myrtle Beach motel designed in this concept is shown below. Today, many examples of these motels and other aspects of Myrtle Beach's early tourist industry have been demolished.

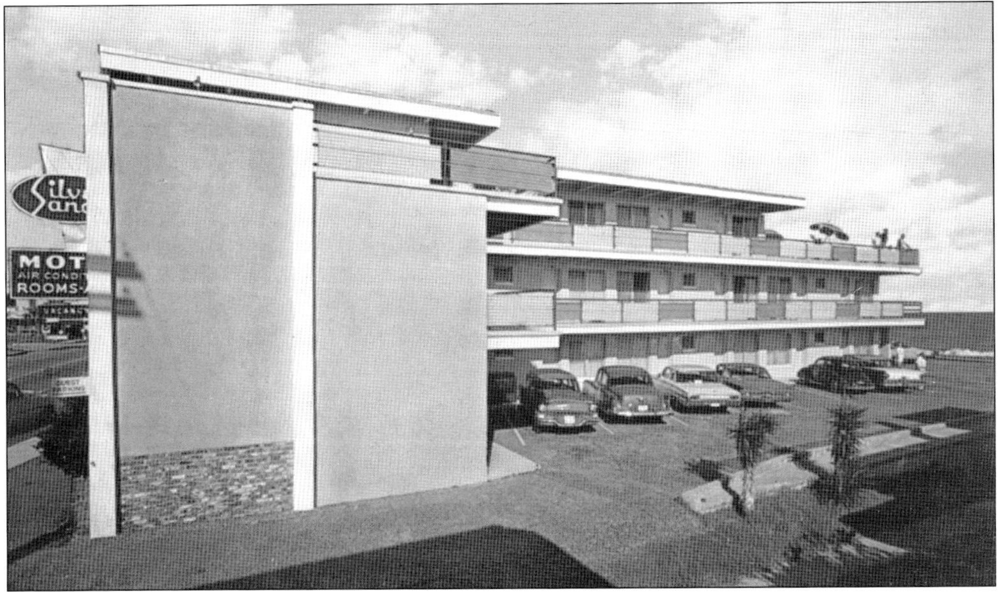

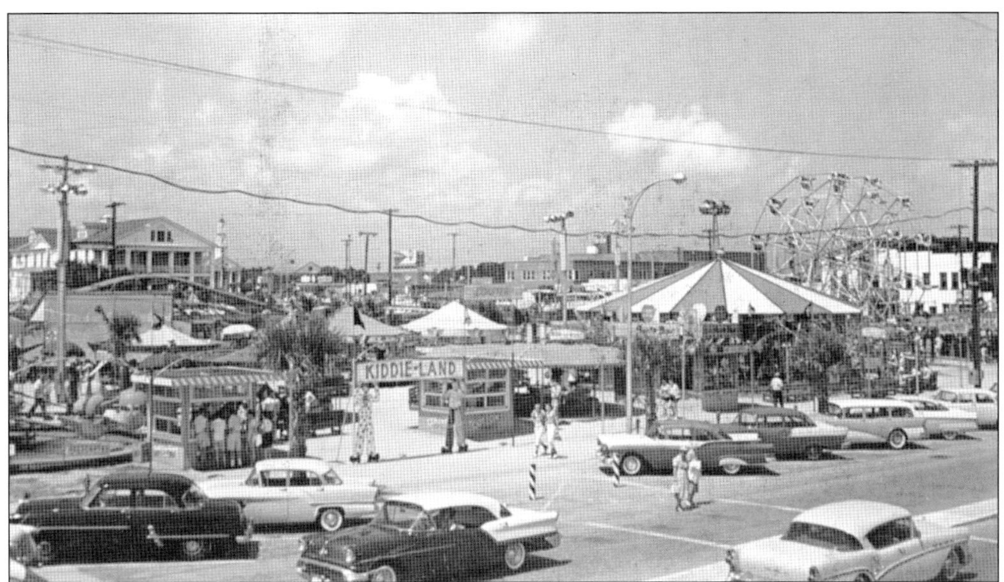

During the mid-20th century, Myrtle Beach continued to experience a population increase fueled by postwar economic growth and increased accessibility to travel. A new city (earning that distinction in 1957), Myrtle Beach added numerous attractions and amusement parks such as Family Kingdom, Pirateland Adventure Park, and Fort Caroline within the next 10 years to cater to tourists. The scene above from 1959 shows Myrtle Beach amusements adjacent to the Pavilion dating to this period. Locals remember this period of time as being representative of the wholesome and family-oriented image Myrtle Beach is remembered for by many, and the postcard image below displaying beach visitors from this time helps display this sentiment. However, this decade especially helped fuel the area's direction going forward, as the aftermath of Hurricane Hazel, the reintroduction of Myrtle Beach Air Force Base in 1956, and increased tourism would lead to further population growth and development.

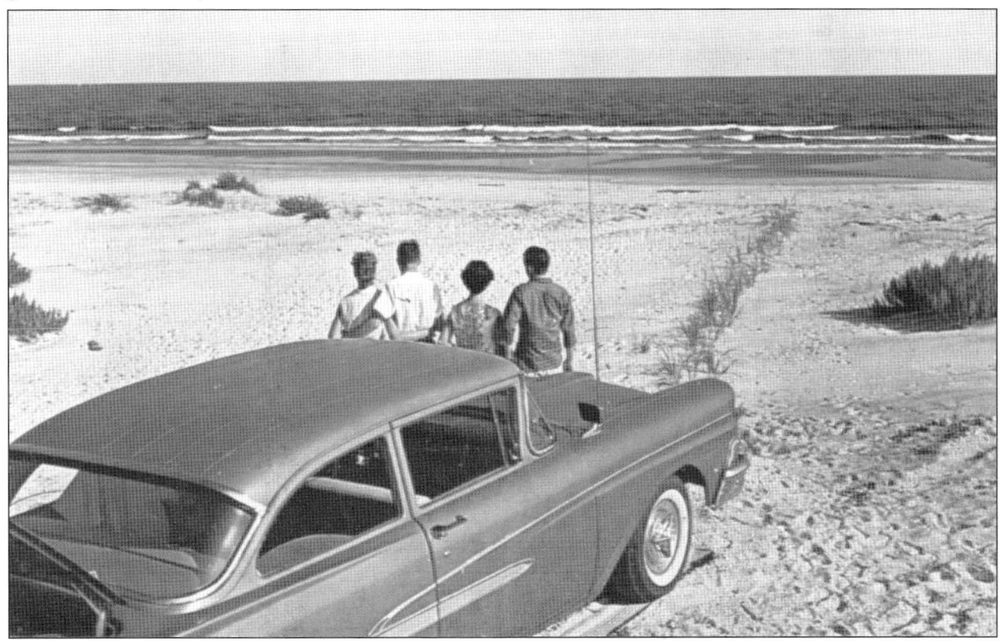

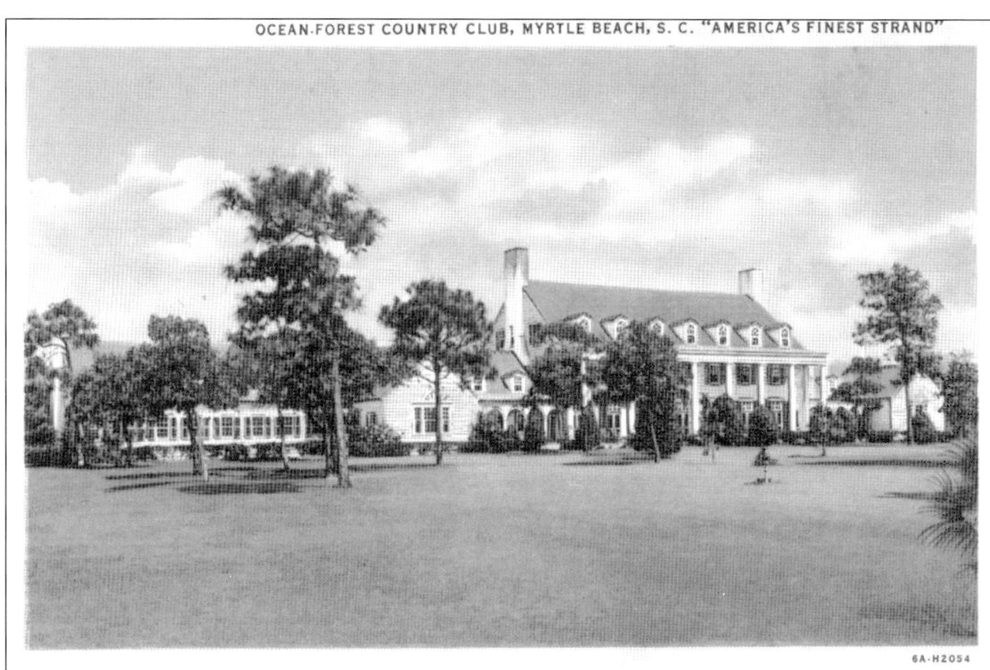

Golf recreation has had a presence in the area that started when the Ocean Forest Country Club, seen above, opened in Myrtle Beach in 1927. Officially renamed the Pine Lakes Country Club in 1946, it is called the "Granddaddy" because it is the oldest golf course in the area. It is also considered the birthplace of *Sports Illustrated* magazine. Though Hurricane Hazel caused widespread damage in 1954, the aftermath required a rebuilding effort in the area that saw much of the property owned by the Myrtle Beach Farms Company sold off to establish golf courses, thus beginning Myrtle Beach's legacy within sports tourism. Throughout the 1960s, Myrtle Beach added new golf courses each year, and a new clientele of tourists, such as athletes and active retirees, seen below, were drawn to the area.

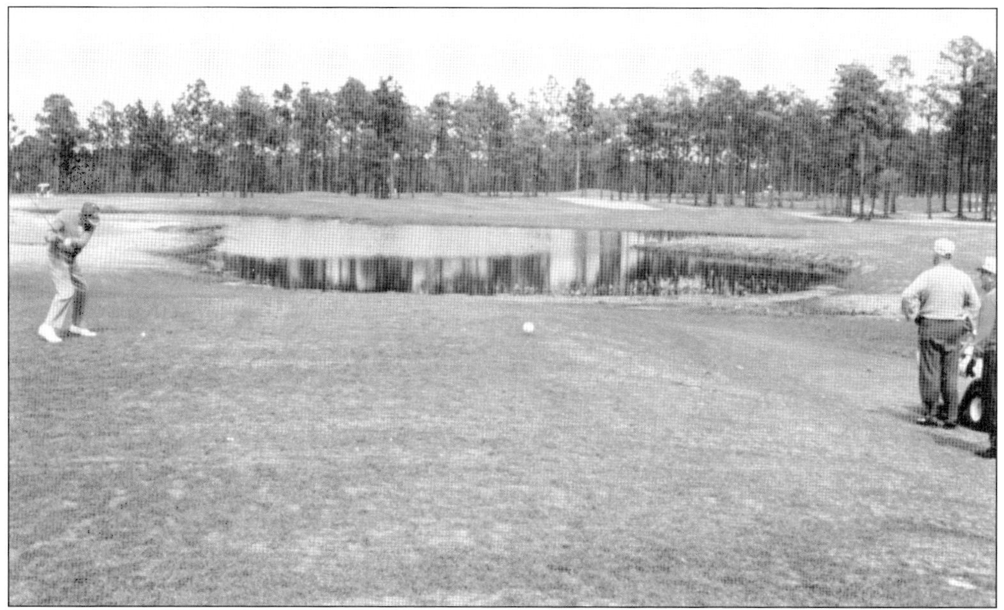

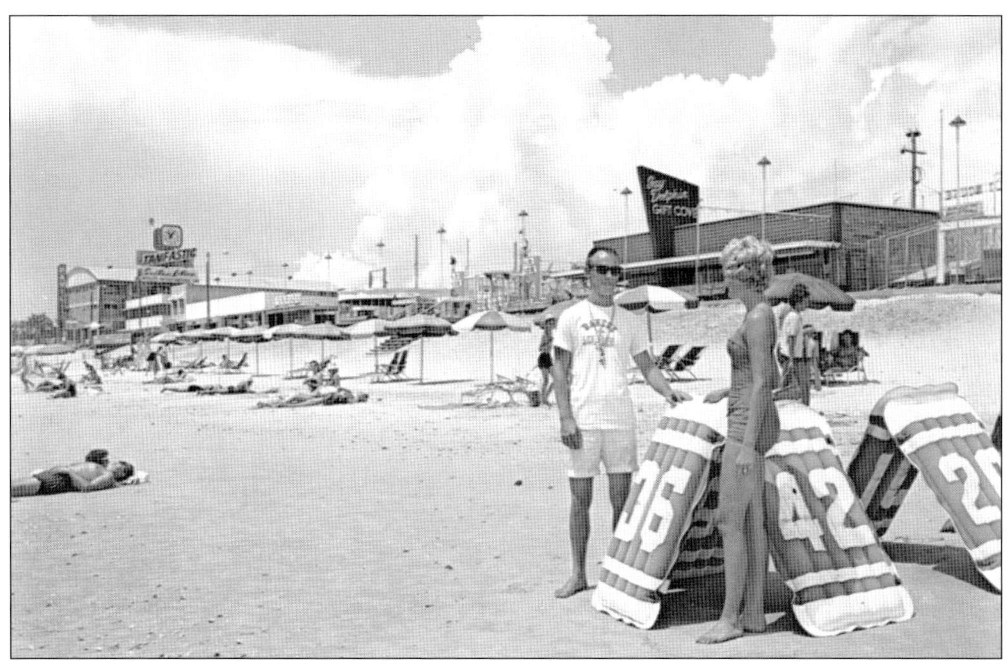

By the early 1970s, Myrtle Beach's population had tripled, and the city created more amenities to accommodate its transformation into a regionally noted city, allowing residents to find necessities and entertainment without having to travel. Some new attractions the city gained at this time include the Myrtle Beach Convention Center and the city's first shopping mall, Myrtle Square Mall, which opened in 1975 but was demolished in 2006. Below, a sign commemorating the 1976 opening of a Sears location at Myrtle Square Mall is shown. Above, Myrtle Beach's shoreline is shown at that time with the Gay Dolphin, a popular gift shop established in 1946, far in the background.

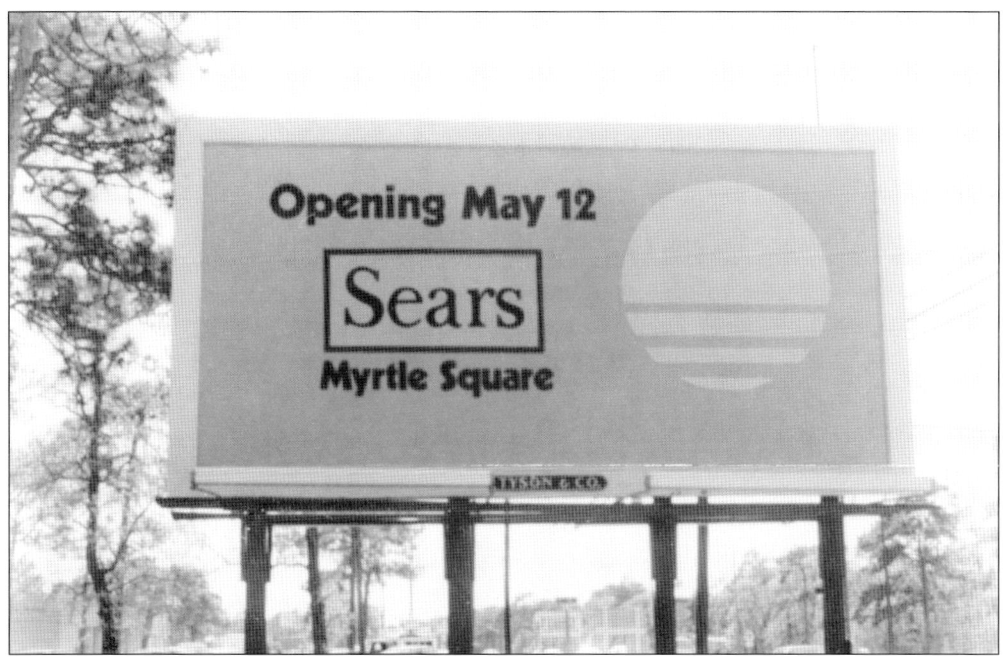

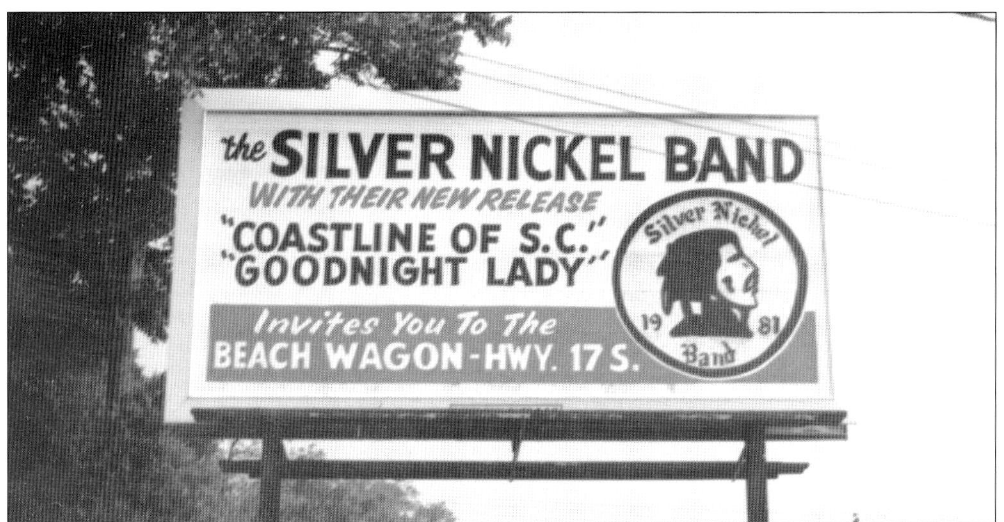

The later 20th century proved to be a turning point in Myrtle Beach's history with further development transforming both the city's atmosphere and its skyline. Though this period marked a prelude to the accelerating growth that came in the 1990s and on, many locals remember this period of Myrtle Beach's history as a time when nightlife, music venues, larger hotels, and other attractions became more present in the city. The image above, a billboard advertisement for a concert at the Beach Wagon (a country music venue) from 1983, gives an idea of the attractions available in Myrtle Beach at that time. The photograph below, taken in July 1990, shows an aerial view of tourists and automobiles cruising Ocean Boulevard adjacent to the Myrtle Beach Pavilion. Once a quiet stretch, Ocean Boulevard's transformation into an energetic street filled with crowds and vehicles over several decades is one that many can connect to Myrtle Beach's immense growth and change.

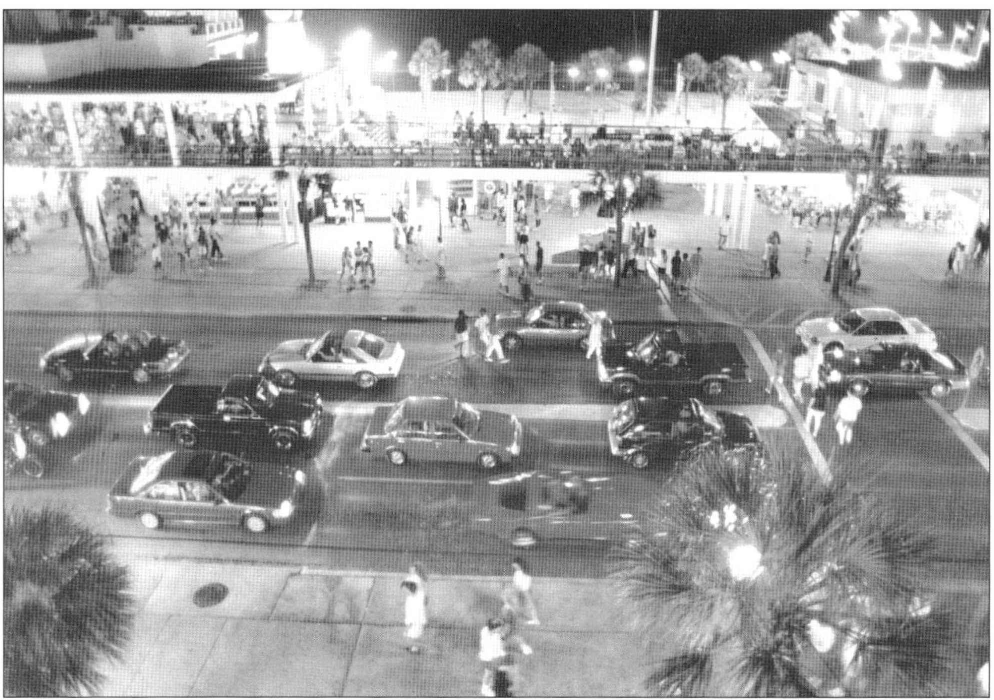

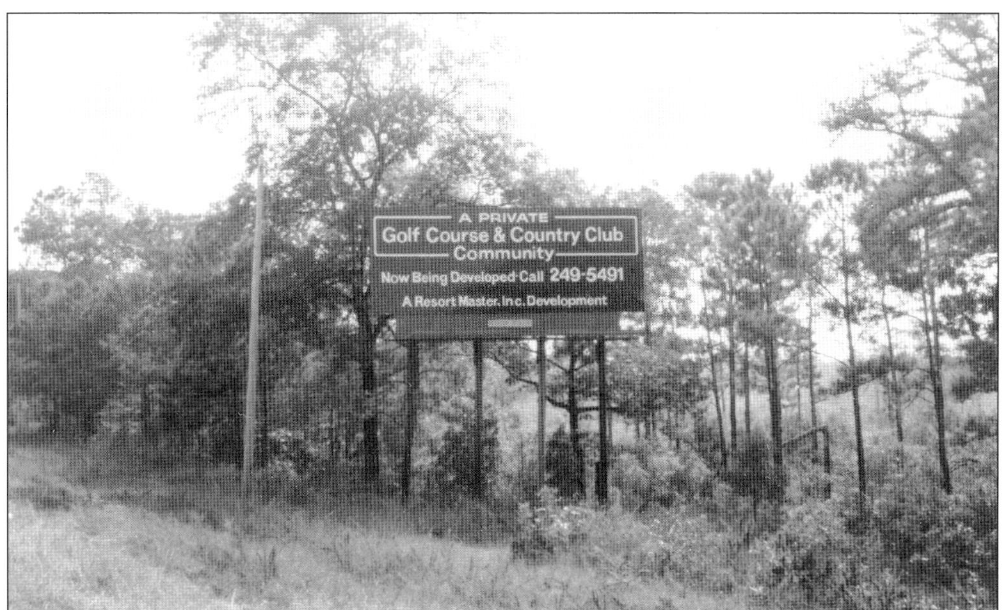

In the past three decades, Horry County has seen a population influx that categorizes the area as one of the fastest-growing regions in the United States. In a scene familiar to those who have lived in or visited Horry County since then, the 1988 image above displays an advertisement for a planned development. This is an early scene that represents the area's transformation from a quiet region to a busy one and is synonymous with the commercialism that has ensued in the region since the 1990s. Just as continued development and economic transformations in Horry County changed the ambience of the area, a decision synonymous with a shift in Myrtle Beach's atmosphere was the closure of the Pavilion, which was shuttered due to financial troubles. In the image below from 2006, the Pavilion's marquee reads its farewell message before it was demolished in 2007. (Below, courtesy of Kevin Fuller.)

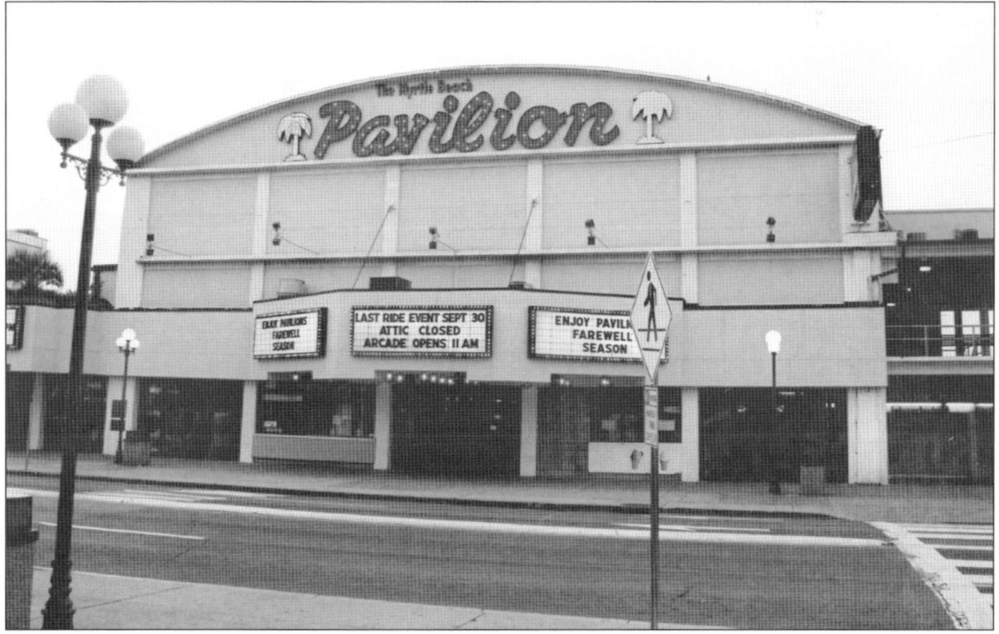

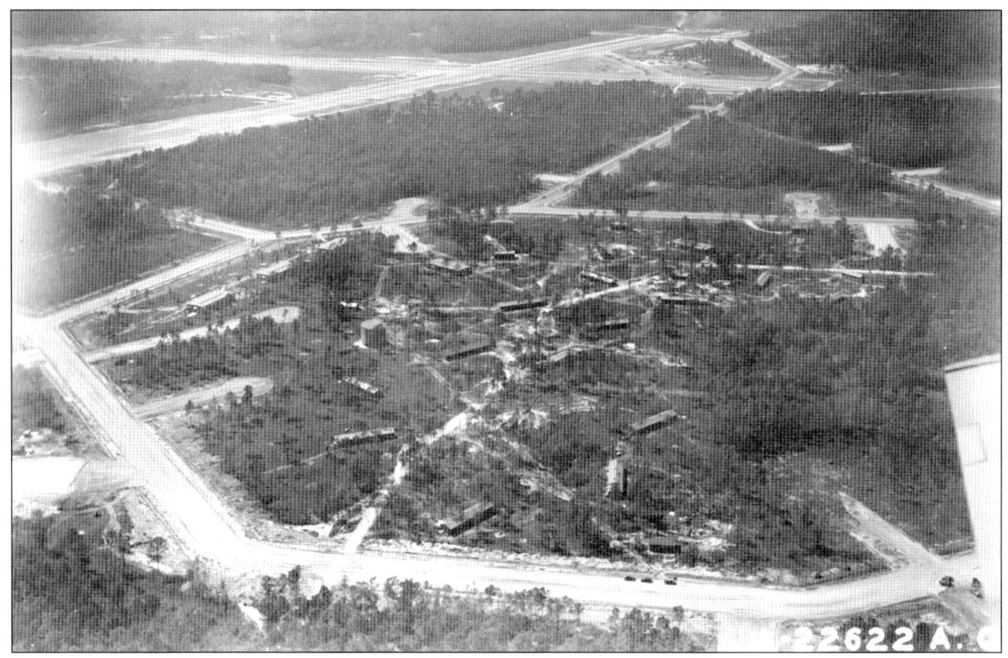

In 1940, the US War Department leased Harrelson Municipal Airport in Myrtle Beach. After roughly two years of the US Army Air Corps maintaining a presence there, the Myrtle Beach General Bombing and Gunnery Range was established in 1942. Over 55,000 acres in Horry County were used for the establishment of this site and the Conway Bombing and Gunnery Range. To make facilities this large, widespread eminent domain took place across Horry County, displacing thousands. Renamed Myrtle Beach Army Air Field in 1943, the base mostly consisted of temporary wooden buildings like the one seen below, which led to the site being nicknamed "Splinter City." A German POW camp was also housed on the base (but also temporarily existed near Seventieth Avenue North in Myrtle Beach). This site closed in 1947, and the property was given back to Myrtle Beach's city government for use as an airport. (Both, courtesy of the City of Myrtle Beach.)

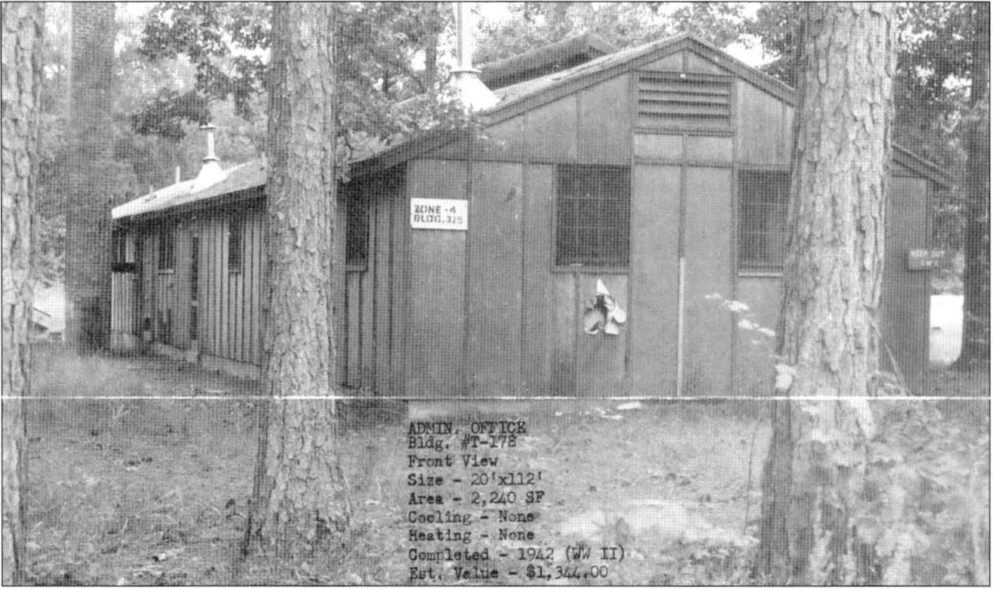

As was customary at the time, the Myrtle Beach General Bombing and Gunnery Range made matchbook covers and other ephemera. Some soldiers were known to tear large matchbook covers from the pack and mail them as miniature postcards. One can note the World War II–era slogan on this matchbook cover, "Keep 'em Flying," which was used by American manufacturing companies and the American military on various types of wartime propaganda. Though the site closed after World War II, within several years, military activities would again make a presence in Myrtle Beach. In 1954, the City of Myrtle Beach donated land to the US Air Force to establish another base there; it opened on December 7, 1956, and the facilities from the old airfield and municipal airport were largely destroyed to create modern amenities. A commemorative postal cover for the base's opening is seen below.

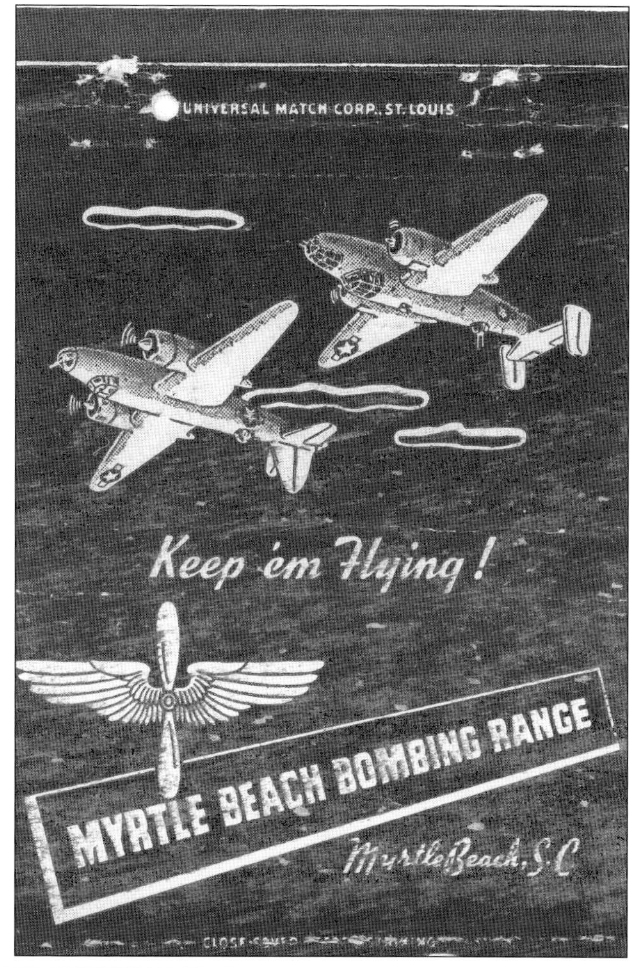

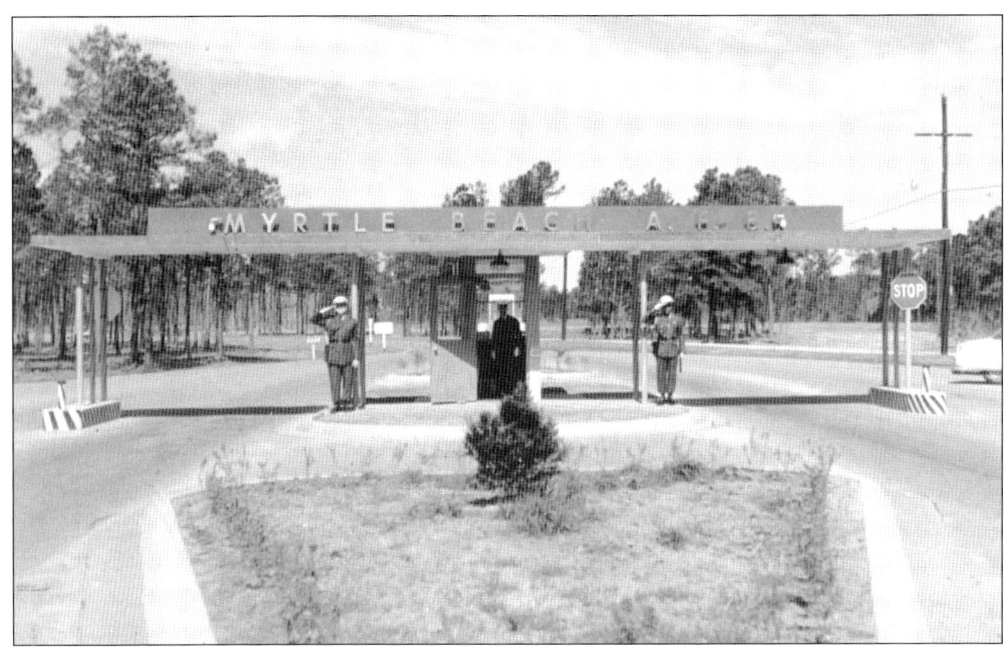

The final Myrtle Beach Air Force Base served as a vital component of the region's economy, and a postcard image of the base's entrance is shown above. For most of this base's history, the 354th Fighter Day Wing/Tactical Fighter Wing was its host unit. The base was vital during Operation Desert Storm and the Vietnam War. The base also gained notoriety for housing A-10 Warthogs, a popular aircraft used by the US military. The Horry County Jetport opened on the site in 1975, beginning shared use of this base between the military and civilians. A Piedmont Airlines advertisement for the airport in 1983 is seen below. Due to government funding cuts, Myrtle Beach Air Force Base closed in 1993. The airfield became Myrtle Beach International Airport in 1999, but much of the former base's land was redeveloped into the Market Common.

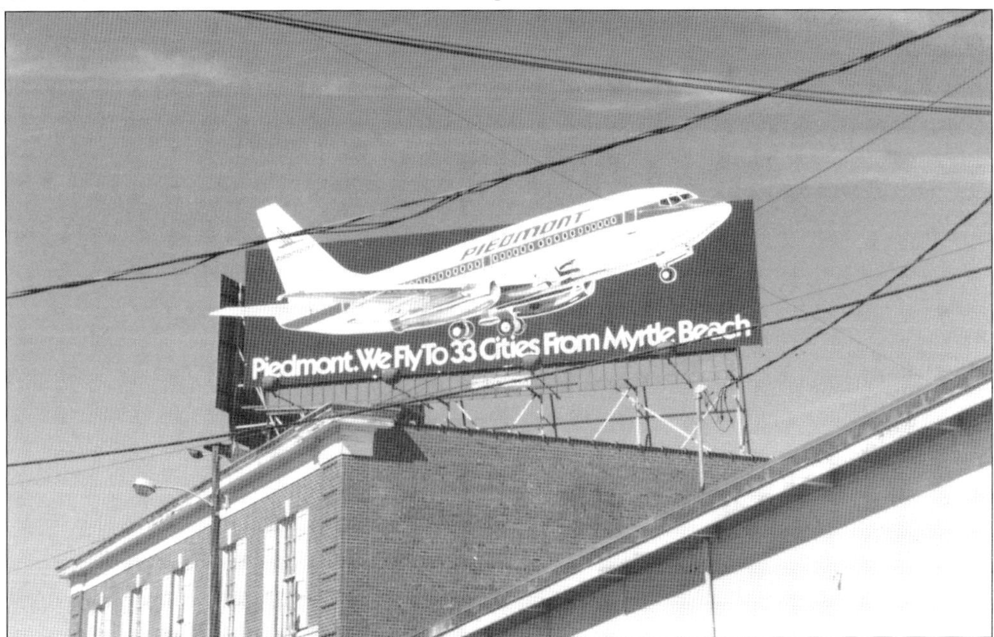

Two

The Foundations of Horry County

Conway and the Surrounding Area

Founded in 1732 as Kingston, the present-day city of Conway is one of South Carolina's oldest settlements and was planned by Royal Governor Robert Johnson. By 1735, when the community's first permanent settlers made their stays, farming had become the main source of economic activity, which continued throughout the 1700s. Initially a strongly pro-Royalist community due to its direct ties to England's monarchy (hence its name), Kingston was home to numerous Tories but was also the site of several encampments led by Gen. Francis Marion, South Carolina's iconic "Swamp Fox." After the Revolutionary War, Kingston, formerly part of the Georgetown District, was renamed Kingston County. In 1801, it was named Horry District for Gen. Peter Horry, a Revolutionary War hero. By the early 1800s, the town's name was changed to Conwayborough in honor of Robert Conway, a general in the South Carolina State Militia and local politician.

At this point, Conway was made up of roughly 100 people, reaching a population of 476 by 1860. It was incorporated for the first time in 1855, at a time when naval stores and related industries were paramount in the region. By the time of the eruption of US Civil War, residents of Conwayborough largely supported the Confederate cause, and two city residents, Thomas Beaty and Benjamin Sessions, signed the Ordinance of Secession in 1860. After the Civil War ended, troops from Maine occupied the town for a short time during the Reconstruction period. Conwayborough changed its name to Conway by 1883 and was reincorporated in 1898. In the ensuing decades, Conway would see its modern history commence with many of its residents serving as founders of Myrtle Beach or as farmers of tobacco, a cash crop that led to the area's economic growth in the early 20th century, both of which have had everlasting ties to the city's heritage and culture.

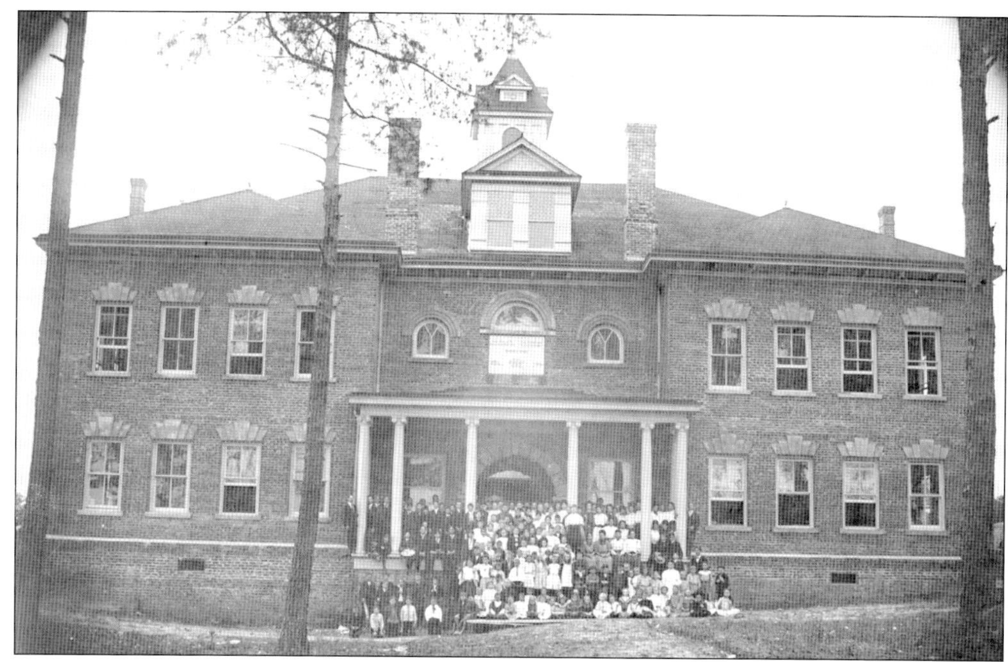

As Horry County is surrounded by swampy terrain, trade by land was limited prior to the development of the railway, which allowed Horry County to develop economically and industrially. In the image below, the Wilmington, Chadbourn & Conway Railroad is seen on Main Street in Conway; many of these wooden buildings in Conway's downtown were later destroyed in a massive fire in roughly 1897–1898. A stark change from a modern view of Main Street today, the train ran through Conway, where laborers transported timber and commodities to various locations. As many working families at this time were impoverished, education was a limited privilege many in Conway could not afford to obtain. At roughly the same time the above image was taken, the Burroughs School opened in 1905 in Conway as one of the city's first public schools for White children. By 2014, its building became home to the Horry County Museum. (Both, courtesy of the Horry County Museum.)

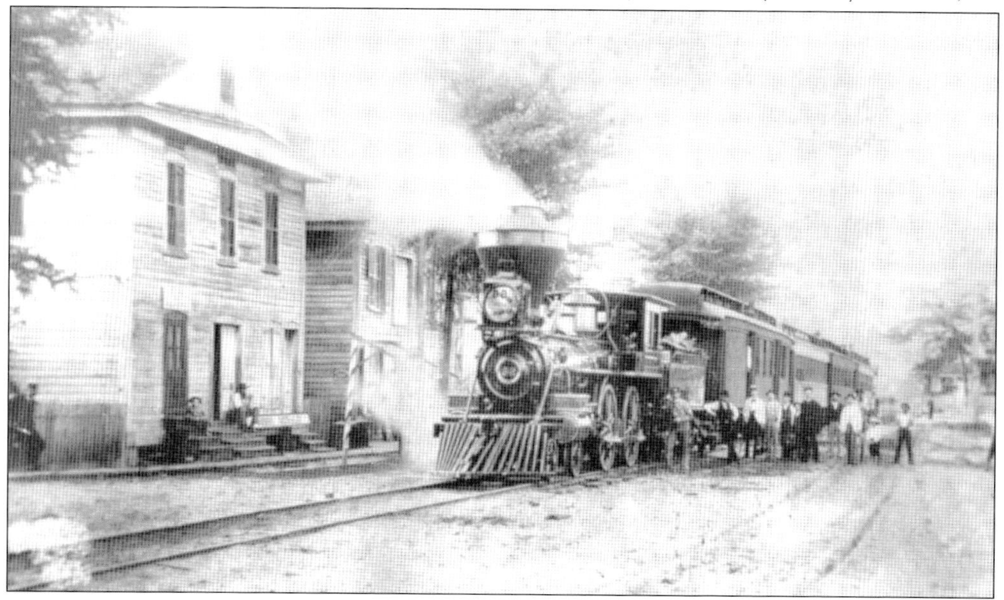

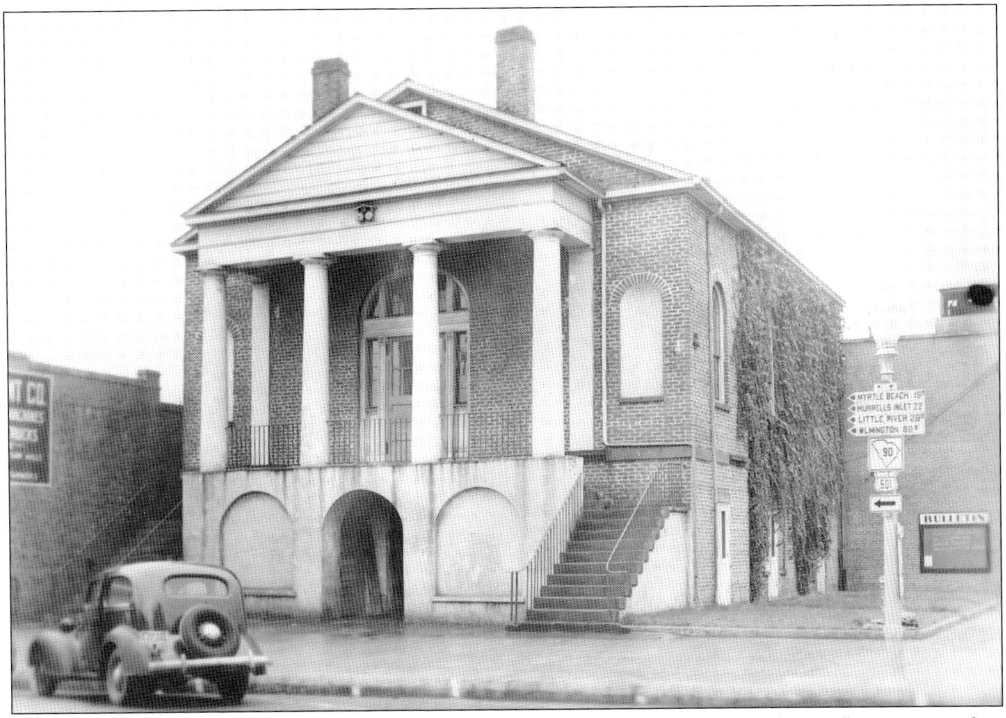

Seen above is Horry County's second courthouse, known as the "Old Courthouse," constructed in 1824. Designed by Robert Mills, a South Carolinian architect, the courthouse is also locally known as the "Mills Courthouse" and was sold to the City of Conway in 1908. As of 2024, it stands as Conway's city hall building. As a railroad once ran through the center of Conway, noise was said to interrupt court sessions, leading to the courthouse being relocated. Built in 1908, the present-day courthouse, seen below, underwent expansions in 1937 and 1964. Like many sites in Conway, both buildings have been placed in the National Register of Historic Places. (Above, courtesy of the University of South Carolina.)

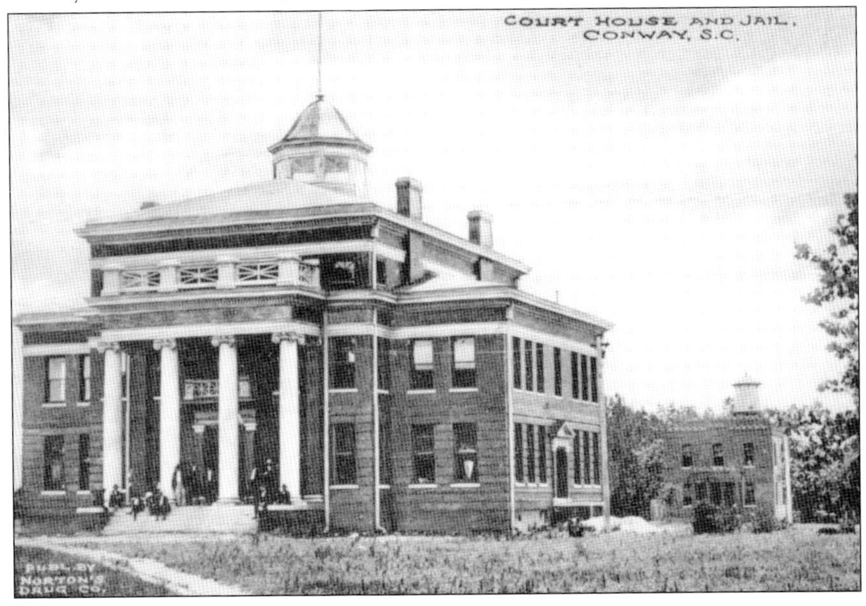

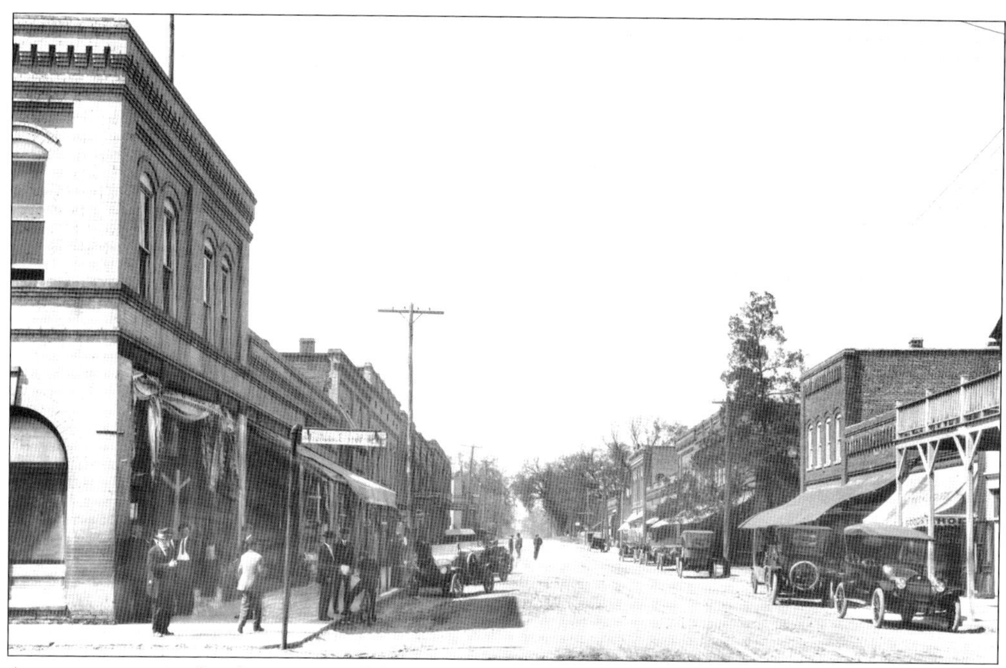

As one can see in the above image, Main Street in Conway by 1910 had vastly changed from prior periods, and new, brick buildings were constructed to replace wooden structures lost to fire. As of 2024, many of them still stand. The image below, from approximately 1928, shows Armistice Day, a holiday that marked the end of World War I, which at that time was the deadliest recorded global conflict. The holiday is now celebrated as Veterans Day. Though the latter image shows this celebration in the form of a postcard, it still allows one to see an example of Conway's general downtown ambience at that time, including the removal of the railroad tracks from Main Street. (Above, courtesy of the Horry County Museum.)

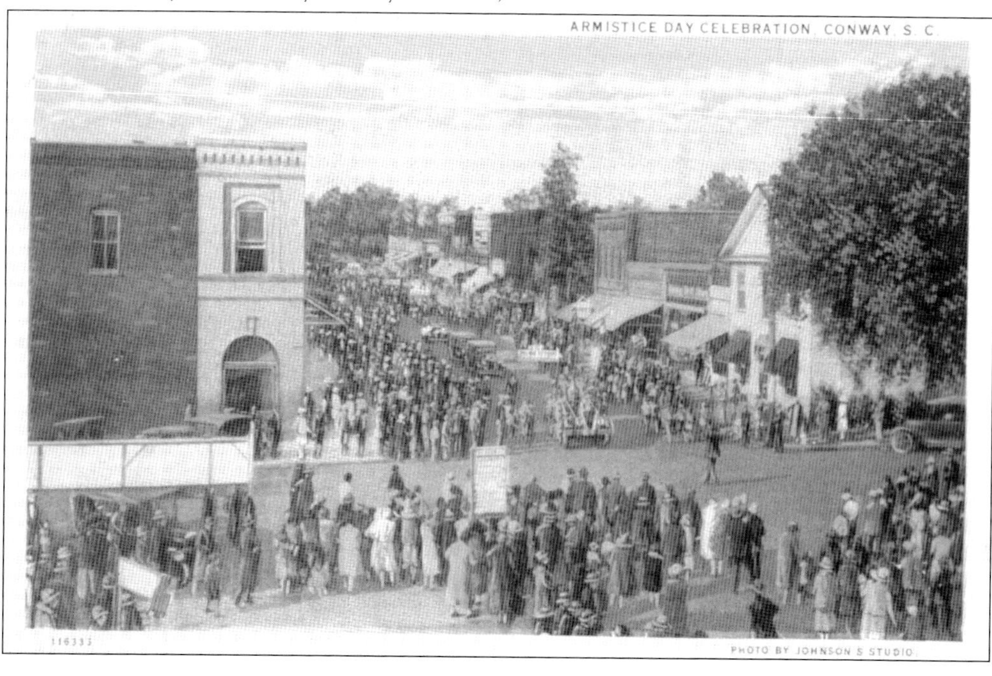

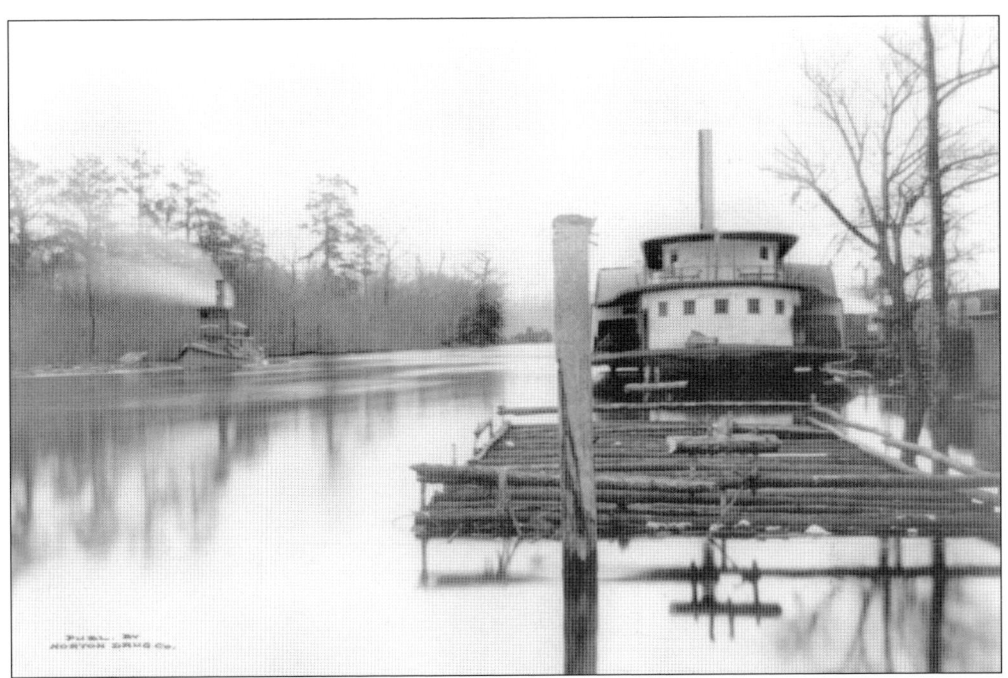

In September 1928, one of South Carolina's worst flooding events occurred as a result of rainfall from the Okeechobee Hurricane. Horry County was not spared, and the flooding that occurred was worse than that of 1924's Bigham's Freshet, another flood remarkably remembered in South Carolina's history due to residents superstitiously blaming the disaster on a local murder. Regardless, the 1928 flood saw local rivers, including the Waccamaw River, seen in these images, reach record heights, causing destruction. For example, the old Conway trestle bridge, a metal swing bridge built in 1912, was damaged and ultimately destroyed in the flood. In the image below from 1928, citizens can be seen sitting on top of the flooded bridge. (Both, courtesy of the Horry County Museum.)

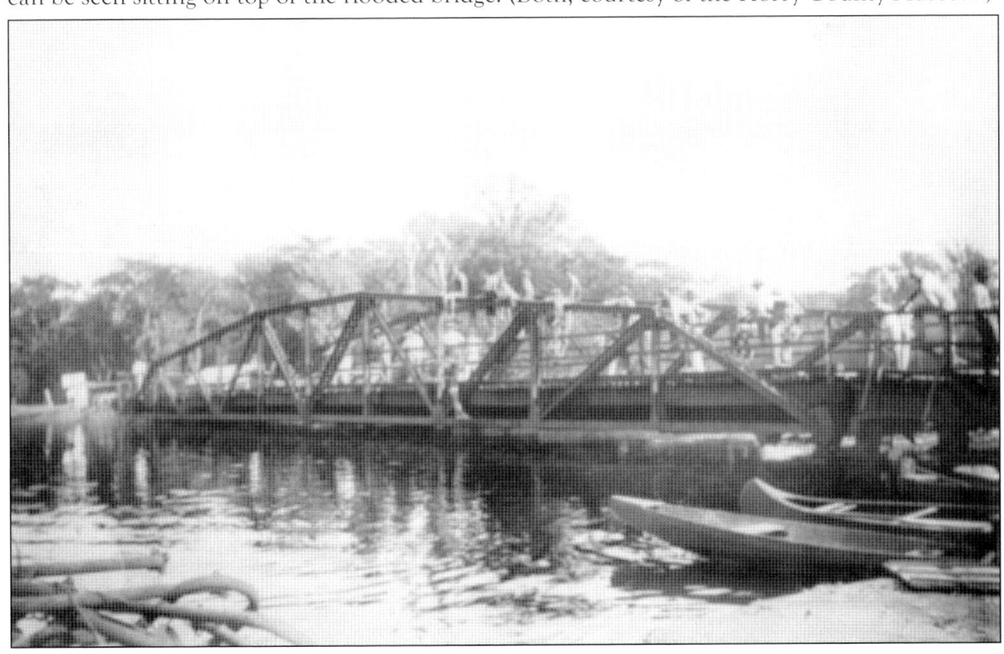

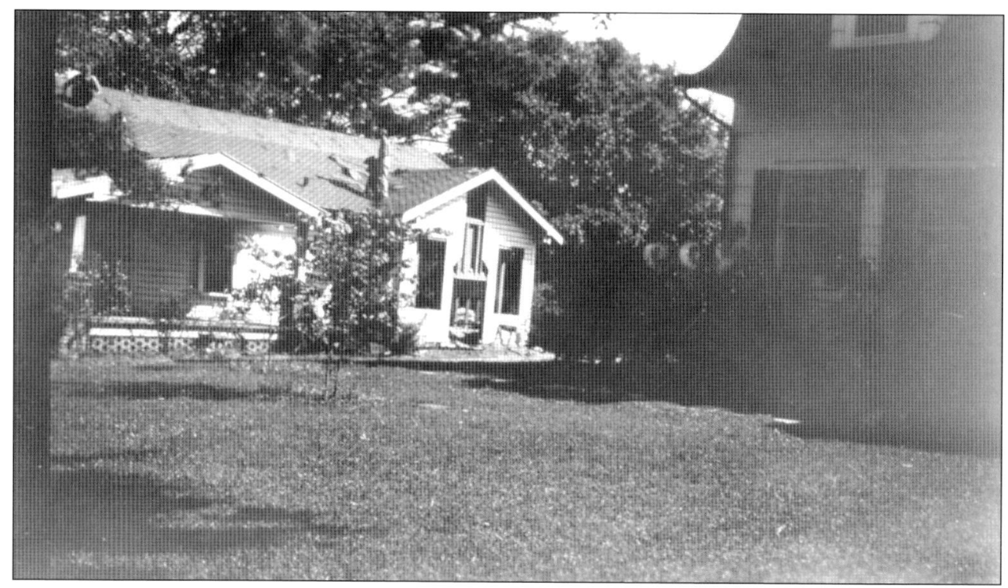

In the image above, construction on Elm Street in Conway is shown in 1928. Laborers can be seen completing construction on a home's roof and saving space to add a chimney. Research shows that this home was later moved to a nearby lot, while the home next to it (with its gilded roof partially shown) was expanded. Conway's residences in the early 20th century were constructed in a variety of architectural styles, but American Craftsman architecture is an especially prevalent design for residences in Conway from the 1920s. To show further infrastructural development Conway had within this decade, the 1928 construction of what appears to be sewage or waste utilities adjacent to the Atlantic Coast Rail line in the Conway vicinity is shown below.

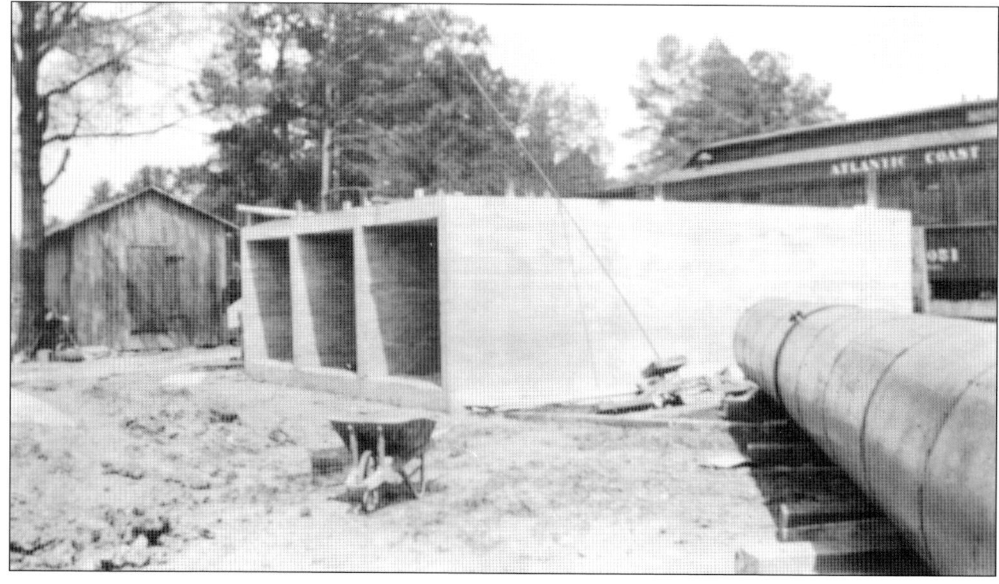

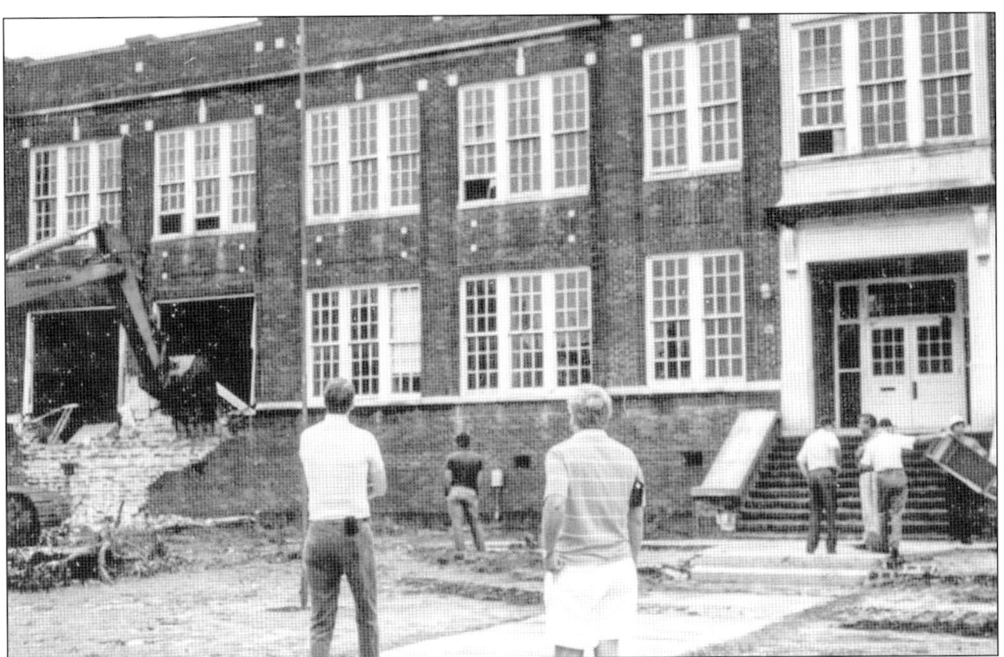

Construction on the original Conway High School began in 1928, and classes started in the building in 1929. Notably, Coastal Carolina Junior College, which eventually became Coastal Carolina University, held evening courses here from 1954 until 1958 when it was a satellite campus of the College of Charleston. The 1979 Conway High School class was the last to graduate in this building before it was demolished in 1988, which is seen here. (Courtesy of Horry County Museum.)

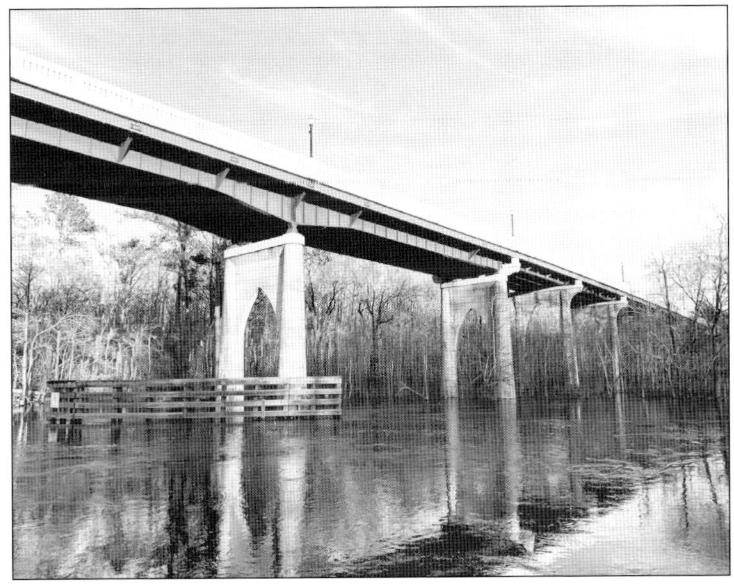

The Waccamaw River Memorial Bridge in Conway was built in 1937 by the Tidewater Construction Company and was designed by W.J. Gooding. The bridge, opened to the public in 1938, was deemed a memorial to Horry County veterans. It has been an essential route for automobile travel, especially as it was once one of the only ways to travel to and from Conway. (Courtesy of the Horry County Museum.)

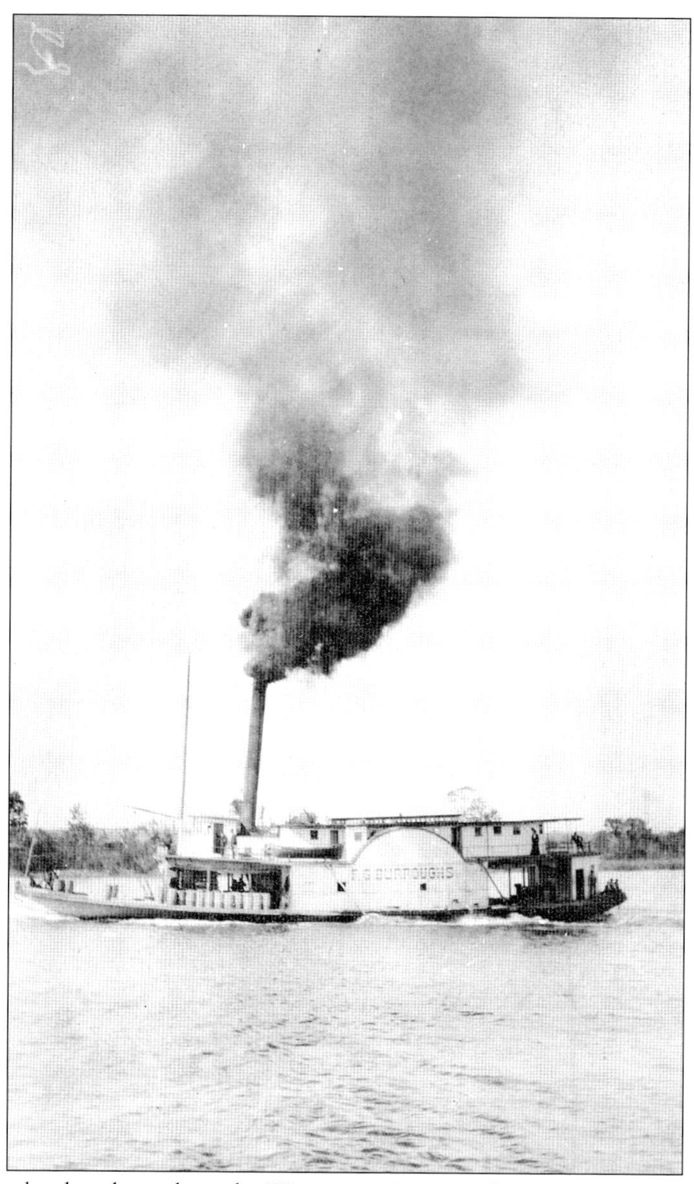

Though various landmarks such as the Waccamaw River and Kingston Lake are hallmarks of Conway's maritime history, the Burroughs and Collins Company, founded by Franklin Gorham "F.G." Burroughs, is largely credited with aiding in Horry County's growth into the 1900s. Founded in 1866, the Burroughs and Collins Company held interests in turpentine production. By 1882, the company acquired its first steamship, which would become part of the company's "Waccamaw Line of Steamers." The *F.G. Burroughs*, one of its iconic steamships, is seen in this image. These steamers allowed people across Horry County to travel to various local sites, as residents had not yet received large-scale access to railroads. These steamships encouraged travel from Conway to other ports, such as Georgetown or Bucksport, and helped aid Conway's (and Horry County's) economic interests. These steamships became obsolete by the 1900s. The Burroughs and Collins Company then turned its interest to railroads, founding the Conway & Seashore Railroad, which allowed travel into Withers, the community that eventually became Myrtle Beach, thus beginning the company's introduction into the tourism industry. (Courtesy of the Horry County Museum.)

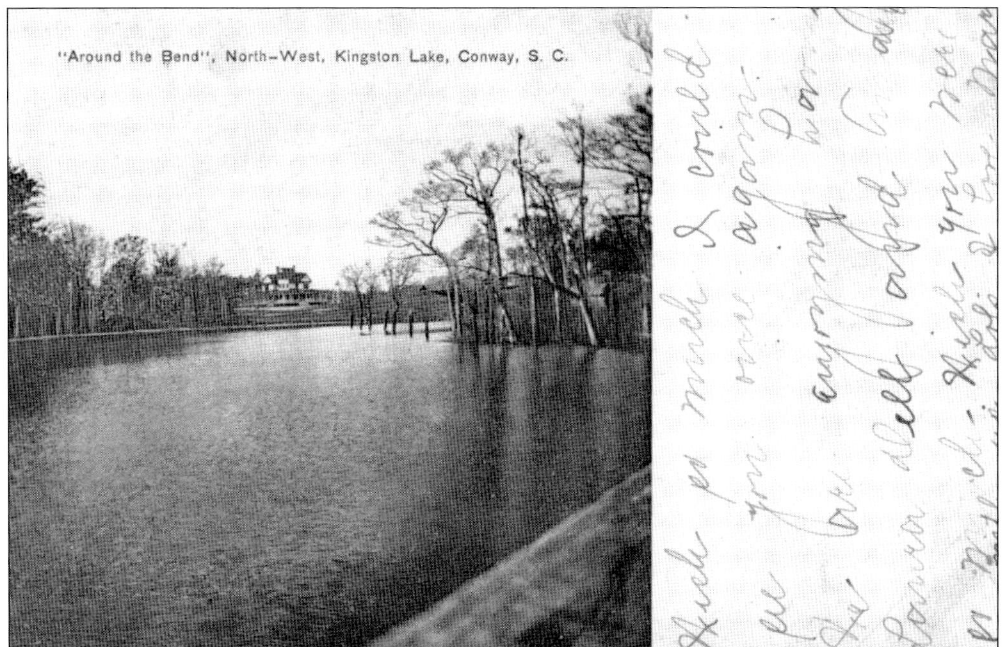

Sitting adjacent to the Waccamaw River is Kingston Lake, which served as a vital waterway for various industries. In this image from between 1900 and 1910, what is believed to be a railroad trestle that sat across Kingston Lake is seen. Though several automobile bridges have been built across the lake, one bridge constructed in the 1920s is infamous for its involvement in a catastrophic vehicle crash.

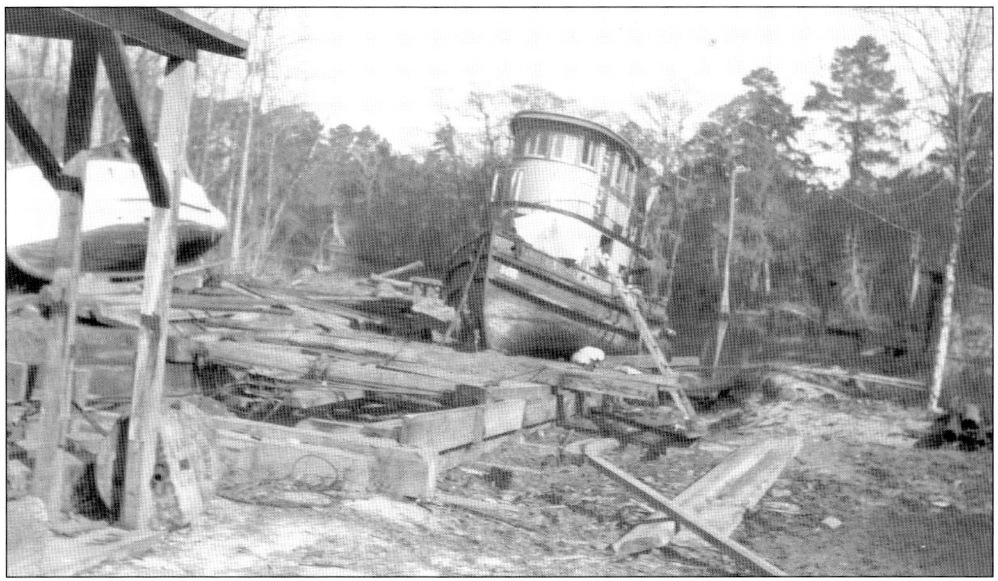

In the days before reliable automobile transport and paved roads, the Waccamaw River provided invaluable transport for locals who could drive vessels to the Atlantic Ocean, Winyah Bay, and other nearby locations. In this 1935 image, members of the Stilley family of Conway are seen repairing their vessel, *Elizabeth*. In the background is a wooden landing that allowed them to guide the boat back on the Waccamaw River.

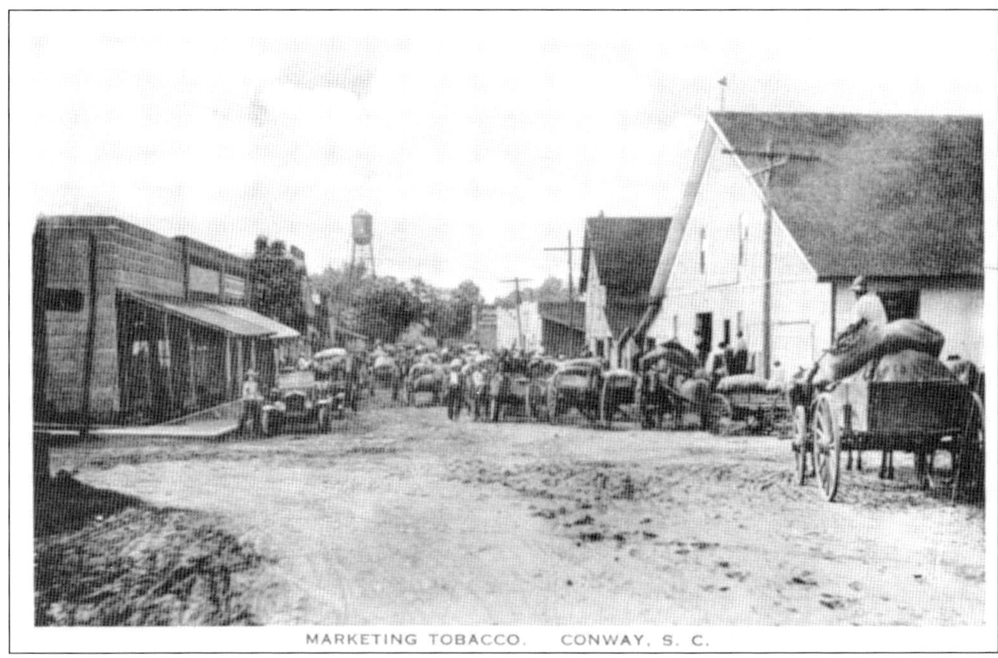

Though the turpentine, naval store, and timber industries were once vital to Horry County, tobacco, nicknamed "long green," quickly became a backbone of the local economy, especially throughout the 20th century. Sources indicate that South Carolina's first tobacco market was opened in Conway in 1899. The community of Galivants Ferry is largely credited with increasing tobacco's relevance in the region, but the crop itself was grown by farmers all across Horry County and the Pee Dee. Though many tobacco farms existed in rural parts of Horry County, transporting tobacco to market in larger towns was the biggest challenge farmers faced to secure a profit from their pursuits. Below, an advertisement for a Conway tobacco market is seen, while the image above shows a general view of a typical Horry County tobacco market in the early 20th century. (Both, courtesy of the Horry County Museum.)

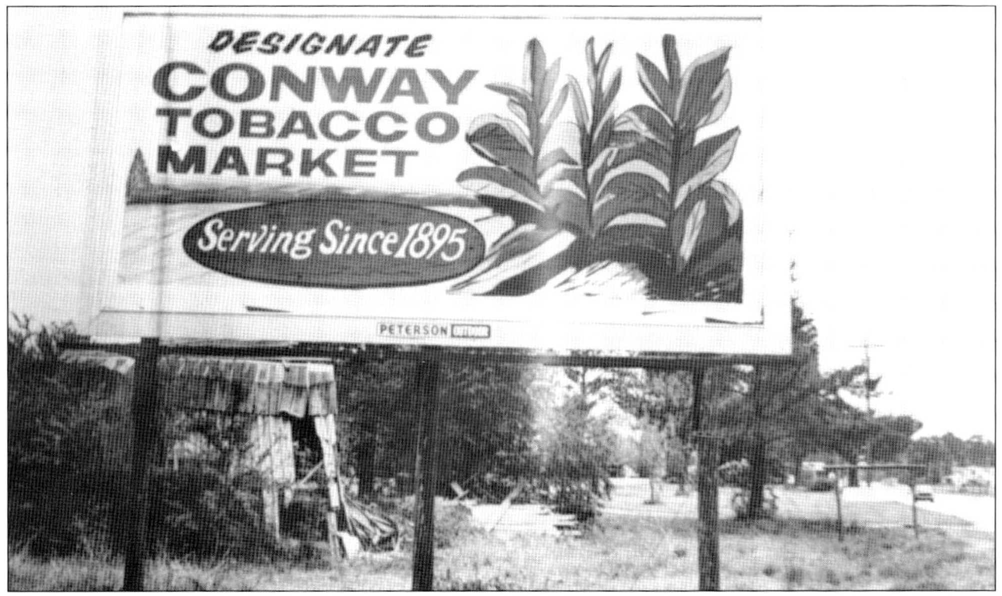

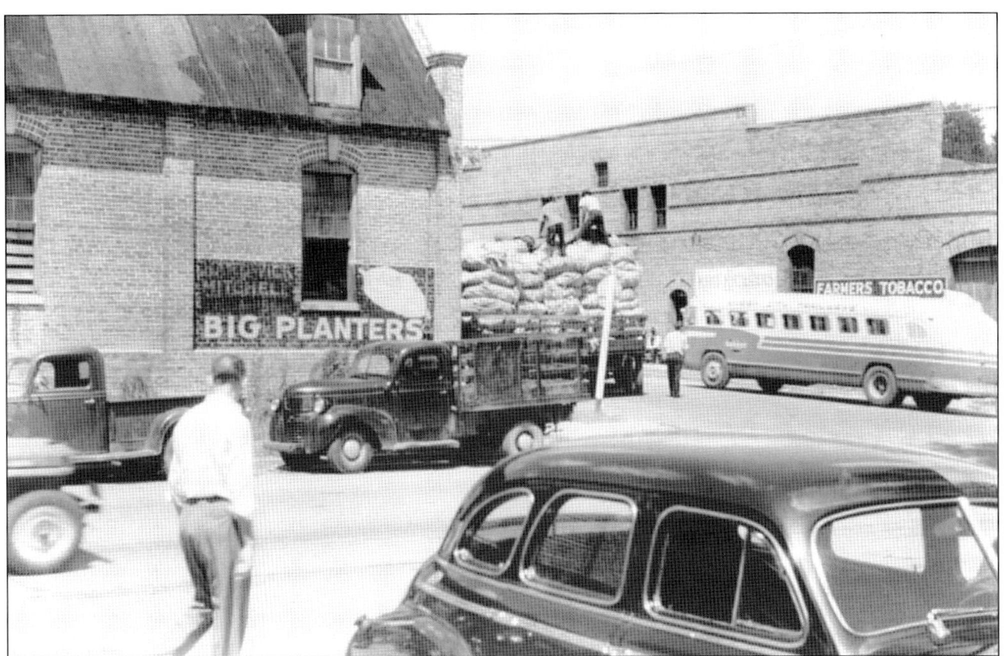

Once the process of drying and curing tobacco was completed, the crop was taken from tobacco barns (also called pole barns), packed, and sold. In the 1937 image above, one can see flatbed trucks used by farmers to bring tobacco to market in Conway. Tobacco markets were normally located close to downtown areas, where farm workers would gather and sell their tobacco to various business owners and manufacturers once their crops were ready to be made into various products. The 1977 image below is a scene from one of Horry County's tobacco markets. (Above, courtesy of Horry County Museum; below, courtesy of the South Carolina Department of Archives and History.)

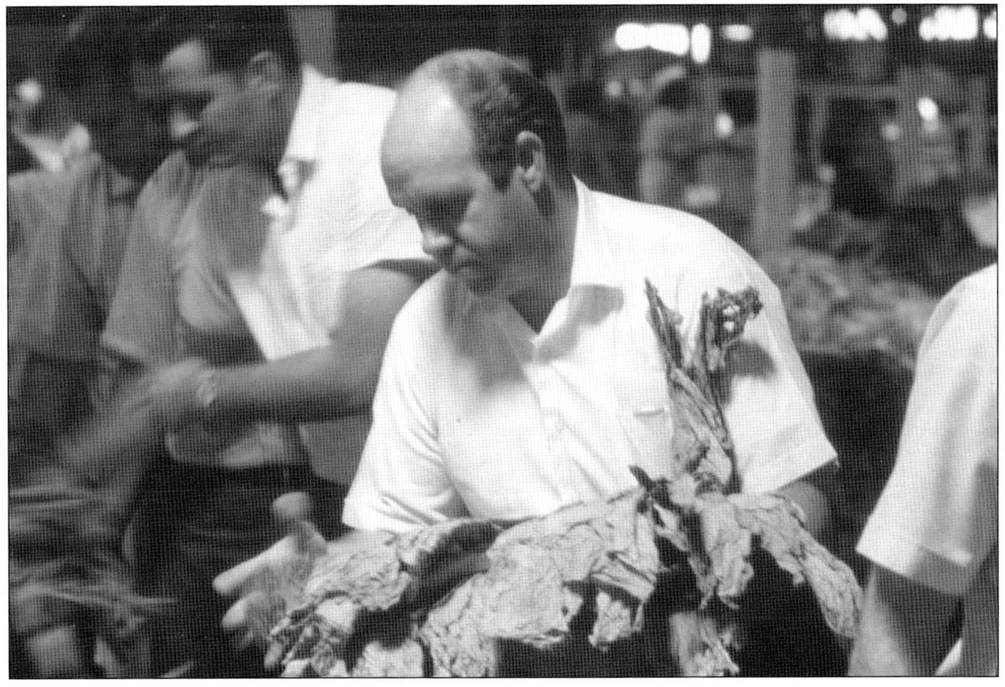

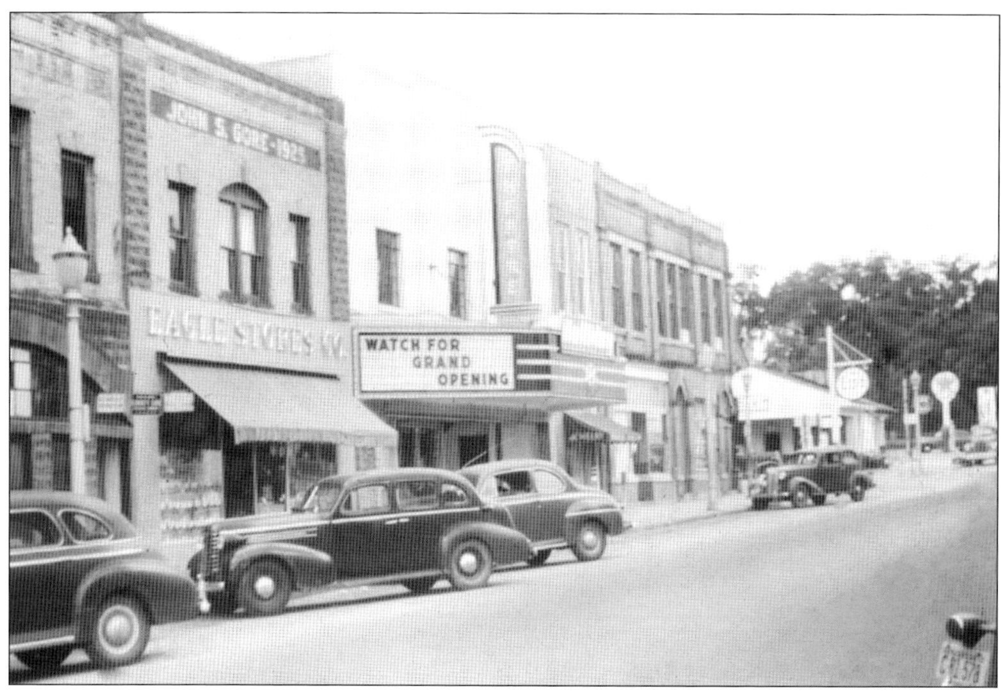

Between 1930 and 1950, Conway's population doubled, and tobacco agriculture continued to have a strong impact on the community. Some of the community's most famed buildings were constructed during this period. For instance, the Art Deco cinema seen above, first called the Holliday Theatre (built around 1940), eventually became Conway's beloved Theatre of the Republic in 1969. Conway's growth trends continued into the 1950s and 1960s, adding roughly 2,500 residents during this period, at a time when most of the region experienced an economic uptick. Seen below is the 1950 Conway Christmas Parade. (Below, courtesy of Horry County Museum.)

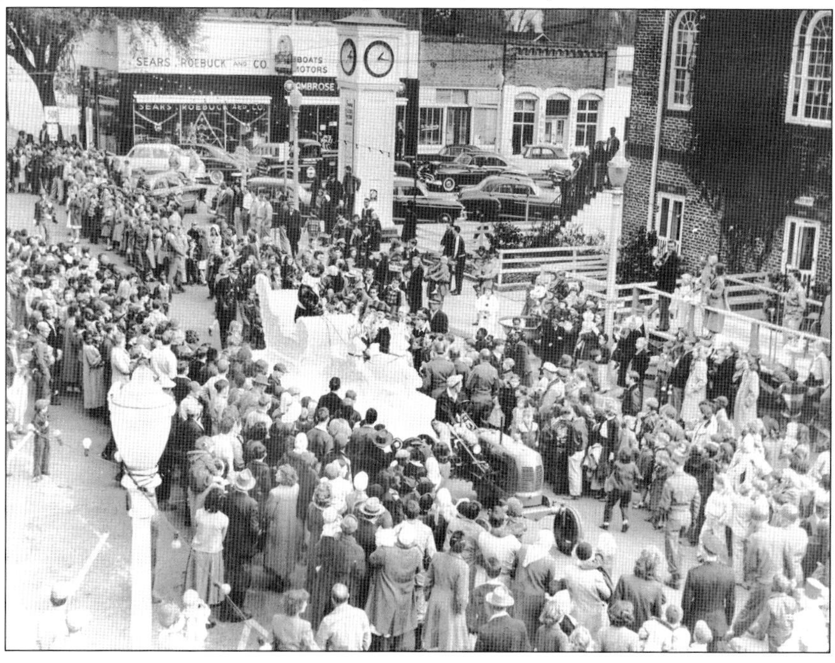

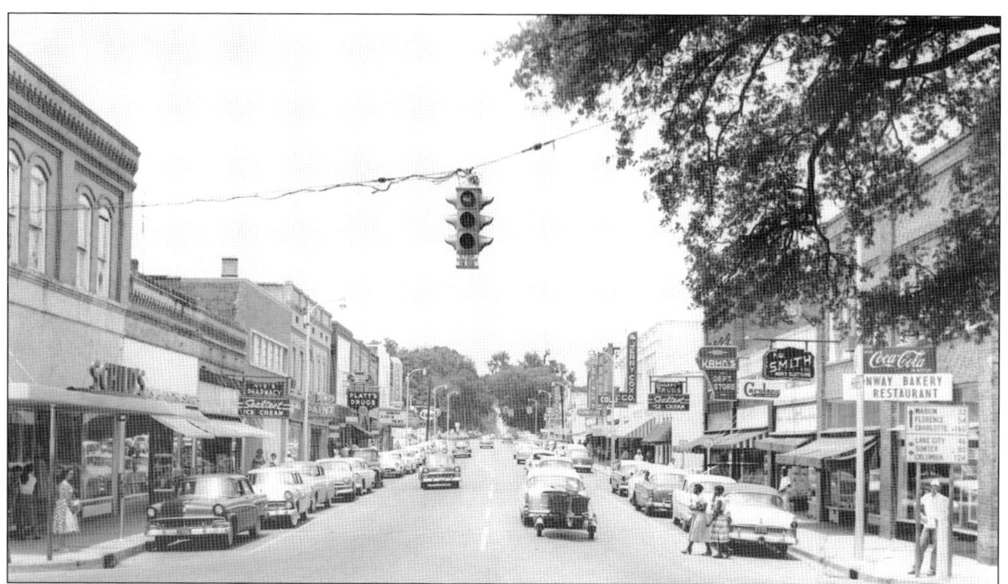

By the 1950s, more buildings were constructed in Conway's downtown area that help constitute the Conway Downtown Historic District, which is in the National Register of Historic Places. A view of a thriving scene of downtown Conway in 1957 is seen above. Below, several of Conway's sites are seen in a mid-20th century view showing Main Street from Fifth Avenue. One major landmark shown is the historic Conway Post Office, built between 1935 and 1936 using funds from the US Department of the Treasury. The first federal post office in Conway, it is an example of New Deal–era buildings constructed during the Great Depression and features architecture in the Classical Revival style. It ceased operations as a post office in 1977 but was subsequently used as the location of the Horry County Museum for four decades. (Above, courtesy of Horry County Museum.)

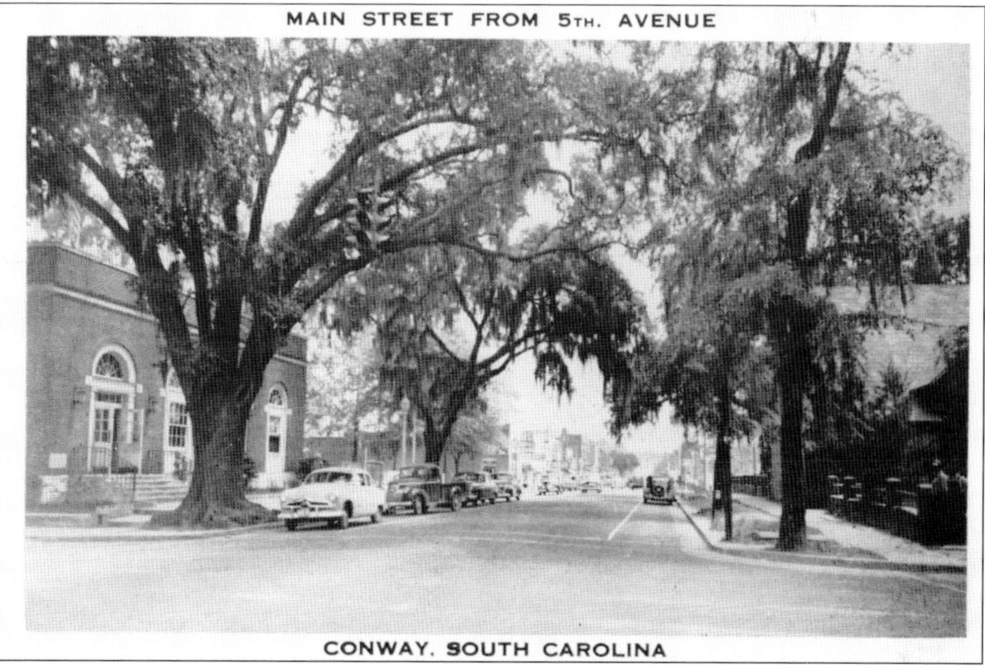

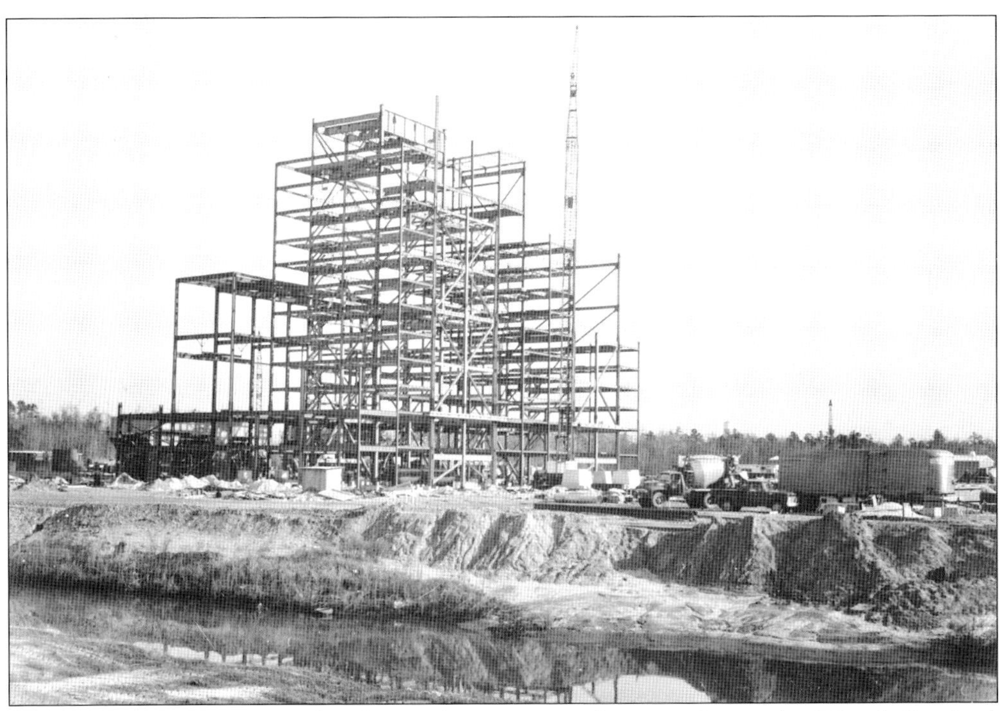

Consistent with the industrial and manufacturing growth Horry County (and South Carolina) saw in the mid-20th century, the Dolphus M. Grainger Generating Station was constructed by 1966 and owned by Santee Cooper, providing electricity to the Conway vicinity. It employed many Horryites in the industrial sector before being closed in 2012 and demolished in 2016. Its cooling source, Lake Busbee, was artificially created from wetlands in the 1960s but was eventually drained in 2018 due to contamination concerns. A man-made reservoir, Lake Busbee also represented Conway's industrial growth in the later 20th century and was an essential component of goals to power the region. (Both, courtesy of the University of South Carolina.)

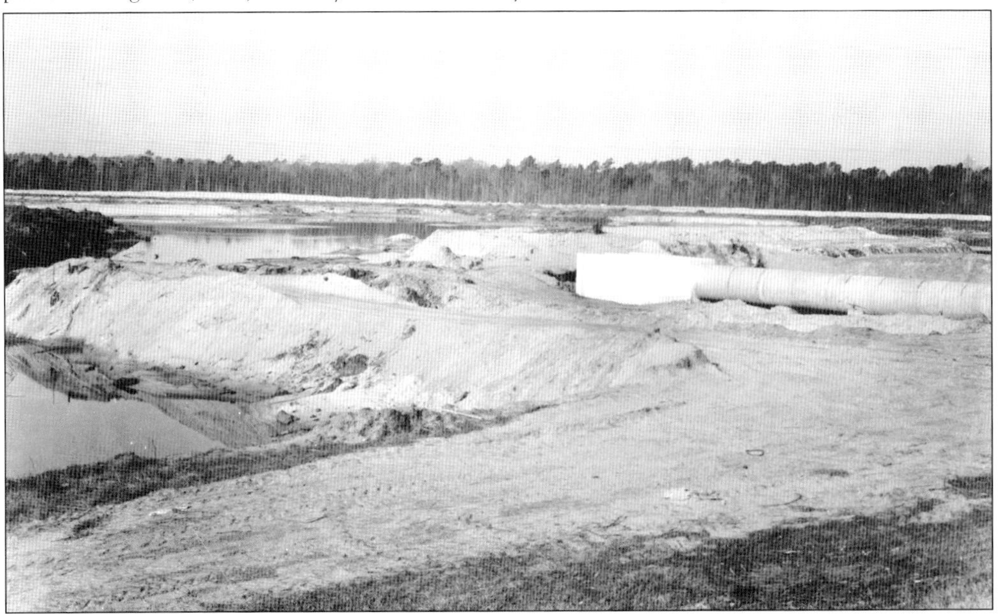

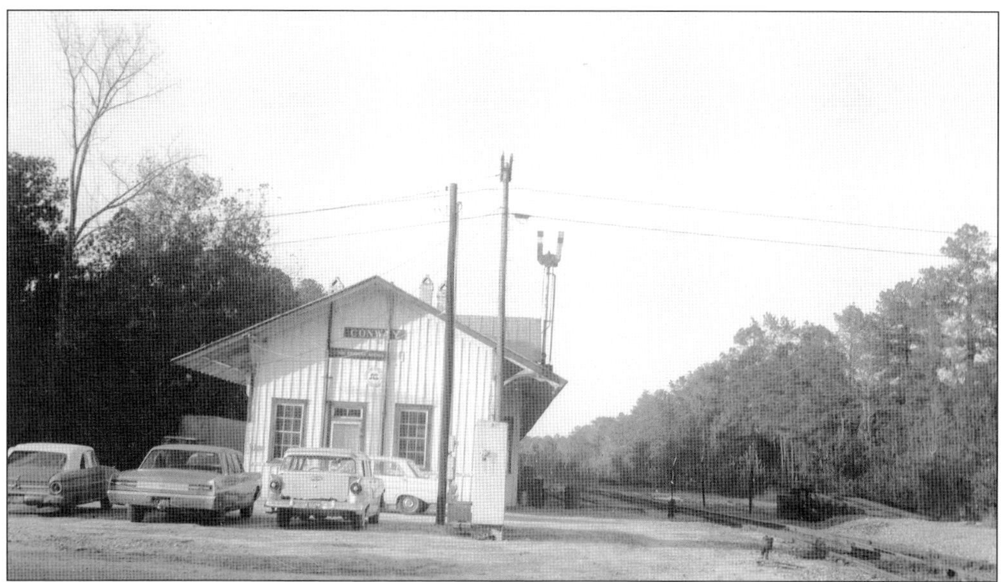

A hallmark of Horry County's history, Conway's Atlantic Coast Line Railroad Depot (above) was built in 1928. The Atlantic Coast Line Railroad bought rail lines into the Conway vicinity in the early 1900s, including the Conway Seashore Railroad and the Wilmington, Chadbourn & Conway line. It is said that pushback caused by the railroad's existence in downtown Conway led to the railroad being rerouted and this depot being erected. Almost a century old as of 2025, it is now in the National Register of Historic Places. In the later 20th century, Horry County's railroads were threatened with closure, leading to momentum to save the historic and economically vital railroad, conveyed in the image below. Horry County subsequently purchased this railroad and leased it to several entities in the following decades. (Above, courtesy of the Horry County Museum.)

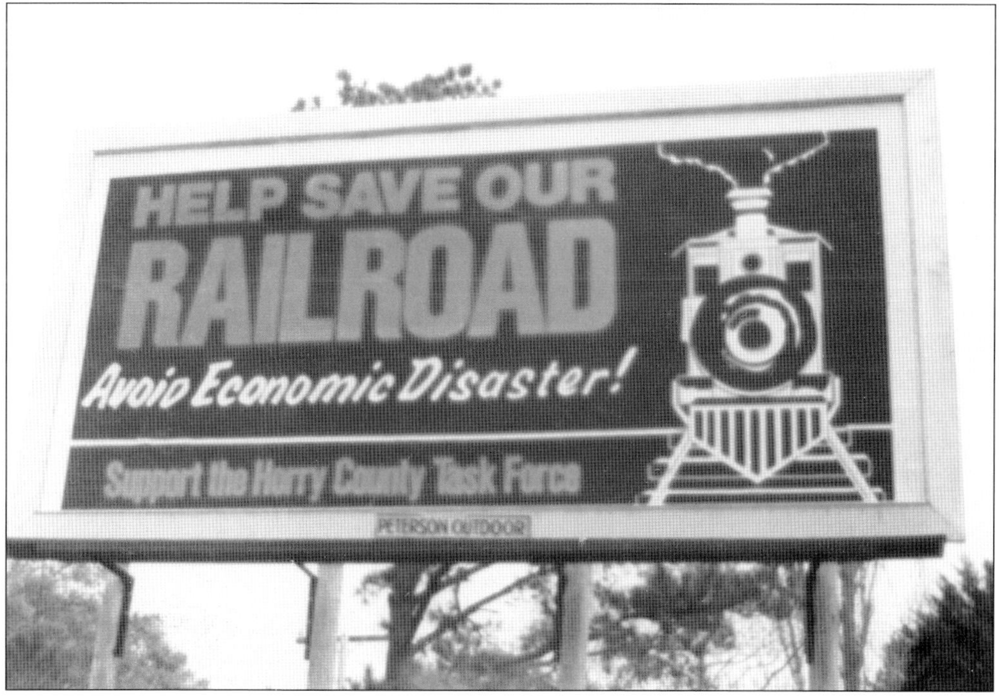

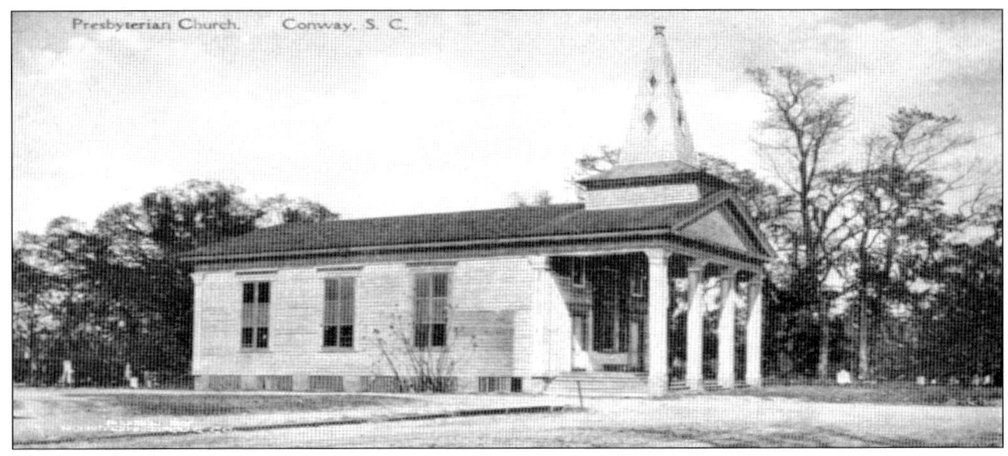

Like many of Horry County's communities, religion is important to Conway's heritage, and the city holds many historic churches. A Presbyterian congregation in this community dates to at least 1756; it disbanded by 1795 but was later reorganized. This reorganized congregation founded the Kingston Presbyterian Church, whose building dates to 1858. The First United Methodist Church of Conway held the historic Hut Bible Class, which was formed during World War I when soldiers from Horry County serving in France worshipped in a building they called the "Hut." After returning to the United States, the class worshipped in several temporary buildings in Conway. Later, the class moved into the First United Methodist Church's original sanctuary after the congregation relocated to an adjacent Mission-style sanctuary constructed in 1934, seen below. In 1987, members of the Hut Bible Class restored the church's original sanctuary to its current state. (Above, courtesy of the Horry County Museum.)

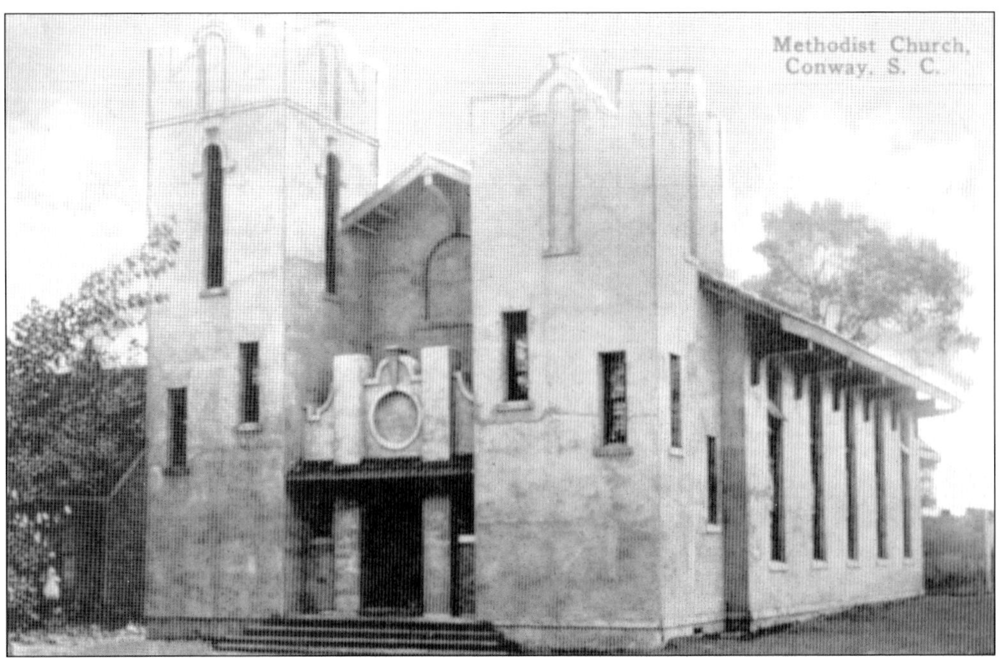

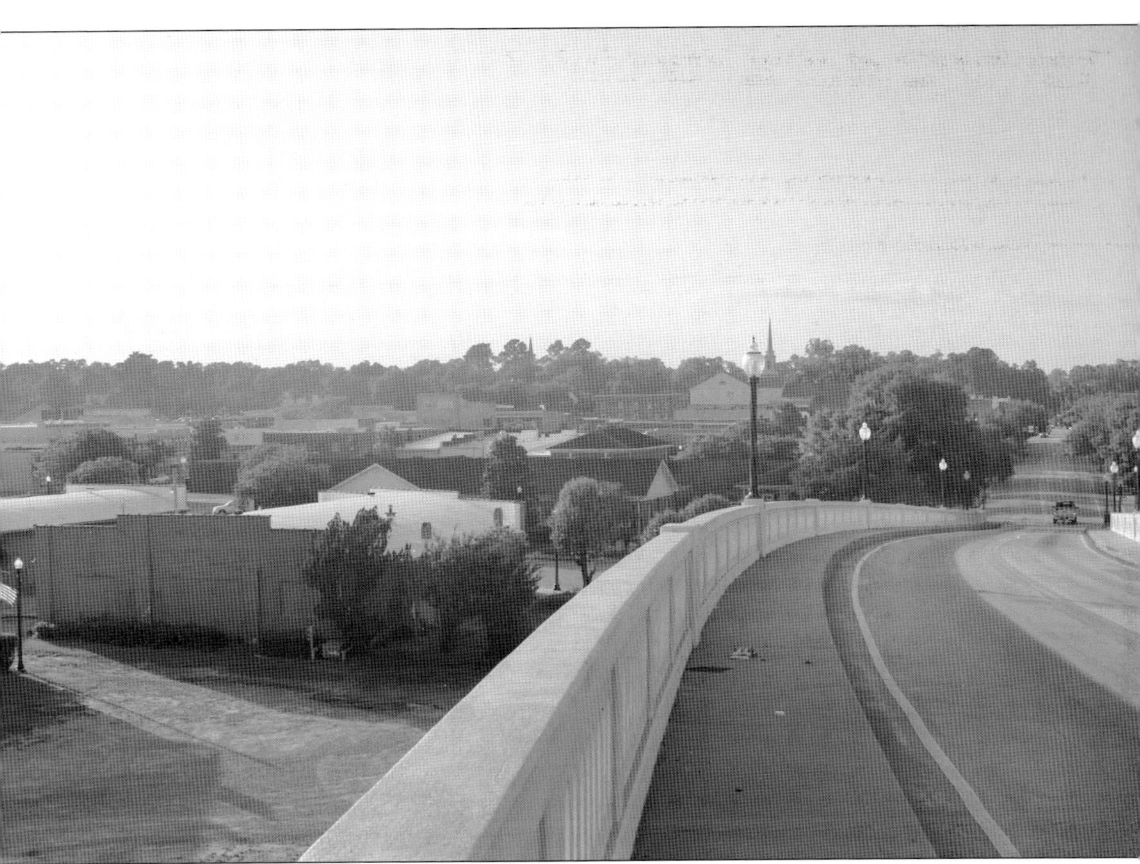

Seen from the top of the historic Waccamaw River Memorial Bridge is an aerial view of the city of Conway in 2021, which captures the city's contemporary atmosphere. One can see the numerous church steeples that make up Conway's skyline and remind one of the community's deep spiritual culture. Near these steeples are also the roofs of numerous century-old brick buildings that housed long-standing businesses and that now hold a variety of enterprises representing Conway's vibrant and diverse community. Conway's former Peanut Warehouse, a century-old historic building, is seen in the left corner. Preservation in Conway has not been a bashful topic, as many locals proud of the city's heritage and culture have supported efforts to preserve Conway's beauty and maintain its historic charm as Horry County's "Rivertown."

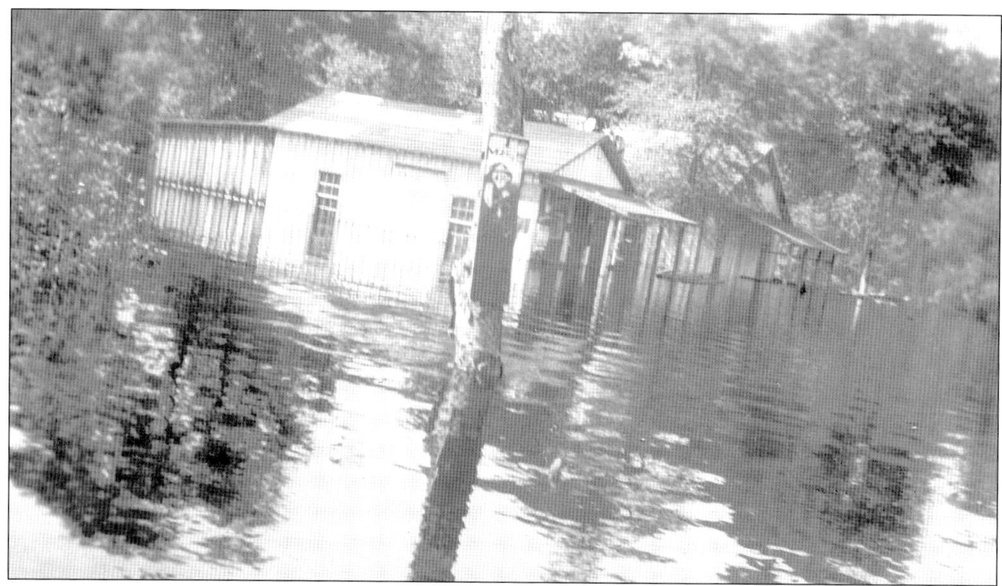

Like many other unincorporated communities in Horry County, Toddville, located southeast of Conway, is largely made up of farmland, and tobacco was cultivated there well throughout the 20th century. Historically, the community was also the site of a turpentine operation. In this image, what is believed to be the Toddville boat landing is seen inundated during the great flood of 1928.

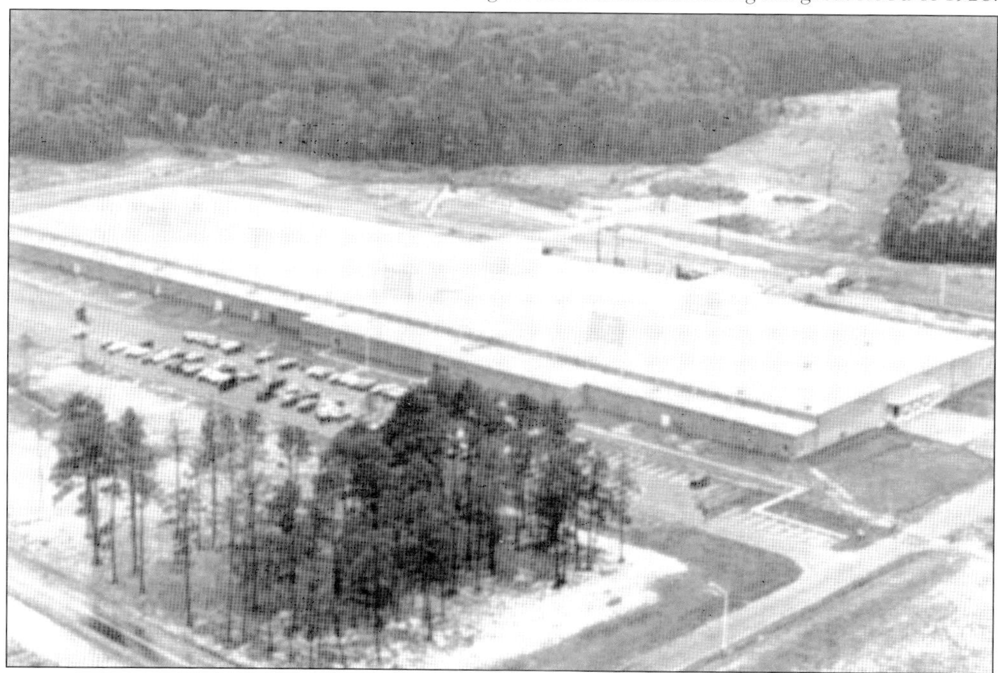

Some of central Horry County's unincorporated places include farming-based communities such as Homewood, Allsbrook, Allen, and Adrian. Though traditionally reliant on agriculture, as farming became less lucrative throughout the later 20th century, people in these communities became reliant on manufacturing work for employment. This textile mill, which was located in Adrian, is one example of factories where local residents found employment. (Courtesy of the Horry County Museum.)

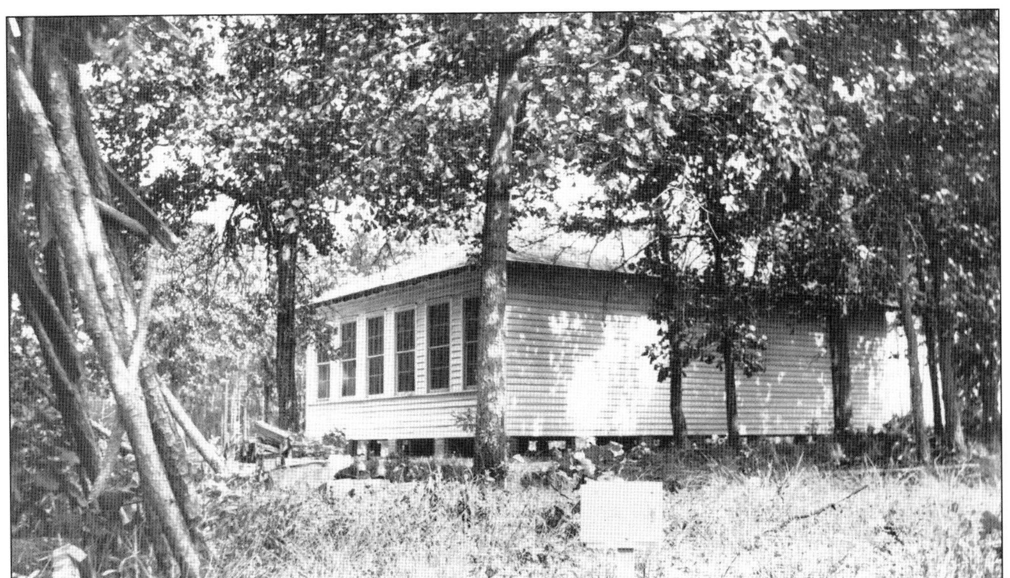

One of several unincorporated communities no longer in existence is Eldorado, which existed from the late 1880s until roughly 1930. Though the origins of Eldorado's name are presently unknown for certain, it was an agricultural community that relied on tobacco cultivation. It also held several businesses and separate schools for Black and White children, including one named the Alligator School. The Eldorado Colored School is seen above in 1936. Though Eldorado reached its peak population in the 1920s, by the onset of the Great Depression, many of its residents left to find more reliable work in neighboring towns, including the former Simpson Creek Township, which was largely made up of farmers. A school in the Simpson Creek community is seen below. (Both, courtesy of the Horry County Museum.)

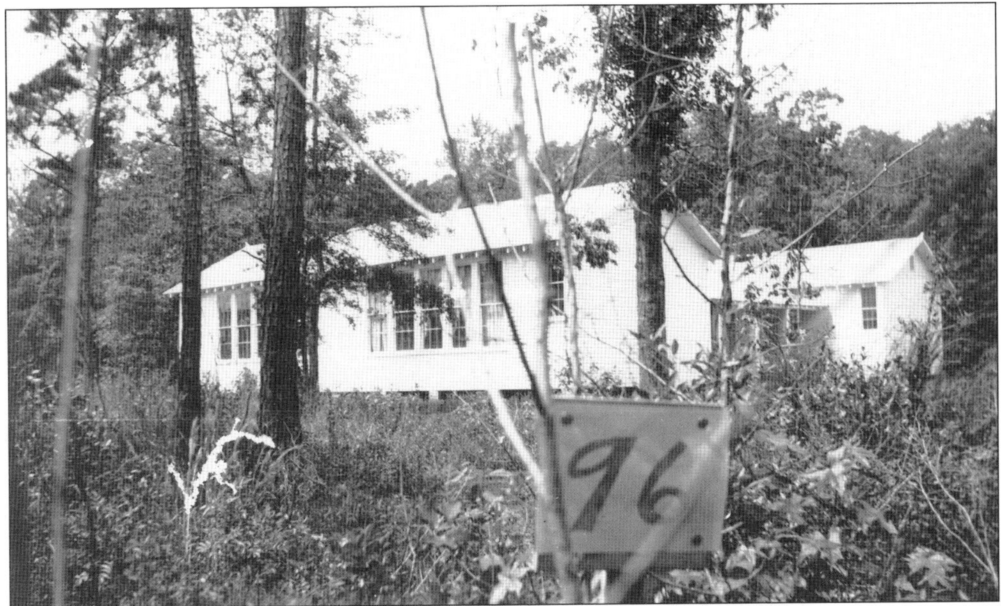

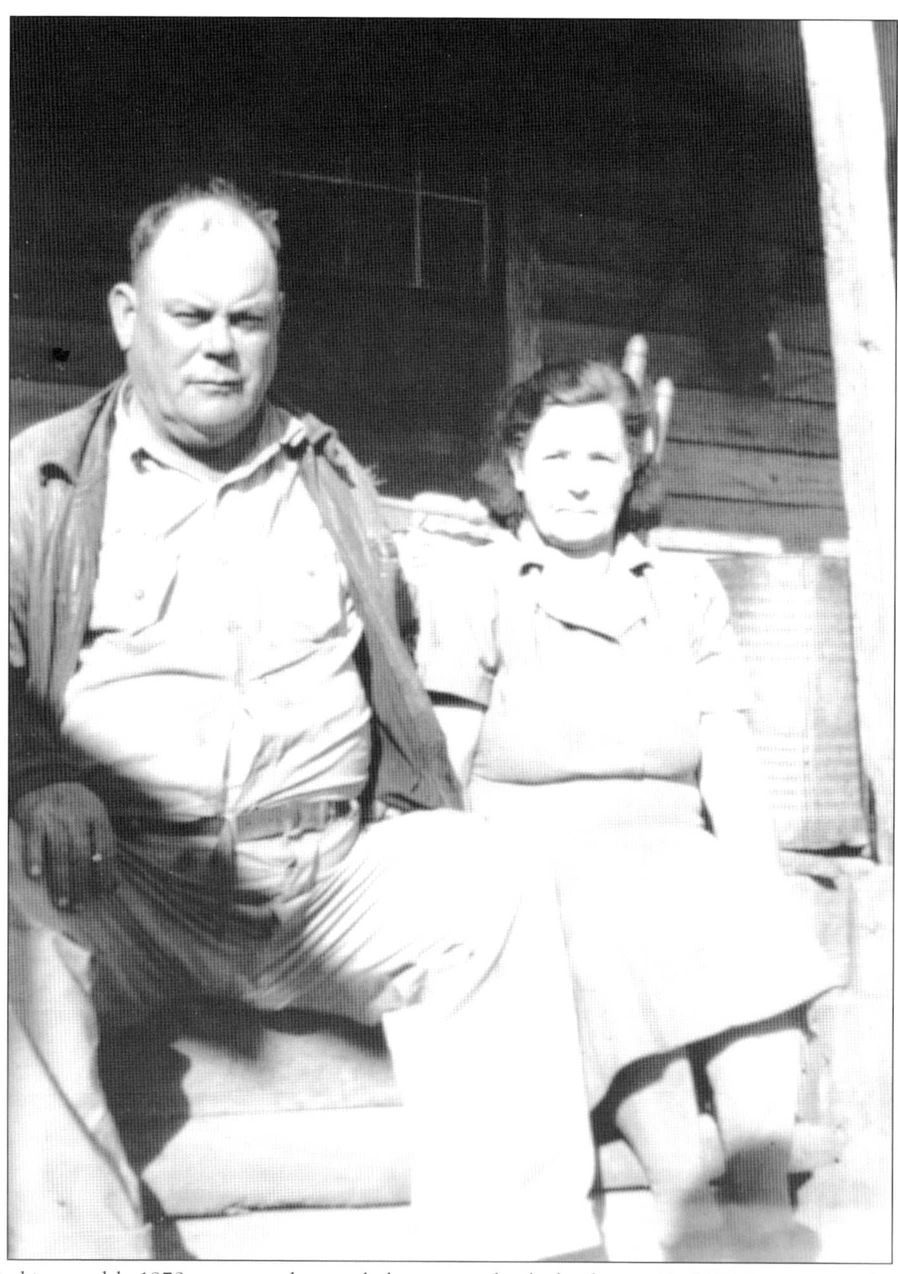

Settled in roughly 1879 on grounds once belonging to both the former R.G.W. Grissette and Beatty plantations, Hickory Grove, an unincorporated community outside of Conway, is said to be named after the hickory trees that once grew in its vicinity. Also known as Fairtraid from 1916 to 1918, the community reverted to its original name by the end of World War I. Hickory Grove maintained a post office that operated from 1906 to 1940, which was known as the Fairtraid Post Office from 1916 to 1918. Following World War I, the community grew. At one point, Hickory Grove was a farming community that strictly focused on tobacco cultivation; farmers in Hickory Grove are seen in this image. Hickory Grove had several businesses during its peak years in the 1940s, though the community's industry declined after World War II, and agriculture became less prevalent in the community through the later 20th century. (Courtesy of the Horry County Museum.)

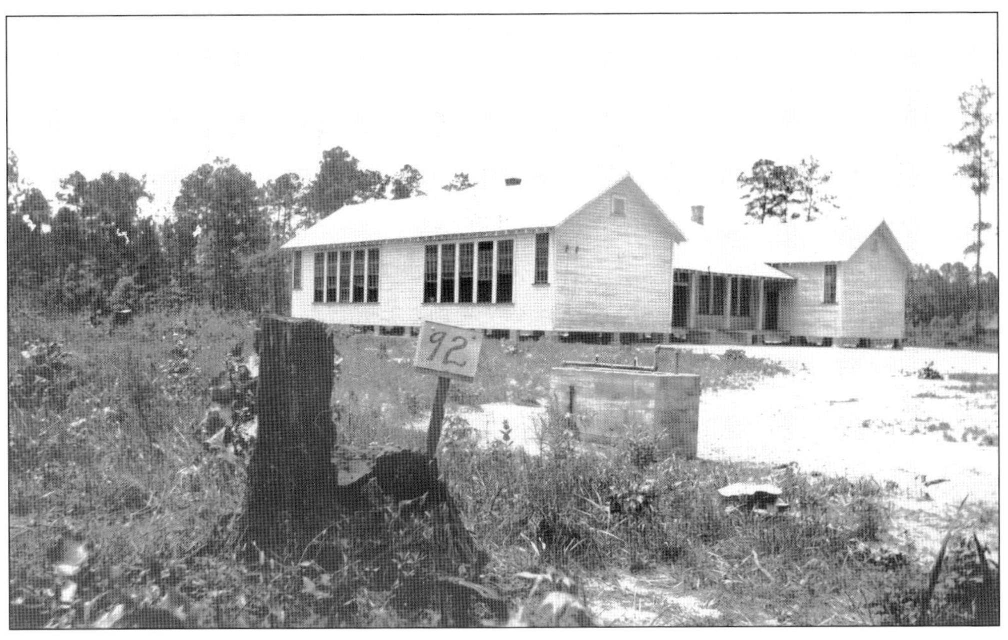

Nixonville, named for early settlers, was founded in approximately 1875. It is also known as the Tilly Swamp Community after the nearby Tilly Swamp. The former Tilly Swamp School, eventually repurposed into a mercantile before being demolished in the 1980s, is seen above. Nonetheless, the community's official name is Nixonville, and the Nixonville Post Office, opened in 1901, operated for 55 years. Hazel Cooper, a Nixonville resident, was Nixonville's last postmaster when the post office closed in 1956. A parcel mailed on the last day of Nixonville's postal operations is seen below. Though Nixonville remained rural throughout the 20th century, it has seen much development since the early 2000s due to its location along SC Highway 90. (Above, courtesy of the Horry County Museum.)

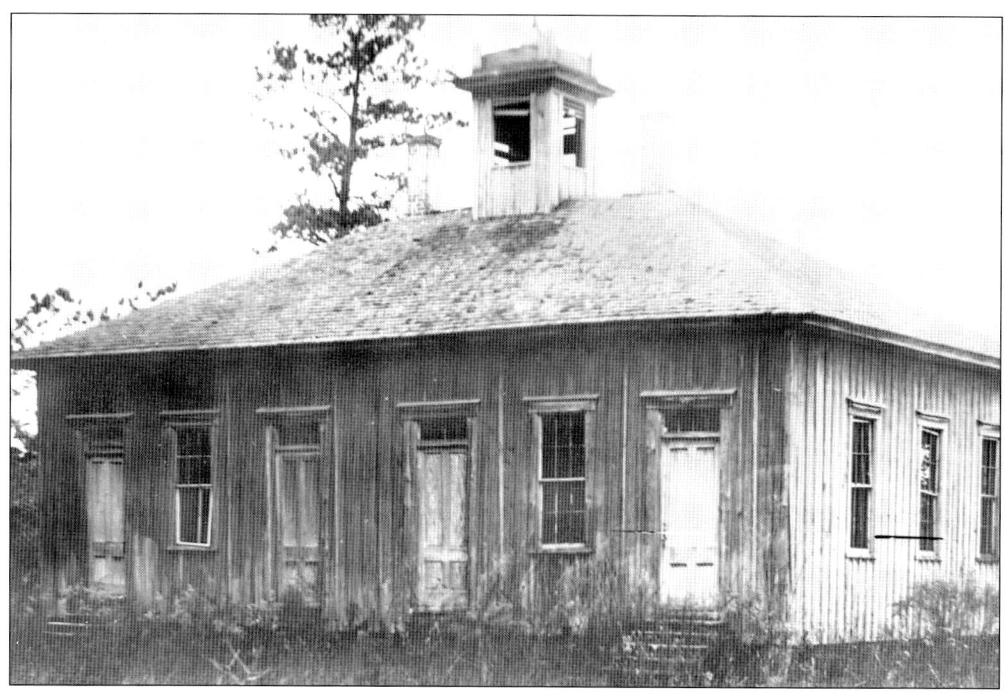

Seen in the above image is Conway's first African American school, the Conway Academy, which was established in 1857. By 1870, B.F. Whittemore, a Boston-born educator, reverend, veteran, and South Carolina state senator, founded the Whittemore School, also known as the "Old Academy," with the goal of educating children of former slaves. Conway Academy was renamed the Whittemore Academy by 1876. In 1911, while called the Whittemore Training School, classes moved to a wooden two-story building along Racepath Avenue, seen in the image below. In the 1930s, the school, which was once Horry County's only school for Black children, gained accreditation, and it moved again in 1936. The third building burned down in 1944, and after using temporary structures for a decade, the new Whittemore High and Elementary Schools opened as equalization schools in 1954. Equalization schools were built in attempts to block educational integration, as lawmakers used these schools to defend the "separate but equal" doctrine. Once schools were integrated, many equalization schools became abandoned or were repurposed. (Both, courtesy of the Horry County Museum.)

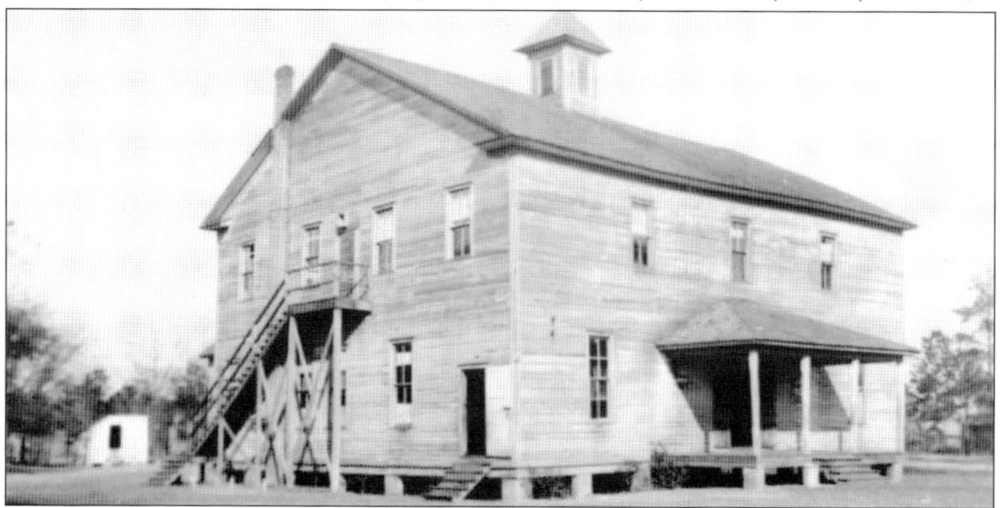

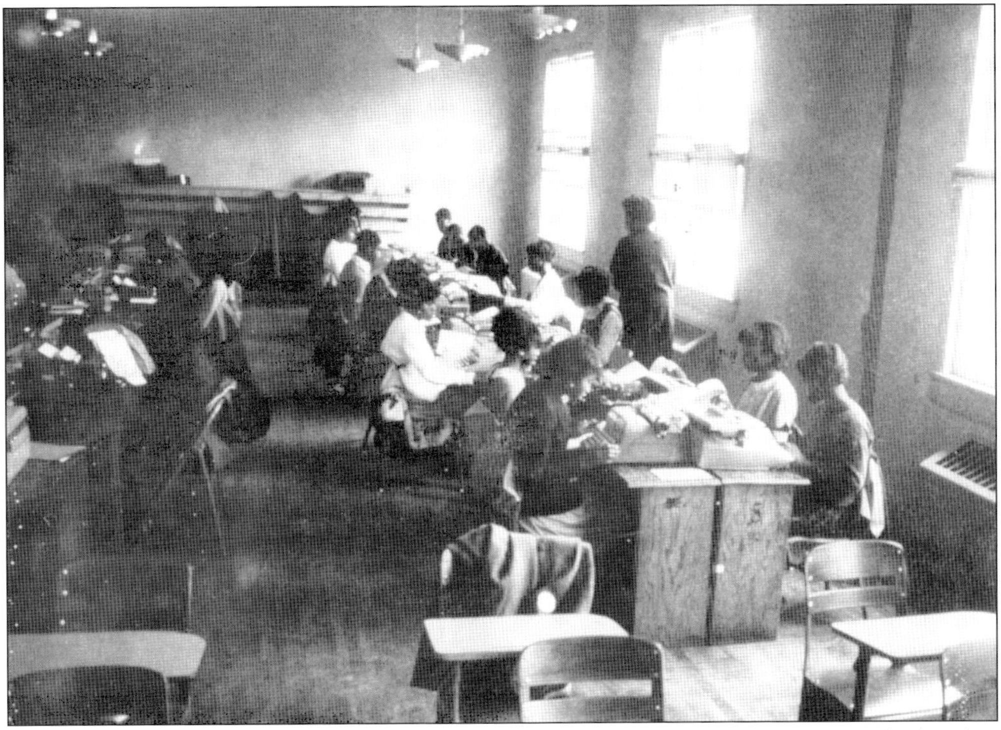

After South Carolina desegregated its public schools, the all-Black Whittemore schools closed in 1970. In the image above, a typing class in the segregated Whittemore High School is seen in the late 1960s. After integration was mandated by law and schools were desegregated, Whittemore High School became the integrated Conway Junior High School. This school also held a technical school for African Americans, Eastern Carolina Junior College, which existed prior to local colleges allowing Black students to attend. Whittemore Elementary School's building became government offices, though it was eventually abandoned and burned down in 2023. Notably, these schools are remembered as gathering places for Conway's African American citizens and for residents of the Whittemore-Racepath community. Cochran, another one of Conway's historic African American communities, held an equalization school that closed upon public school integration and was subsequently used as government offices. Seen below is the Cochran Colored School in the 1930s. (Both, courtesy of the Horry County Museum.)

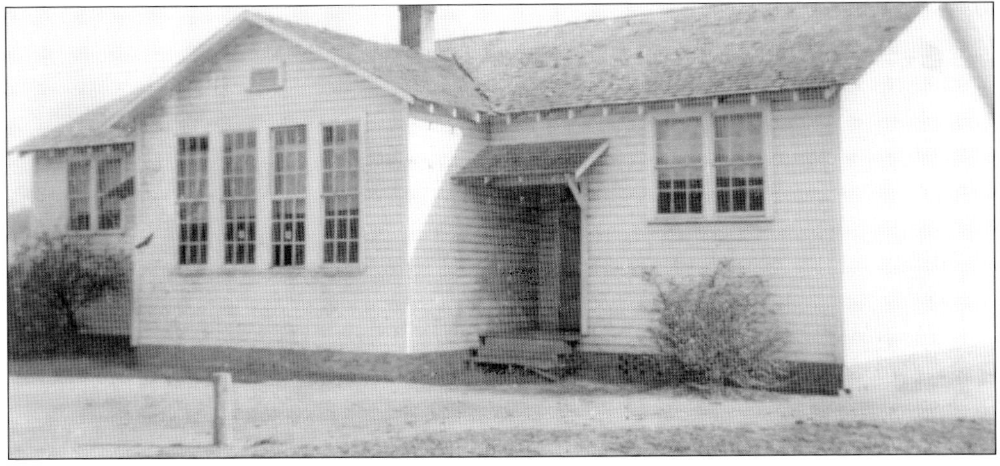

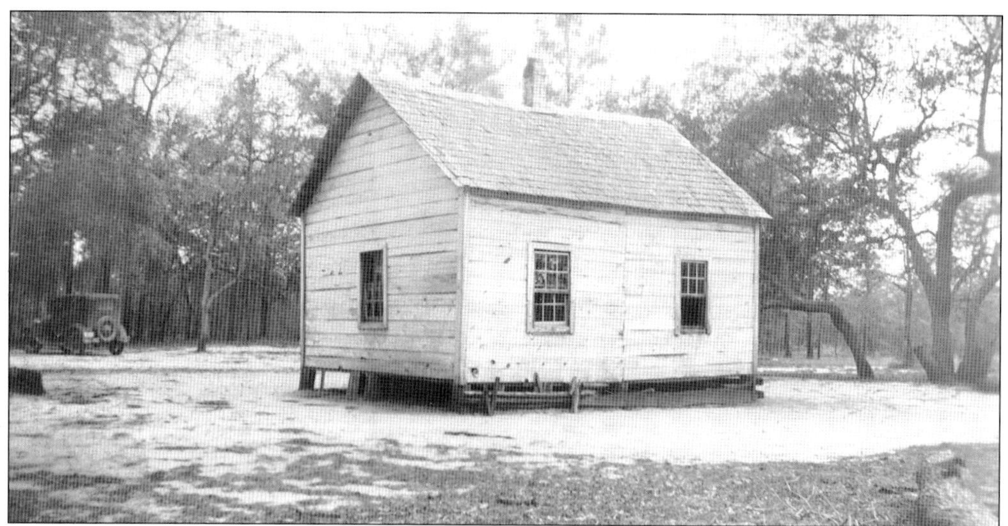

The late 18th century brought a national movement for accessible education, and "common schools" began to be implemented in South Carolina beginning in 1811. However, throughout the ensuing century, churches and community schools, especially in rural areas, often educated children before they went to work to help their households, and students commonly stopped their education in what present-day standards consider the middle grades. In Horry County, prior to the 1940s, church congregations or rural community schools, such as the Gunter's Island School, seen in these images, educated numerous children. Community schools also acted independently, and Horry County technically held 88 independent schools before public schools were consolidated into the Horry County School District in 1941. Though community schools taught students basic skills, limited education opportunities led to issues of illiteracy, and greater pushes for secondary education therefore commenced in the early 1900s. (Both, courtesy of the Horry County Museum.)

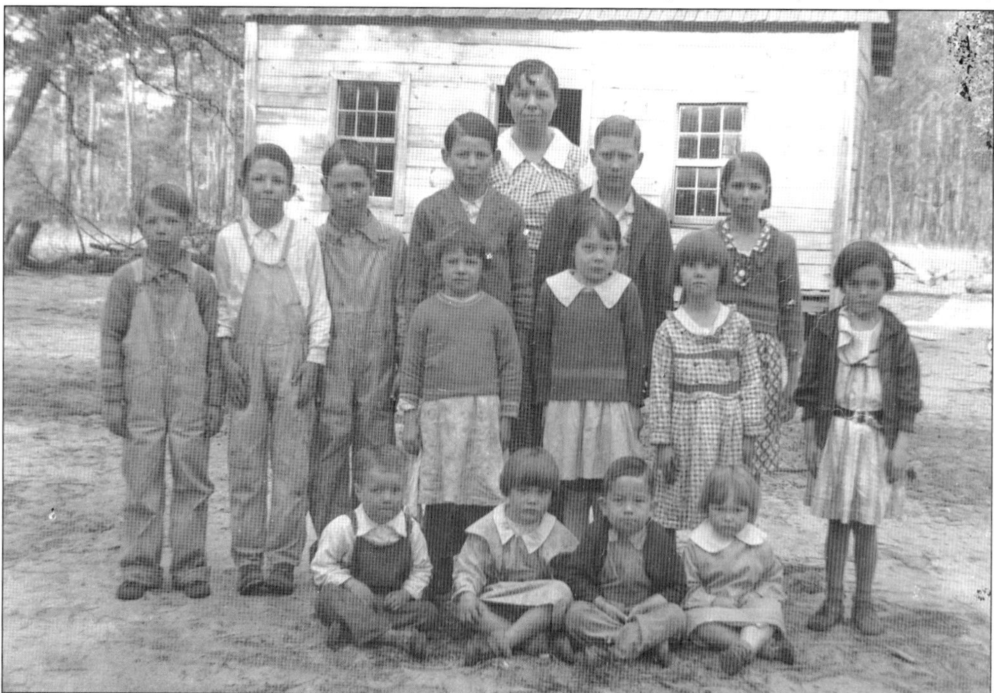

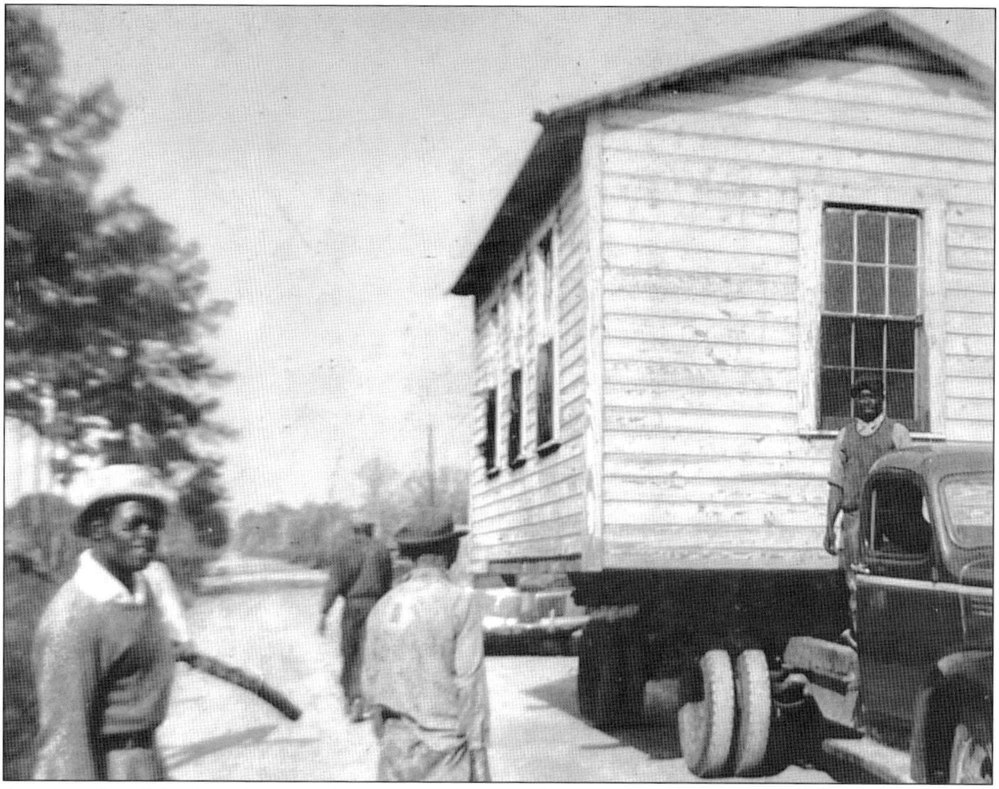

As educational facilities began to be improved, this led disparities between White and Black schools to be rather evident as students of color were left with poorer-quality schoolhouses, materials, and other resources compared to White children. The image above shows a small building, obviously without any amenities, being transported for use as a school in St. John's in western Horry County. Black students were also educated at training schools, segregated high schools that taught elementary and secondary-level curriculum and were often funded by philanthropic donations, especially by the Slater and Rosenwald Funds. Teachers at a Horry County training school are seen below. Continued disparities between White and Black educational facilities led to further movements for educational equality (especially the equalization school movement in South Carolina) and eventually school integration. (Above, courtesy of the Ambrose family; below, courtesy of the University of Virginia.)

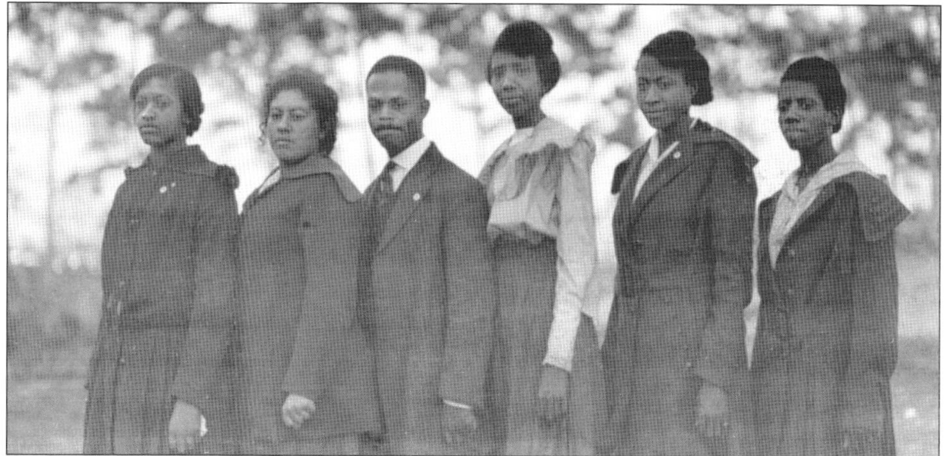

-6-

New Industries Worked With:

Crown Cork and Seal
Jeffery Manufacturing
Tetra Pack
Cryovac
Firestone Steel Products
Hercules Powder Company
Spartan Tool and Die

Expansions:

Beverage - Aire
Arrow Armature

York County TEC:

York County TEC began operation October, 1964 and has now completed eight months of classes.

Cost of Building	$500,000.00
Value of Land (25 acres)	74,000.00
	$575,000.00

Equipment:

State Equipment	$173,000.00
Federal Surplus	115,000.00
Total equipment installed	$288,000.00
Equipment on order	20,201.00
	$308,201.00

Student Enrollment:

1964-65	2,599

This fiscal year attendance amounted to 134,284 student contact hours or 186 FTE.

All centers have expansion plans either underway or in the planning stage. Greenville's addition of 63,000 sq. ft. will be completed by October 15th. Present plans are to operate a heavy equipment operators course under MDTA which can be used to clear the additional land acquired by Greenville TEC. The "annex" building at Sumter will be sold to the public schools for $50,000 and these funds applied toward construction of additional space at Sumter TEC. Richland TEC is working on plans for an approximate $25,000 addition to present facilities.

Horry/Marion bid has been let. A recent visit to Mr. R. D. Anderson, State Director for Vocational Education, revealed that at least $200,000 surplus funds from the Vocational Education Act of 1963 would be available for transfer to Technical Education. The State Board of Education transferred these funds with the recommendation that they be used to assist in construction of Horry/Marion.

Motion made by Dr. Anderson and seconded by Mr. Funderburk that "Funds allotted by the State Board of Education and recommended for Horry/Marion use shall be transferred for use in the construction of the Horry/Marion Technical Education to be matched by local funds." Unanimous.

240

In the mid-20th century, South Carolina's illiteracy rate became a top concern for legislators. Poor educational outcomes for South Carolina students worsened at this time because many came from impoverished backgrounds, leading to high dropout rates. This led to a statewide crisis that caused students to essentially be trapped in a cycle of sporadic or low-paying employment due to a lack of satisfactory education. This, in turn, led further generations to repeat this cycle, causing a mass illiteracy epidemic in the southern United States (and in South Carolina) that most often affected underfunded, rural, or minority communities. In 1960, a commission to combat this illiteracy epidemic was founded by the South Carolina Educational Commission, featuring delegates from all counties. Soon, commissions to explore the construction of technical colleges in regions across the state were founded. In this 1964 image, meeting minutes that approved the creation of the Horry-Marion-Georgetown Technical Education Commission are shown. (Courtesy of the South Carolina Technical College System.)

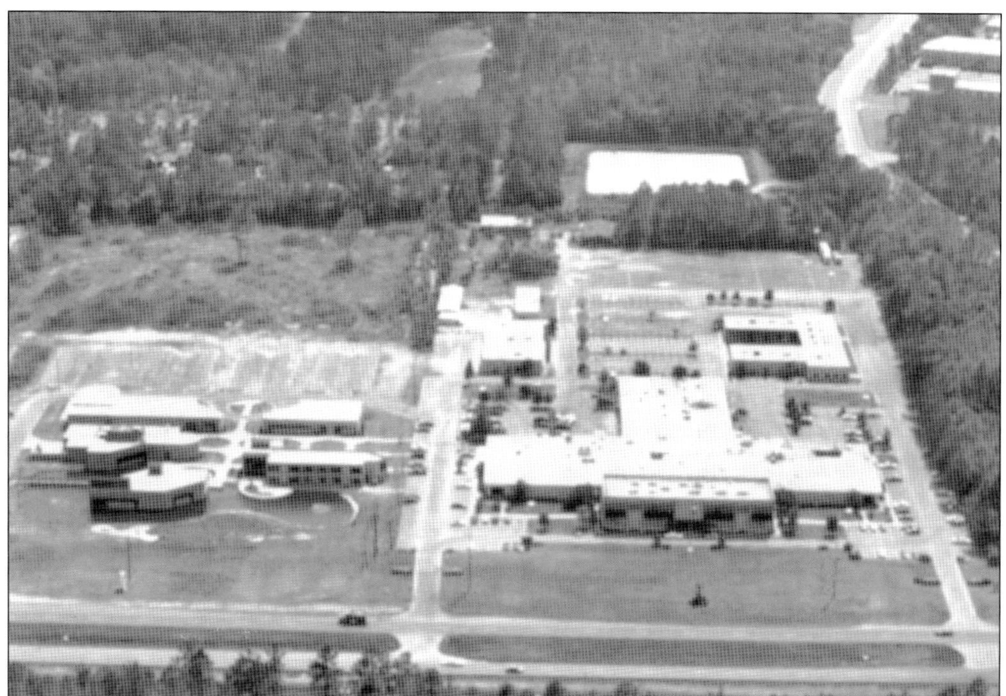

After the South Carolina Technical College Commission founded the Horry-Marion-Georgetown Technical Education Commission in 1964, the latter board began the process of establishing the Horry-Marion-Georgetown Technical Education Center. A location off US Highway 501 in Conway, seen in the above image from the 1980s, was chosen for its central proximity between the three counties. Construction by the Dargan Construction Company began in July 1964 on land acquired with federal government funding. After construction ended in January 1965, the Horry-Marion-Georgetown Technical Education Center commenced classes in July 1965 in one large building called TEC 101, which housed all academic classrooms and faculty offices and is seen in the image below. (Both, courtesy of the Horry County Museum.)

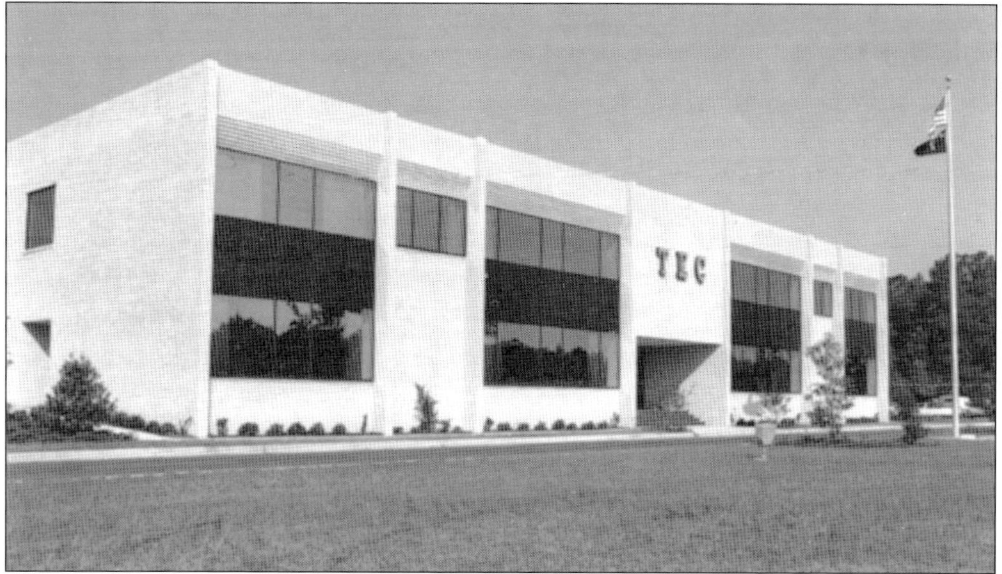

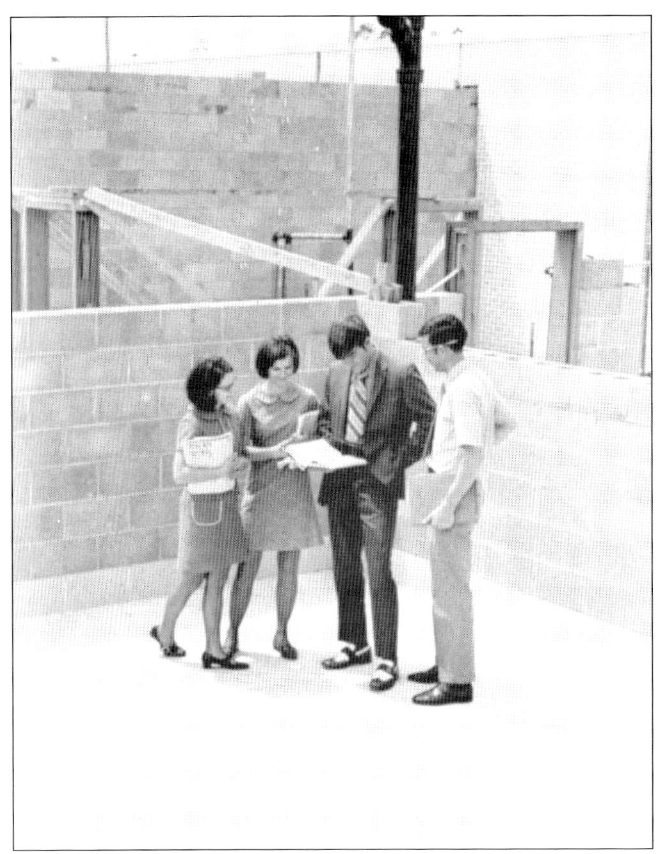

Regardless of the local concern over the survival of Horry-Marion-Georgetown Technical Education Center, the first students earning certificates completed their programs in 1967, and the first associate degree class graduated in May 1968. These graduations helped boost community support and optimism toward the school. Marion County left the institution in January 1969 and eventually joined the Florence-Darlington Technical Education Coalition. The school then became the Horry-Georgetown Technical Education Center (known as Horry-Georgetown TEC) and underwent a major expansion in 1970. Images of this expansion are seen here. (Both, courtesy of the Horry County Museum.)

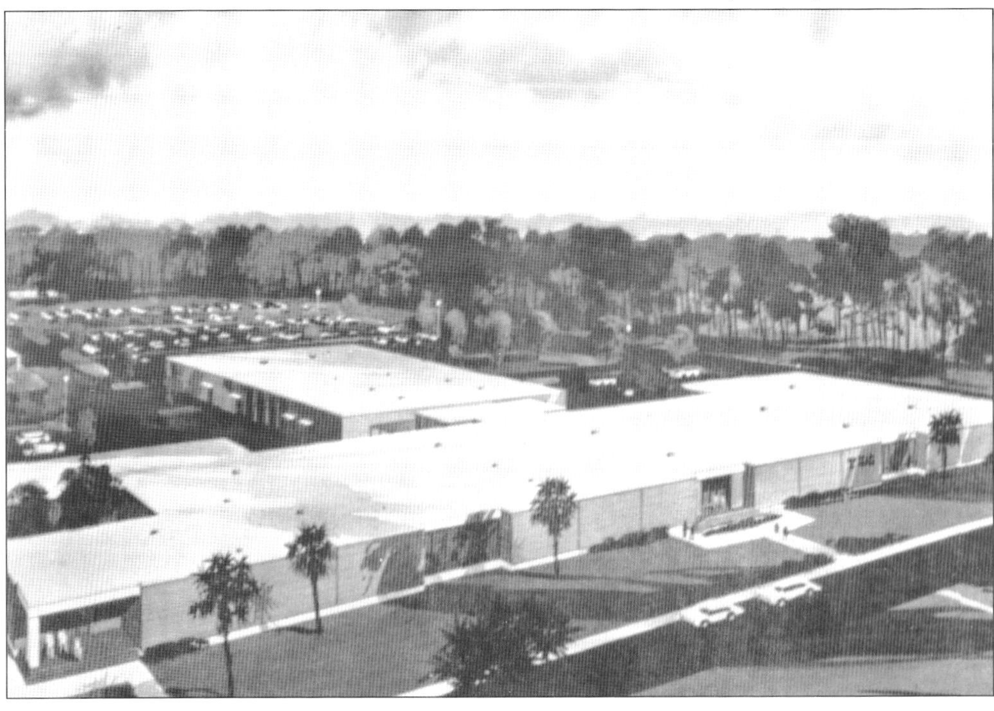

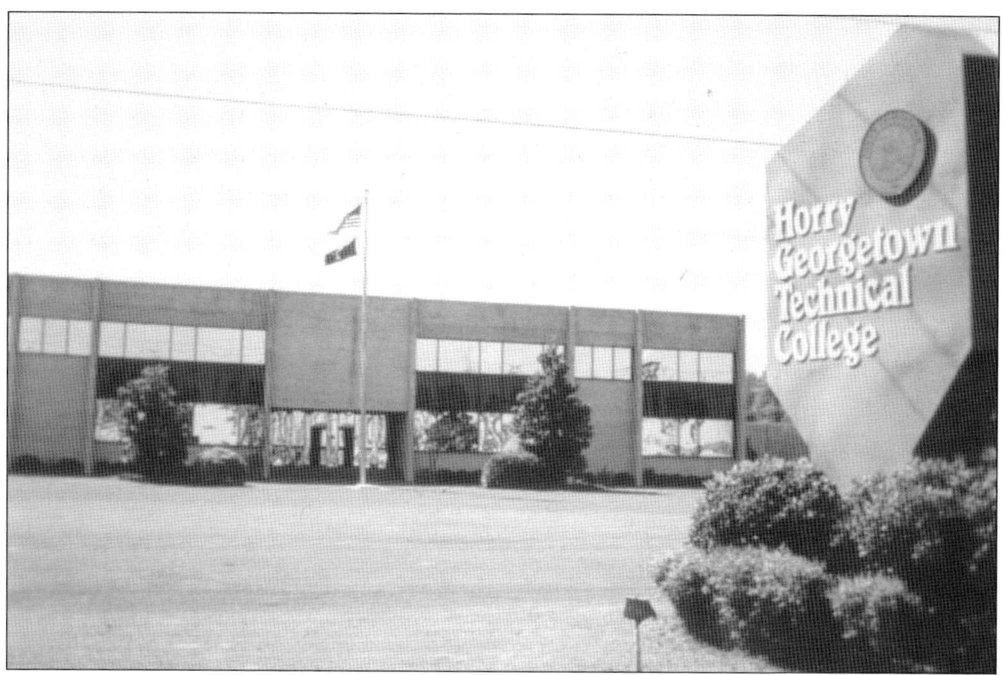

The Horry-Georgetown Technical Education Center earned accreditation in 1972, and momentum to rename the school began in order to reflect its degree programs and credentials. The institution was officially rebranded as Horry-Georgetown Technical College in 1975, as shown above. In 1976, another campus was opened in Georgetown. After further expanding in 1978, Horry-Georgetown Technical College gained a stronger reputation for its academic programs, which appealed to numerous local residents of all backgrounds. In the image below, the 1981 Horry-Georgetown Technical College commencement ceremony shows several graduates, including veteran Homer "Bill" Heaton, during graduation. In the 1990s, the institution's Grand Strand campus was founded, and lands once belonging to Myrtle Beach Air Force Base were acquired by the school for use as part of that campus. (Above, courtesy of Horry County Museum; below, courtesy of Angela Heaton McRae.)

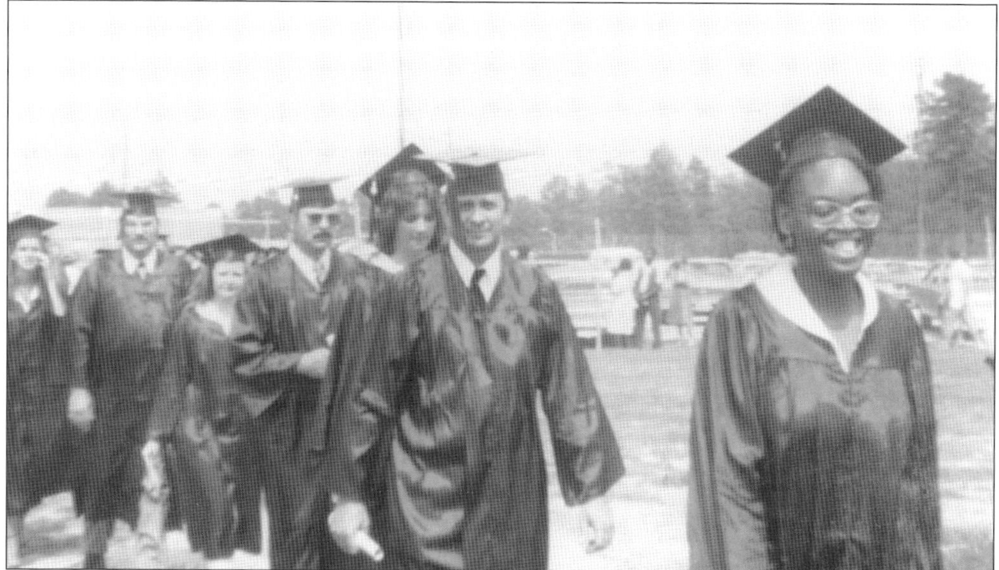

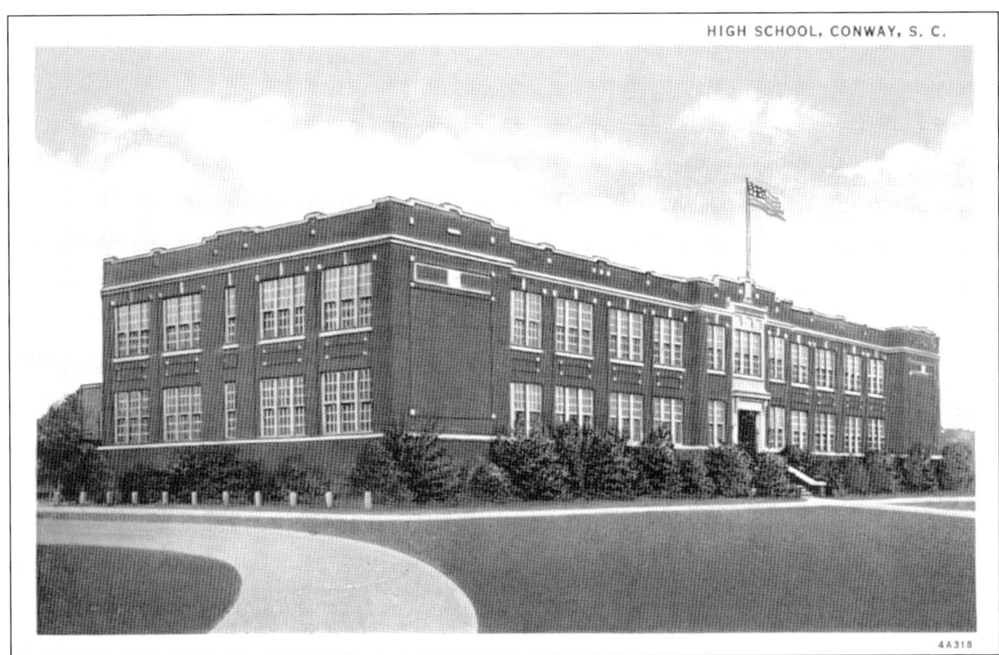

By the 1950s, the need for a higher learning institution in northeastern South Carolina became evident. As South Carolina's technical college system had not yet been founded, the closest colleges and universities were more than an hour distant from Horry County. Coastal Carolina University's origins began in 1954, when the Coastal Carolina Junior College, founded by the Coastal Educational Foundation, began holding evening classes at the original Conway High School building (seen above) as an extension of the College of Charleston, which sponsored the program. By 1958, the College of Charleston disassociated with the school, and Coastal Carolina Junior College was then supported by Horry County taxpayers. The Horry County Educational Commission was founded in 1959 to oversee the school's financial affairs. (Below, courtesy of Coastal Carolina University.)

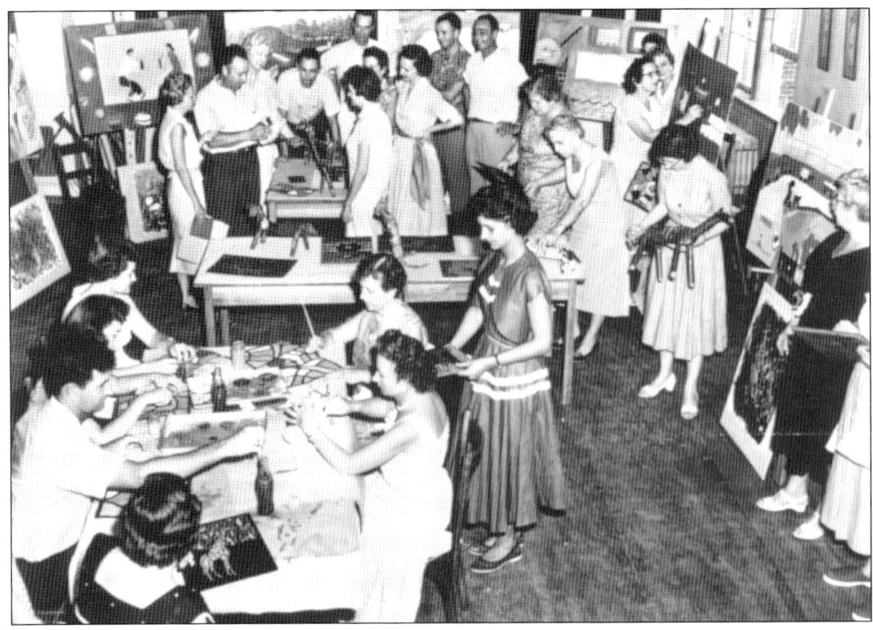

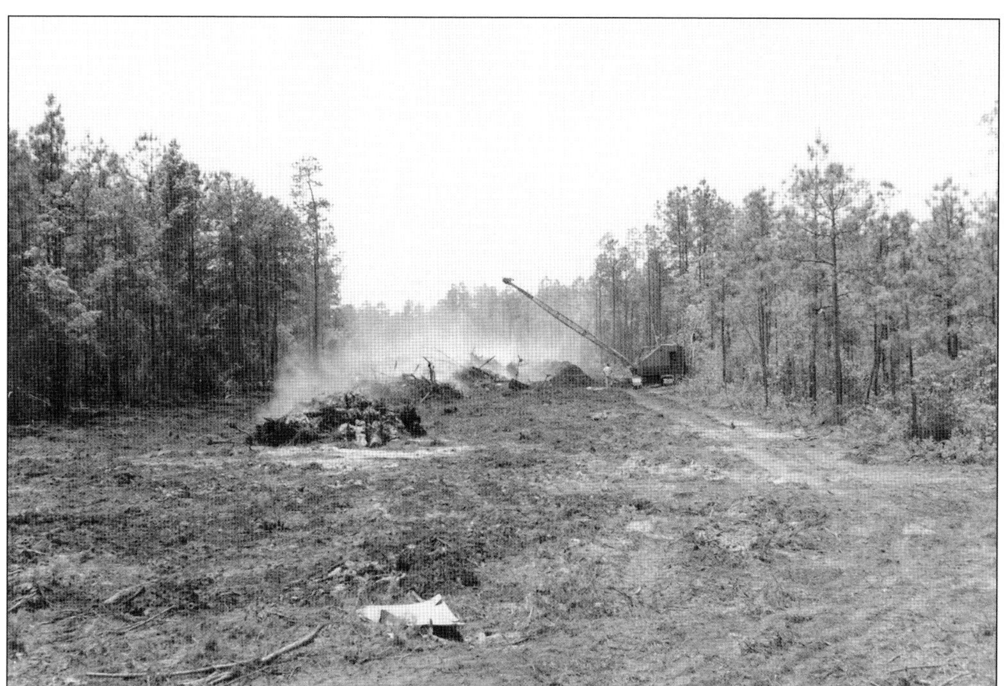

In 1960, the Horry County Educational Commission established a contract with the University of South Carolina to make Coastal Carolina Junior College a part of the University of South Carolina system. That same year, the school's name was changed to USC–Coastal Carolina College, and a location for a formal campus was chosen by the Horry County Educational Commission on land along SC Highway 544 and US Highway 501 that belonged to the International Paper Company and the Burroughs Timber Company. Construction, as seen in the above image, began on the campus in 1960, and in 1963, the college's first structure, now known as the Edward M. Singleton Building, seen in the image at right, opened to students. (Above, courtesy of Coastal Carolina University; right, courtesy of the South Caroliniana Library.)

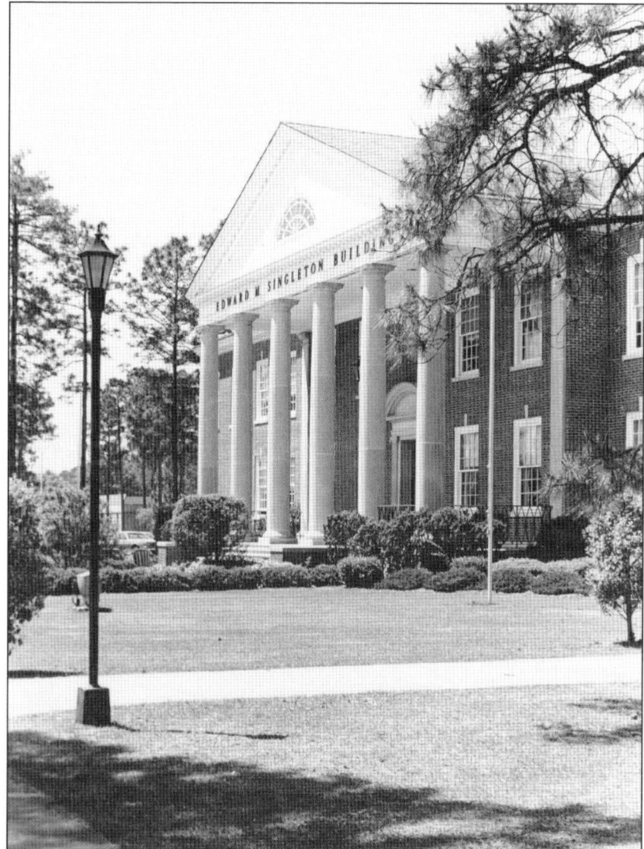

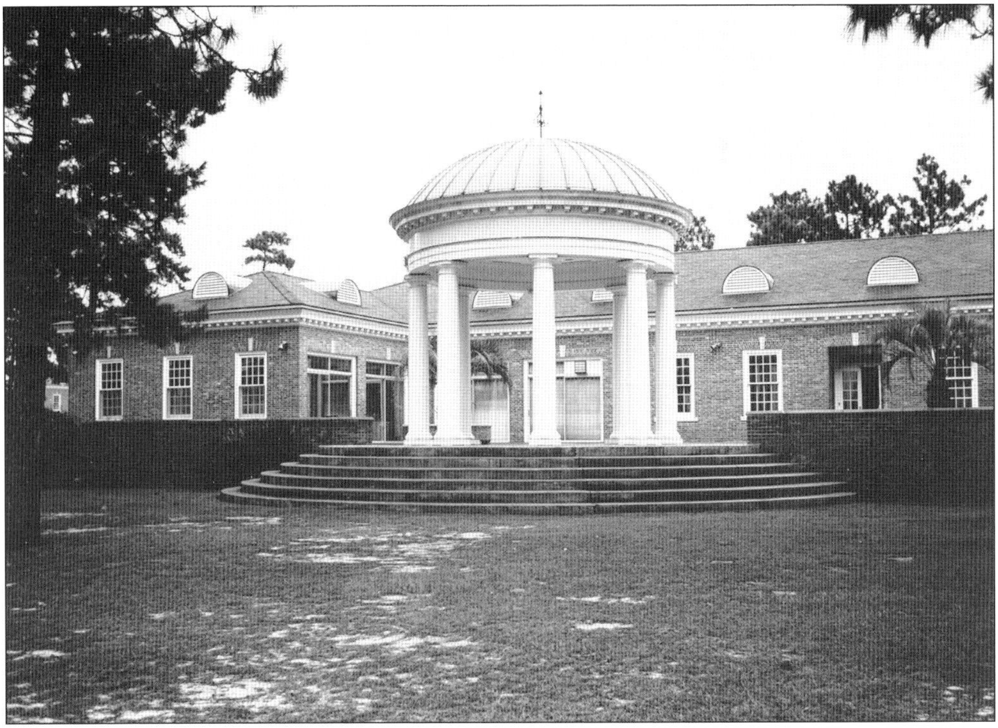

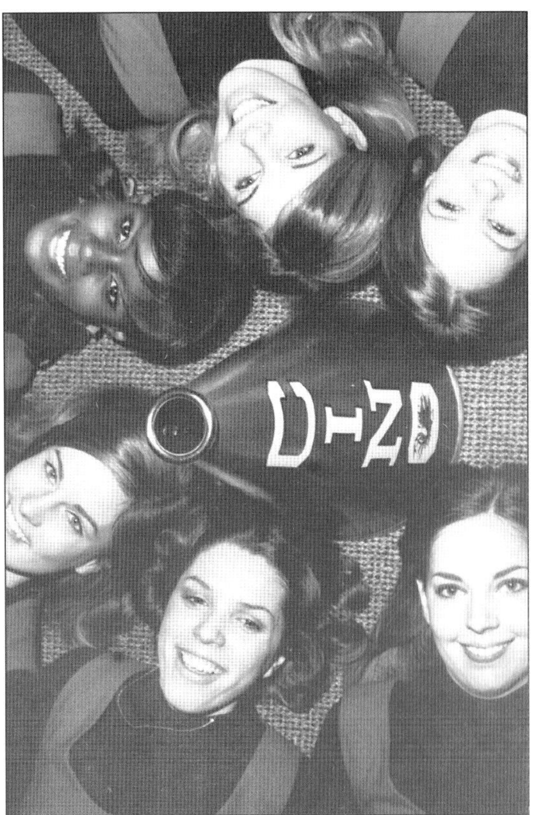

Initially, USC–Coastal Carolina College remained small, and though always coeducational, it began admitting Black students in 1965. A previous institution for African Americans, Eastern Carolina Junior College, briefly existed in Conway in the immediate years before USC–Coastal Carolina admitted non-White students. The college grew slowly in the 1960s, but in 1966, one of the school's most iconic sites, the Athenaeum, seen above, was built. The school's morale increased as its independence grew. In a move representative of its independence, basketball coach Cal Maddox and several students selected a new mascot for the school. Originally the Trojan, by the early 1960s, USC–Coastal Carolina College's official mascot became the fierce Chanticleer (another name for a rooster). It was chosen for its similarity to the University of South Carolina's Gamecock, and the mascot's former design, remarkably similar to the Gamecock's, can be seen in the image at left of a horn among school cheerleaders in 1971. (Above, courtesy of the South Caroliniana Library; left, courtesy of Coastal Carolina University.)

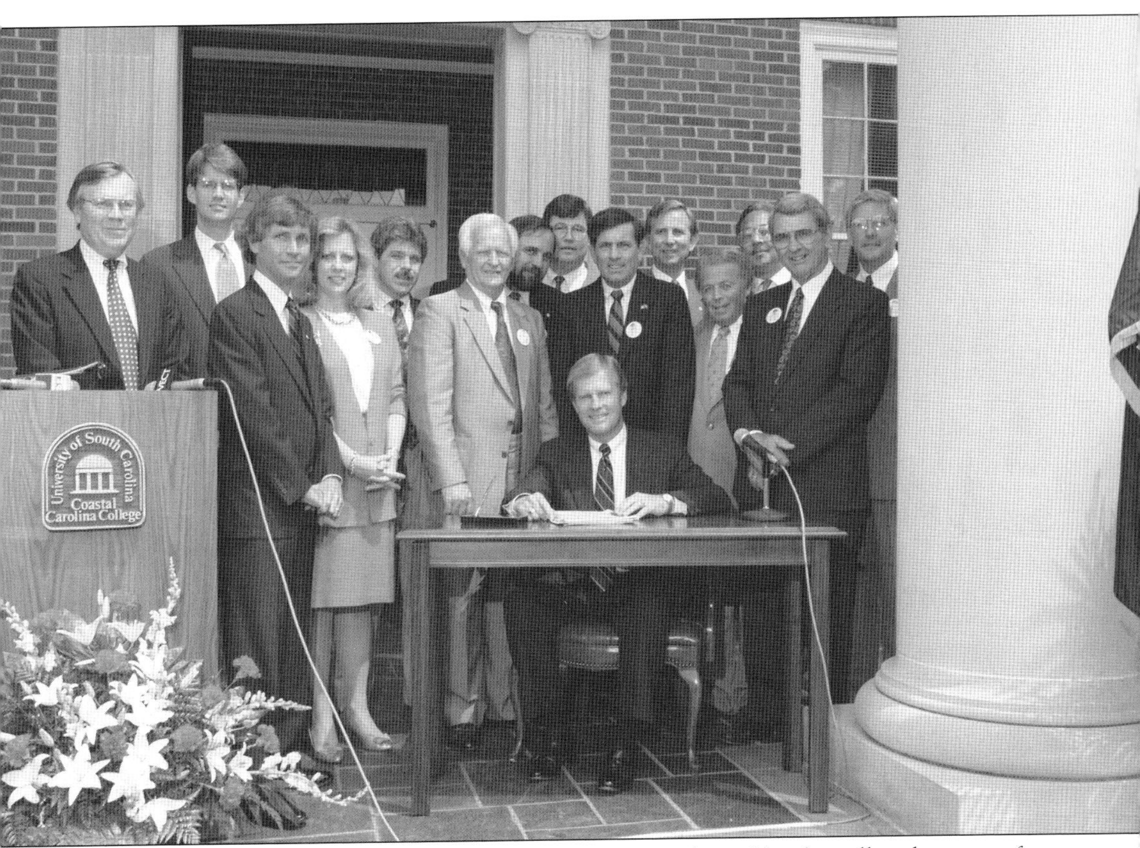

USC-Coastal Carolina continued to grow in the 1970s, and notably, the college became a four-year institution in 1974, providing local students with the opportunity to earn bachelor's degrees. Though the 1970s were a pivotal point in the school's history, the 1980s saw the construction of more academic facilities and dormitories and an increase in the student population. By 1991, USC-Coastal Carolina College had reached a student body of 4,000. At this time, both the Coastal Educational Foundation and the Horry County Educational Commission sought for the school to obtain its independence. In 1992, the University of South Carolina gave its support to grant the school independent status. Subsequently, the South Carolina Legislature passed legislation which established Coastal Carolina University as an independent institution beginning on July 1, 1993. South Carolina governor Carroll Campbell signed that legislation on May 14, 1993, at the institution, which is shown in this image. Ronald Ingle, the former chancellor of USC-Coastal Carolina College, became the university's first president. (Courtesy of Coastal Carolina University.)

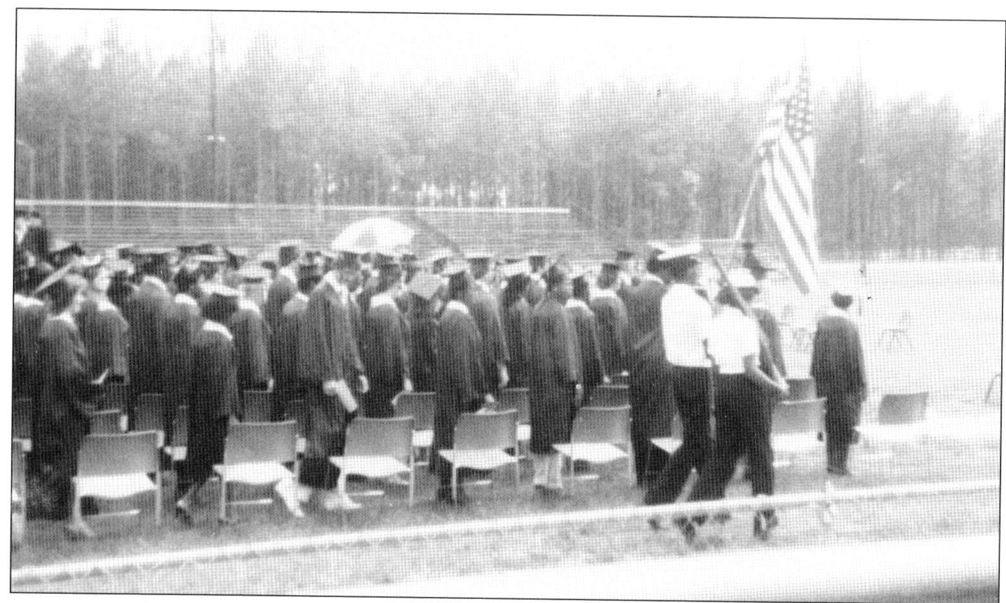

After Coastal Carolina University gained its independence, the institution saw unprecedented growth. A $68-million master plan for the university's campus was unveiled in 1996, and in 2003, Coastal Carolina University was granted its own football team. A source of pride for locals, the Coastal Carolina Chanticleers have achieved national fame, and Coastal Carolina University joined the Sun Belt Conference in 2015. The Chanticleers currently play in Brooks Stadium, which was built in 2003. A sketch of its intended design from the time of its inception is shown below. Above, the institution's first athletic field is shown in 1981, when it hosted the graduation ceremony for Horry-Georgetown Technical College. The differences between these two images show the immense growth and transformation this institution saw in those decades, especially regarding the quality of its facilities. Combined with Horry County and the Myrtle Beach Metropolitan Area's rapid growth, the school's development has only continued, and with a student body of over 10,000, Coastal Carolina University has become one of South Carolina's premier higher education institutions. (Below, courtesy of Coastal Carolina University.)

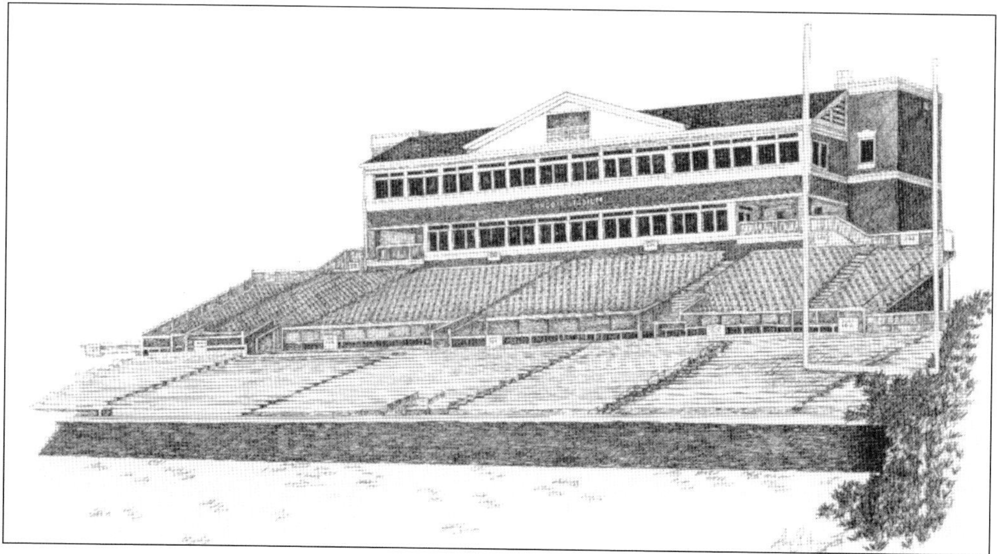

Three

From Beaches to Lumber Mills

Southern Horry County

In similar fashion to Conway, southern Horry County boasts a unique and distinctive history largely steeped in maritime heritage and culture. Heavily forested, this area of Horry County was essential to the timber and naval store industries. The bountiful pine forests of southern Horry County spurred the entrepreneurial spirit of many early Horry County settlers in the 1800s. One of these settlers, Henry Buck, began a lumber and shipbuilding business that would become nationally famous and would see lumber processed through its mills used in ships making worldwide voyages (like *Henrietta*) and on nationwide projects, including the construction of the Brooklyn Bridge in New York City in the late 19th century.

The lumber industry in this section of Horry County also led to the establishment of several communities, including Bucksville, Bucksport, and Port Harrelson. These communities, especially Bucksport, have strong African American heritage. Most of the prevalence of African American culture in this region is spurred by Henry Buck's ownership of slaves, as many generations of these slaves' descendants remain in the vicinity.

Other communities in southern Horry County with strong African American histories also include Burgess (originally called Marlow) and St. James, which were both farming communities in early years. Additionally, several modern communities sit on the grounds of the former Ark Plantation, last owned by John Tillman, which was sold and parceled after Tillman's death in 1865. One sold parcel became known as Roach's Beach and was later sold to George J. Holliday, a tobacco producer who renamed the area Floral Beach in honor of his wife, Flora, and daughter Floramay Holliday. In the 1920s, developers from Columbia, South Carolina, partially developed the land, and in 1952, the land was sold again and became known as Surfside Beach, thus beginning the community's modern history. Garden City, located on the southern border of Horry County, was also a rural community that continued to grow with the development of the tourism industry throughout the 20th century.

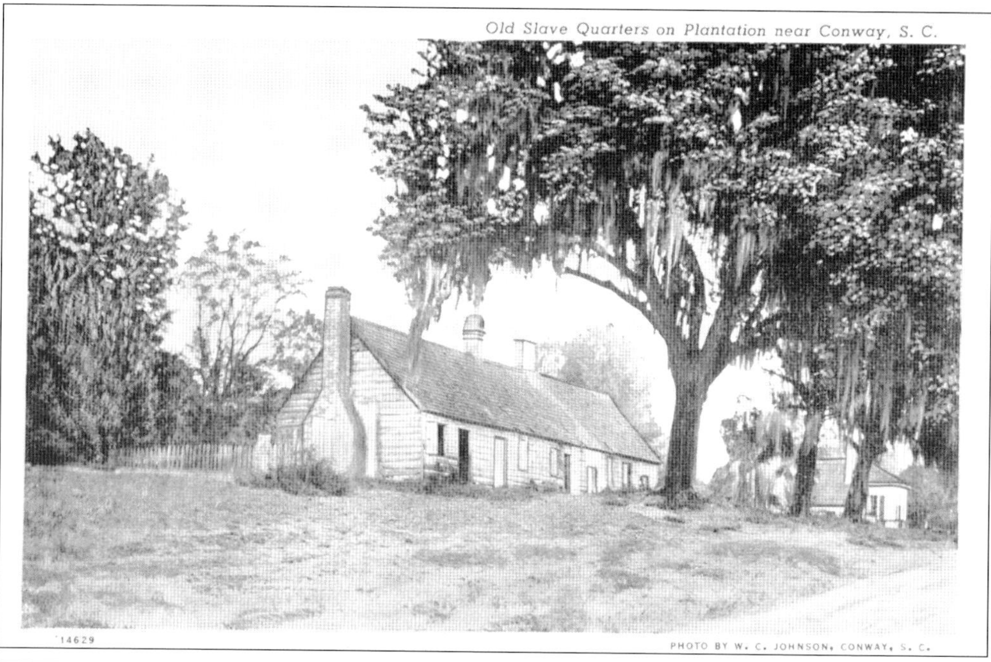

Henry Buck was the founder of a large lumber company that gave Bucksport and Bucksville, South Carolina, their names. Born in Maine to the noted Buck family (who are the namesake of Bucksport, Maine), Buck relocated to Horry County in the 1820s and owned a vast amount of land and slaves. His lumber company is attributed to making the area a timber-producing haven before his death in 1870. Slave cabins on his plantation are shown in this postcard image.

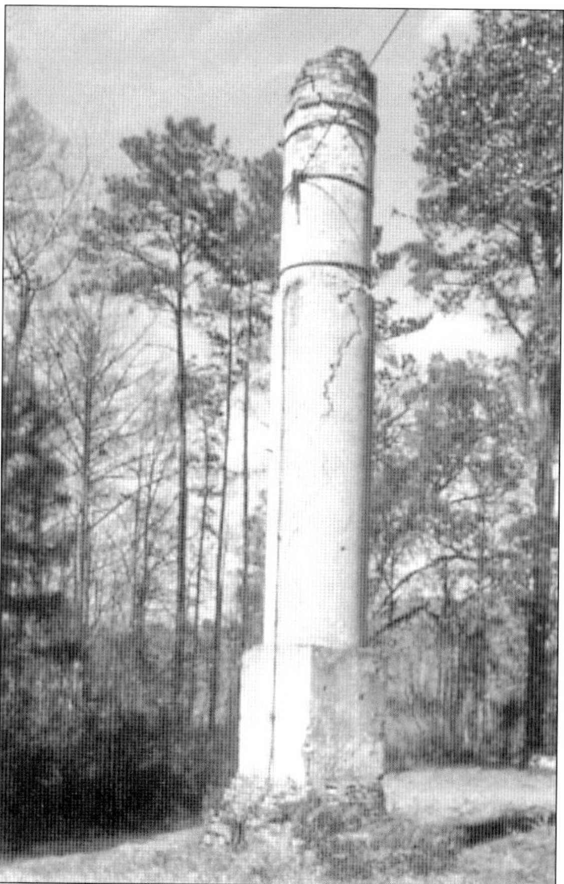

Seen on Henry Buck's plantation property, the Buck's Mill Farm in Bucksville, is the ruin of an old smokestack or chimney from Buck's Upper Mill, which was one of the lumber mills Buck's company operated. Buck's Middle Mill was known as Bucksville, while the Lower Mill served as the origins of the Bucksport community. (Courtesy of the South Carolina Department of Archives and History.)

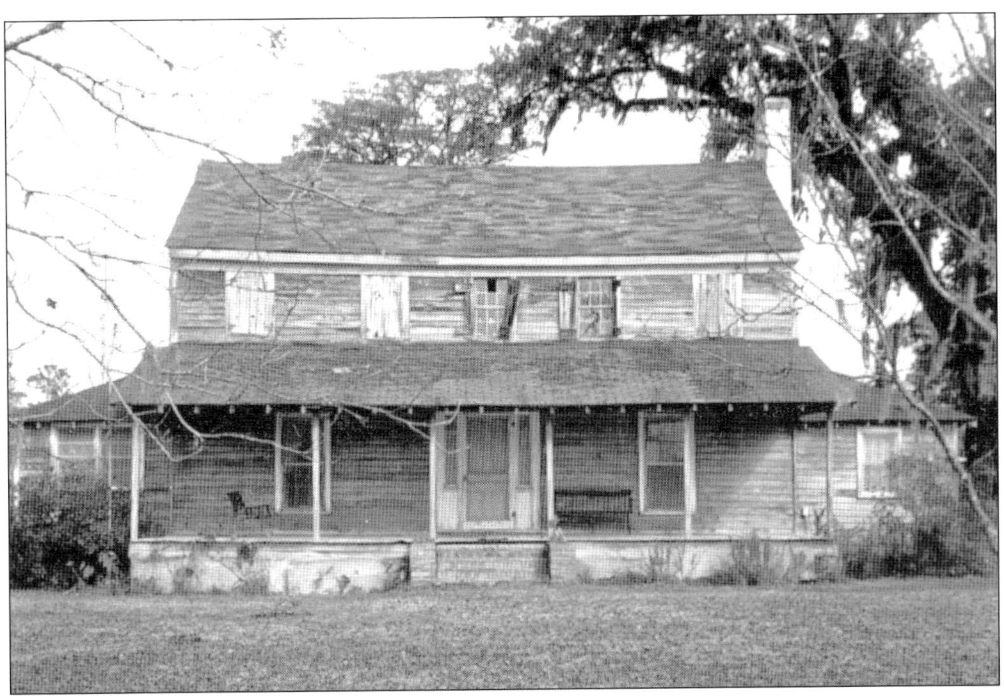

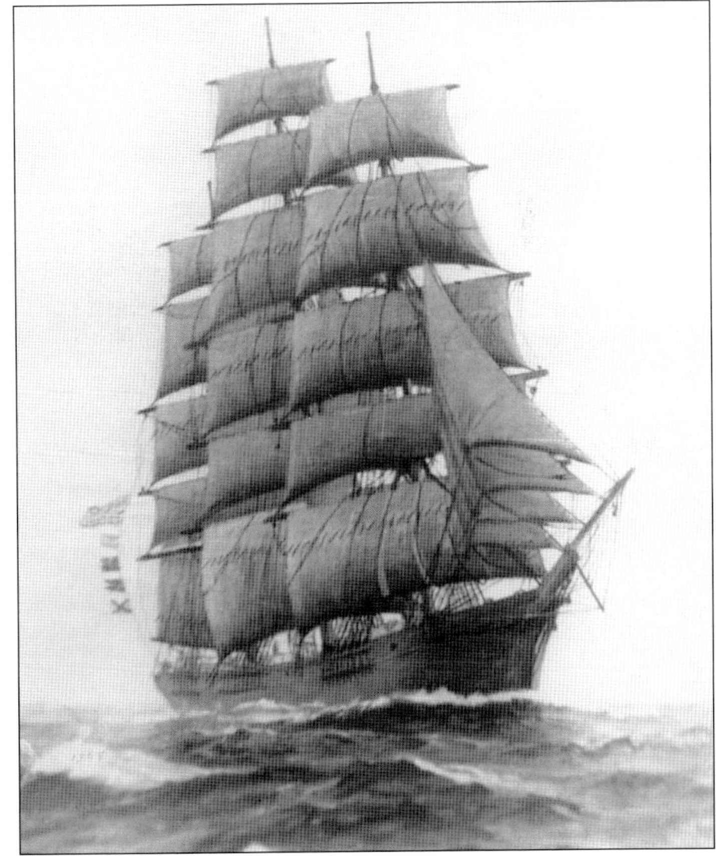

Seen above is Henry Buck's plantation home (part of the Buck's Mill Farm), which was built in 1838 and renovated in the 1980s. Here, Buck became one of Horry County's largest slaveholders. The plantation sat in Bucksville (known as the Middle Mill), Buck's most notable community, where numerous ships built by the W.L. Bucks Company were also launched. One Bucksville-built ship in particular, *Henrietta*, seen at right, sailed worldwide and brought fame to Horry County's shipbuilding and timber industries before being lost in a shipwreck off the coast of Japan in 1894. (Both, courtesy of the Horry County Museum.)

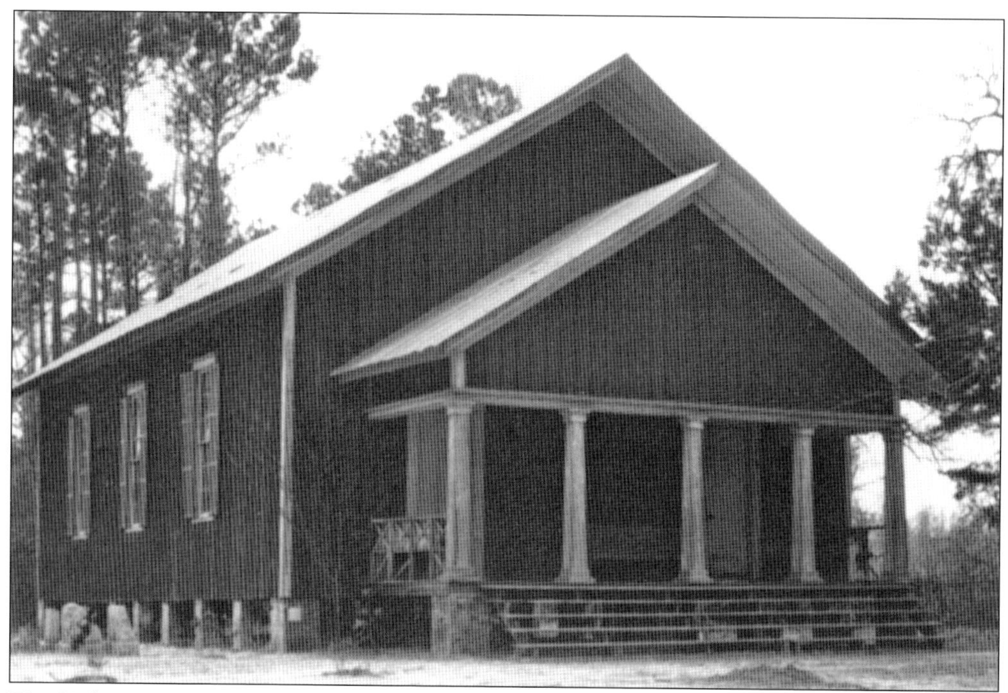

The Hebron United Methodist Church's roots date back to 1762, when it was built by John Singleton. Construction on the present church, seen here, began in 1848 for a cost of $1,700, and sources vary on the year it was finished, but the most credible estimates conclude it was completed in 1851. (Courtesy of the University of South Carolina.)

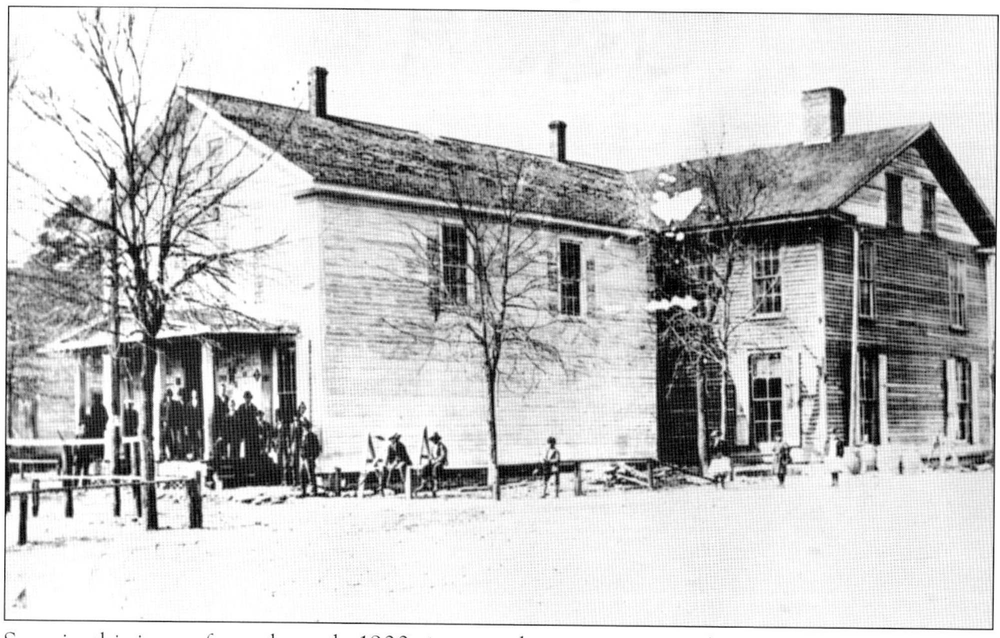

Seen in this image from the early 1900s is a naval store operation that existed near Bucksville. Naval stores are products such as turpentine and tar used to preserve wooden ships. Created from longleaf pine trees, these products were made across the southeastern United States for consumers worldwide due to the area's abundance of pine trees. (Courtesy of the Horry County Museum.)

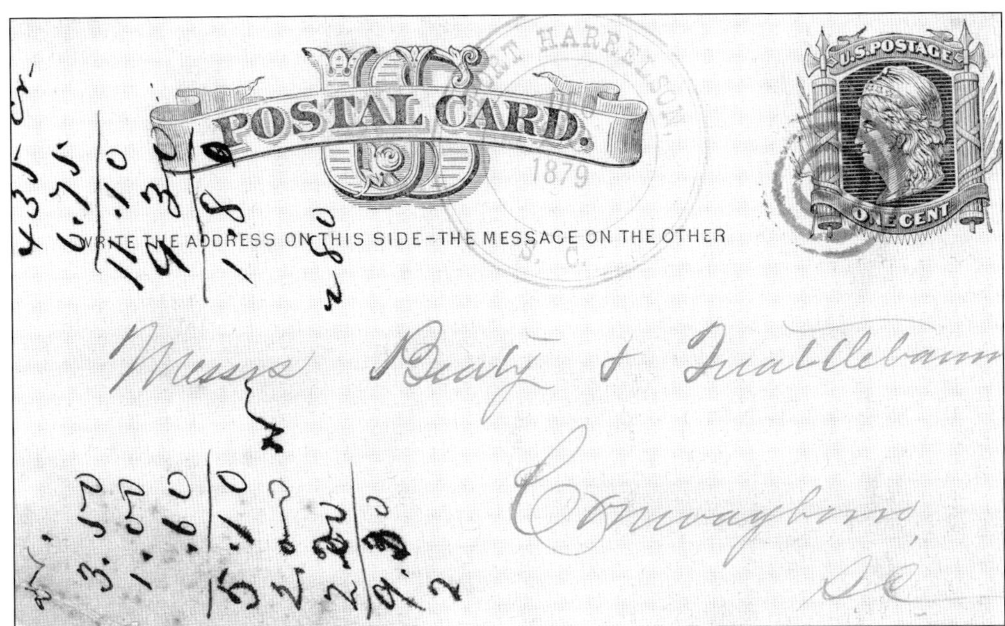

Port Harrelson, located near Bucksport, was another community that once saw great success with the lumber industry. The community was also referred to as Yauhannah and Bull Creek and held a post office from 1870 to 1916 under the Port Harrelson and Bull Creek names. Henry Buck was its first postmaster. Seen above is a Port Harrelson postage cancel stamp from an 1879 postcard sent to Conwayborough, spelled here as Conwayboro. Another postal cover referencing Buck's Lower Mill (which later became Bucksport) and Port Harrelson is also seen below. Aside from these communities, Eddy Lake was also a lumber-producing village that existed between Bucksport and Port Harrelson and housed the Eddy Lake Cypress Lumber Company. Once a rather successful village with a grocery store, church, and cabins for workers, the community's success collapsed when its mill burned down in roughly 1909. The community was subsequently largely abandoned.

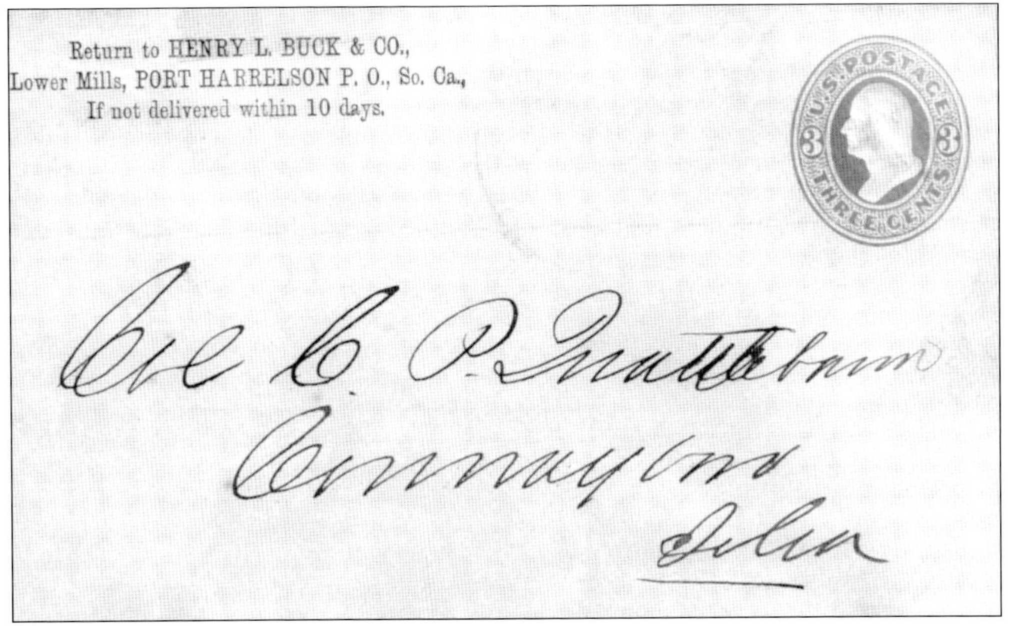

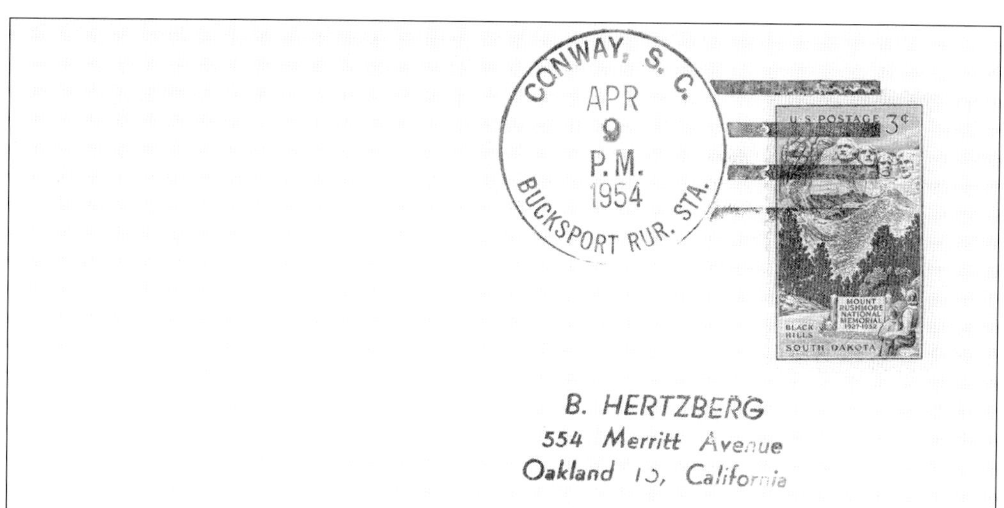

Buck's Lower Mill, vital for transporting locally produced lumber-related goods worldwide, is believed to be the last of Henry Buck's mills founded in Horry County. It was first known as Murdock's Landing. In 1837, Capt. Samuel Pope and Henry Buck purchased land here, and a sawmill named Pope's Mill was then established. After Pope sold his share of this enterprise, the vicinity became known as Buck's Lower Mill by the 1840s and was subsequently renamed Bucksport in ensuing decades. This community's first post office was built in 1854 as Buck's Lower Mill. Known as the Bucksport Post Office after 1894, it was the first post office in Horry County to gain electricity. It operated independently until 1926, when it became a rural station under Conway's post office, as it is referred to above. It closed permanently in 1956. As the lumber industry lost prevalence in Bucksport, the community primarily relied on farming after the 1920s. Bucksport's marina remains active, as seen in the 1950s image below, and is especially popular for water recreationalists.

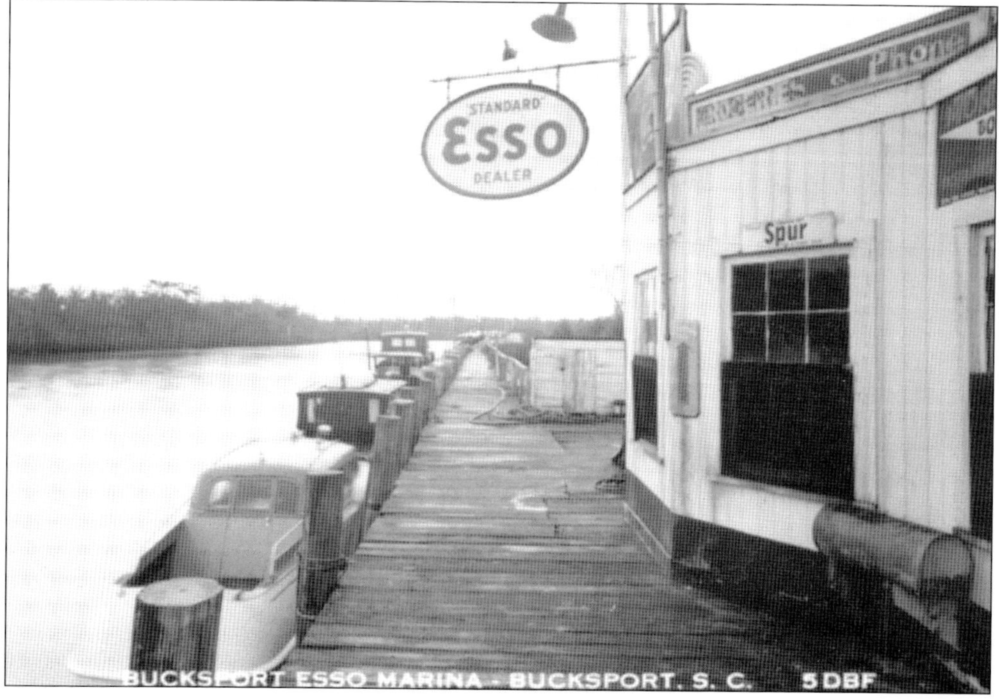

As Bucksport is a historically African American community, many residents are the descendants of Henry Buck's slaves and were raised in sharecropping families. Education has therefore been a hard-fought resource in Bucksport due to racial and economic barriers. One early public school in Bucksport built for the African American community that provided all grade levels was the Richardson Training School. It closed in the 1950s. Bucksport Elementary School, built in 1954 and seen below, also holds a history as an equalization school. Once schools were integrated, many of these buildings were abandoned or were repurposed. Bucksport Elementary School's building became a community center. A map of the Bucksport area with neighboring communities is seen at right. (Right, courtesy of the University of South Carolina.)

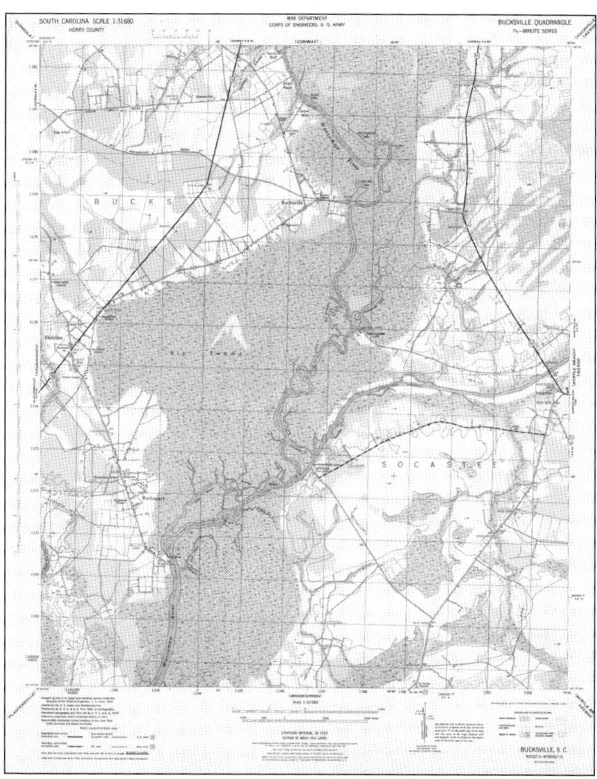

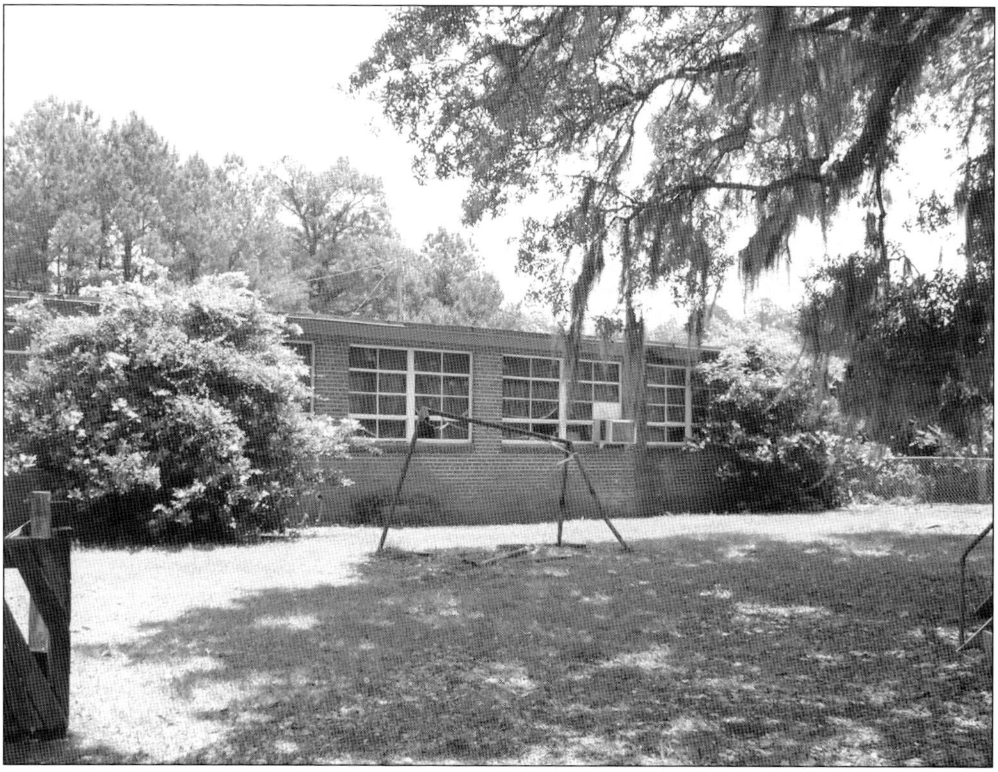

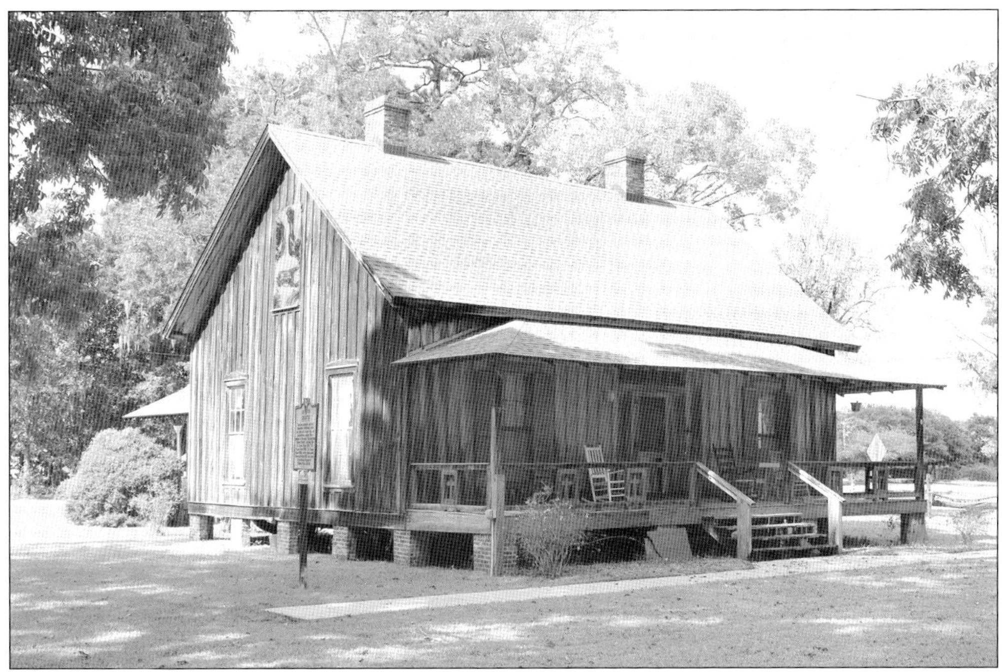

The Sarvis-Ammons House is Socastee's oldest standing building. The residence was built largely with cypress wood by Samuel Scarborough Sarvis, a Socastee turpentine businessman and Civil War veteran. Construction finished on the home in 1881. After remaining in the Sarvis family until 1975, it was purchased by Jane Sarvis Ammons in 1983 and eventually renovated before being sold to the Socastee Heritage Foundation.

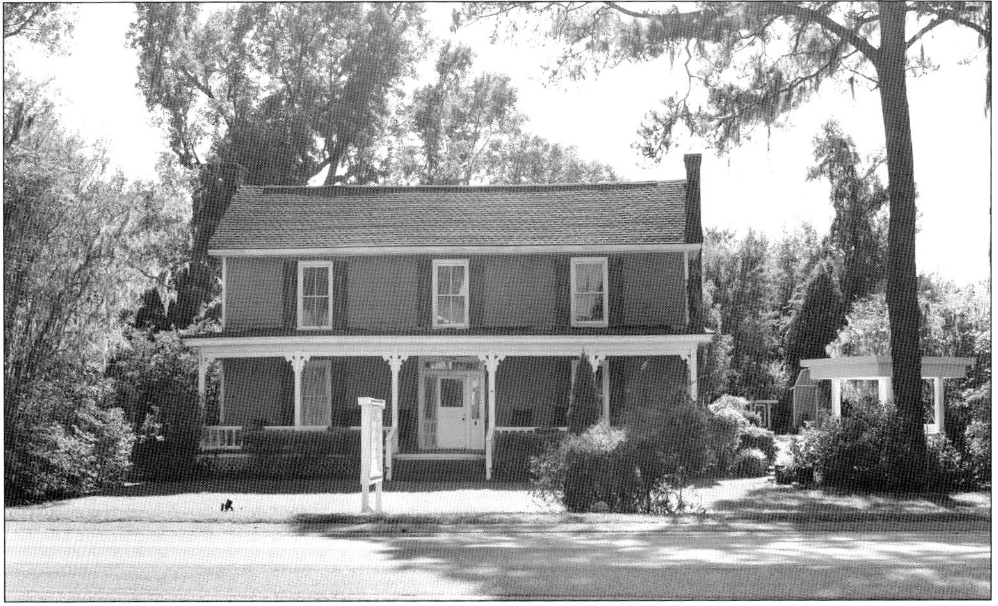

The Thomas B. Cooper House was built in approximately 1908 by Robert H. Price and was constructed for Thomas B. Cooper, a Socastee community postmaster and turpentine businessman who also owned the T.B. Cooper Store. In the century since its construction, the home has been renovated. A century-old pecan grove also sits on the property.

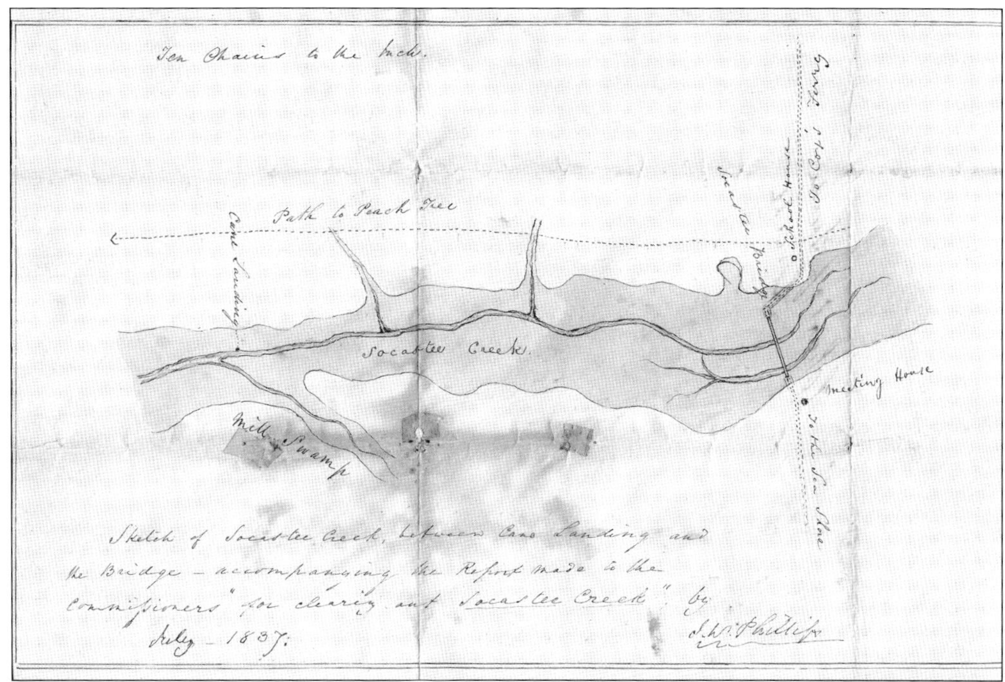

On this 18th-century map, early plats in the Socastee vicinity are shown, and it portrays the landscapes where many early settlers resided. Socastee was first called Sawkestee, a Native American term that can be found in various land deeds from the 1800s. The spelling "Sawkestee" was anglicized to "Socastee," which remains the community's moniker today. (Courtesy of the Horry County Museum.)

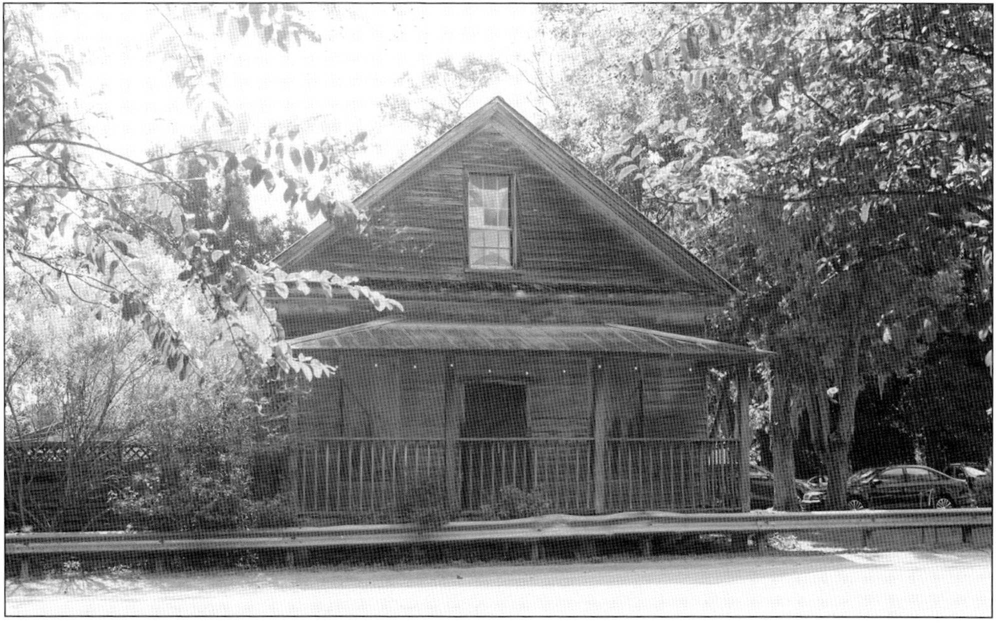

The T.B. Cooper Store was constructed in 1905, and a general mercantile operated in this building until roughly 1930. Located adjacent to the Thomas B. Cooper House, the store was an early gathering place for many in this formerly rural vicinity, and notably, the store also housed a post office in its early years.

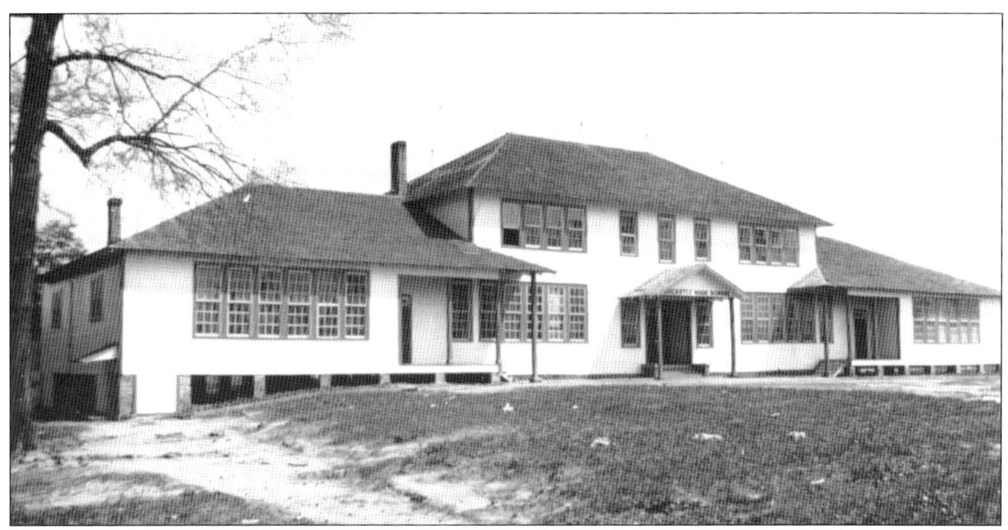

Socastee High School has a unique history as it was one of Horry County's largest public high schools. In this 1930s image of Socastee's first high school, a two-story building used by generations of Socastee students is shown. Socastee High School also held several other structures on its original campus, including a teacherage and science building, before this schoolhouse burned down in 1953. (Courtesy of the Horry County Museum.)

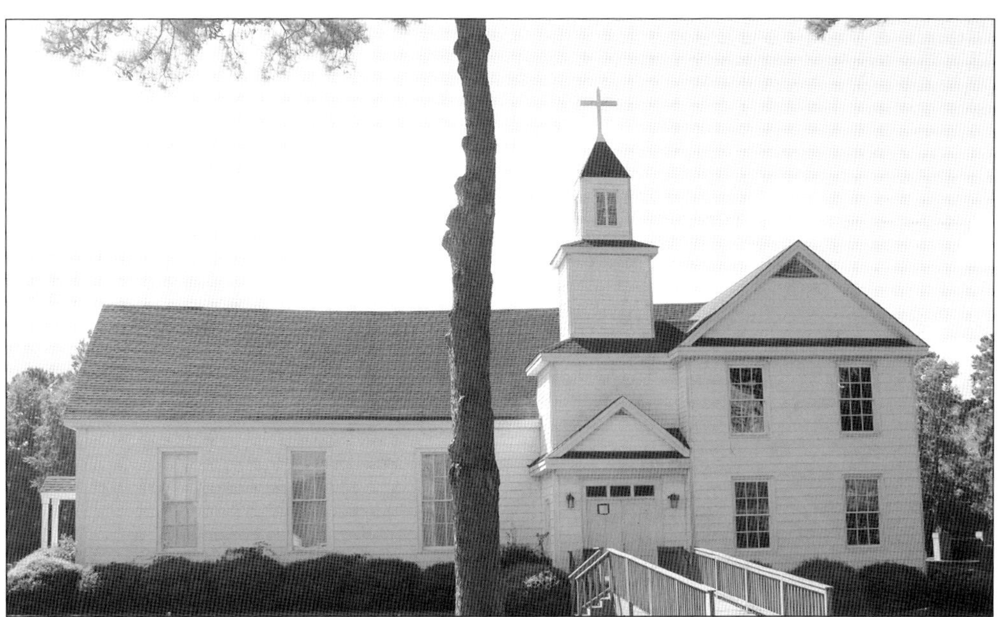

Religion in Socastee is another important aspect of the community's culture and heritage. Socastee United Methodist Church is the community's oldest church, and the congregation was established in the early 1800s. Though several fires and disasters have destroyed buildings on the church property, structures and graves from the 19th century can still be found. A church sanctuary built in 1875 is seen in this image.

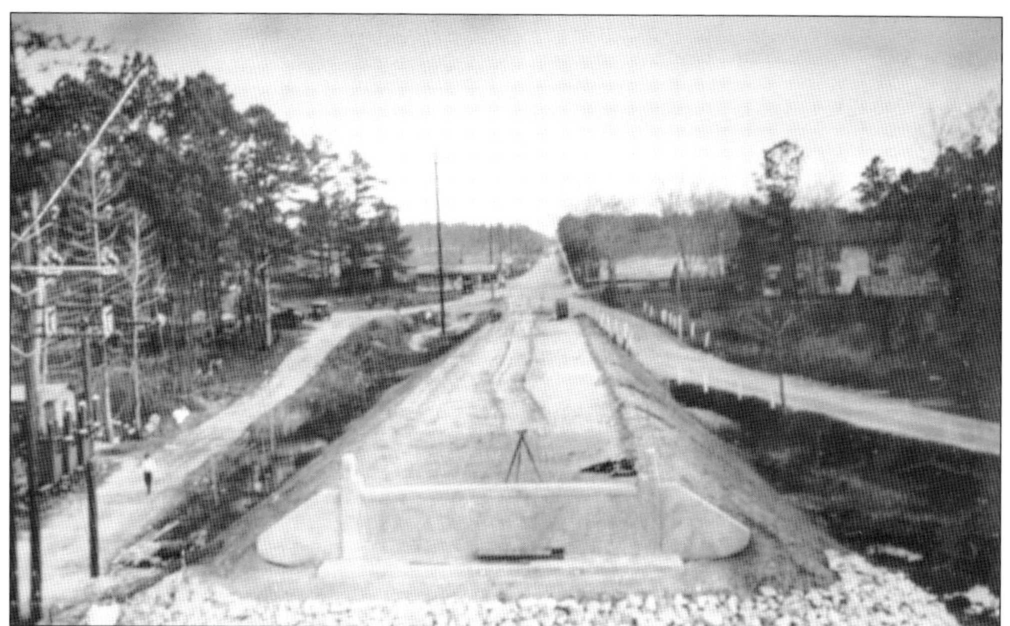

The Atlantic Intracoastal Waterway, a man-made water channel that runs from Massachusetts to Florida, is a major part of Socastee's maritime heritage. In 1929, the US Army Corps of Engineers was assigned with maintaining the whole waterway, and these engineers constructed Horry County's portion of the canal during the Great Depression. An image of the waterway's construction in Socastee is seen in the above image. The Socastee Swing Bridge, opened in 1936, is another important aspect of Socastee's history. Constructed from steel, the bridge operates on a swing trestle that allows the bridge to move for oncoming boat traffic along the Atlantic Intracoastal Waterway. In recent decades, the swing bridge, seen in the modern image below, became the topic of preservation efforts and underwent significant renovations. (Above, courtesy of the Horry County Museum.)

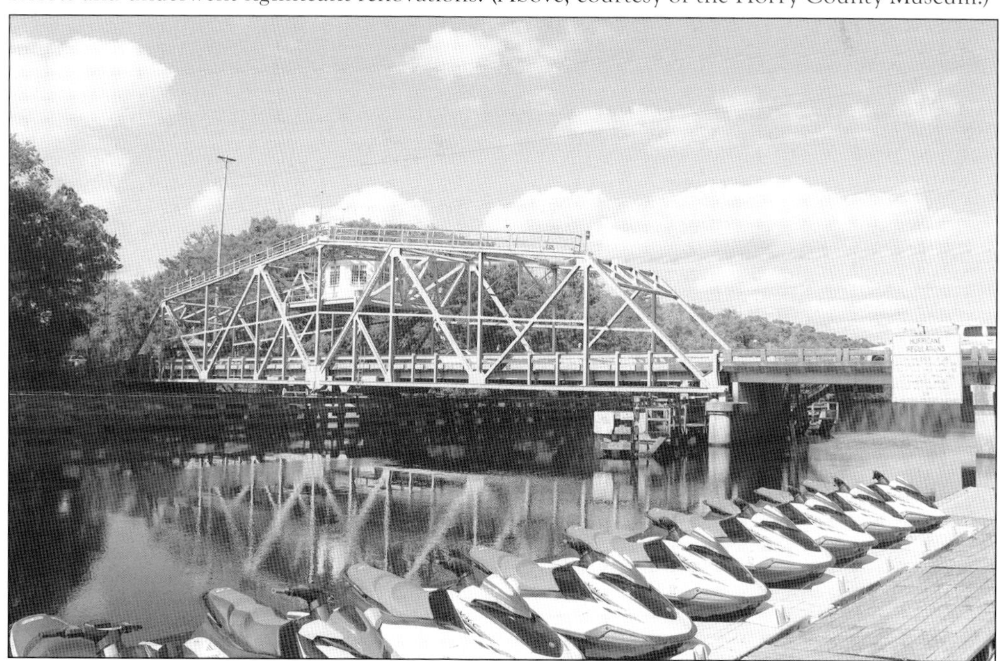

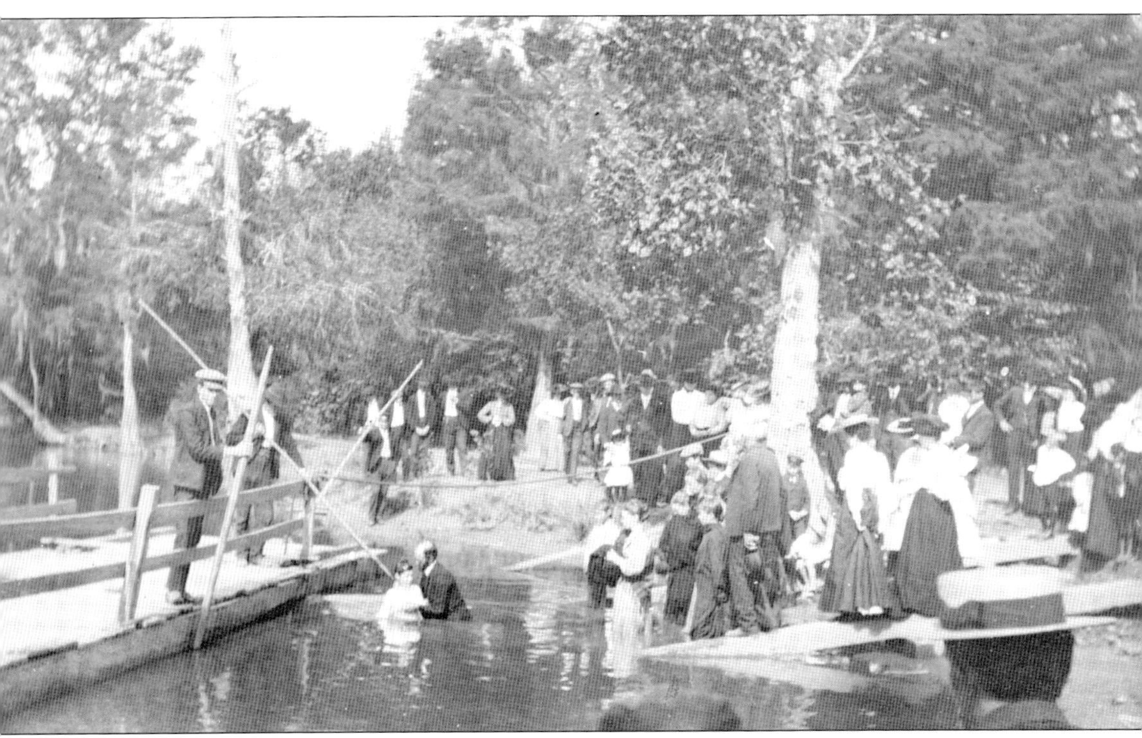

Peachtree Landing is a small recreational port located along the Waccamaw River in the Socastee community. A vital boating port in Horry County's early years, many goods were traded from here to various destinations. Peachtree Landing also once held a locally noted ferry that allowed people to travel from Socastee to Conway at a time when land travel was not always readily accessible due to a lack of adequate roads in Horry County. Beachgoers especially utilized Peachtree Landing's ferry at this time to travel to coastal locations such as Murrells Inlet. Christian groups in the area, mostly of the Baptist faith, also used Peachtree Landing for baptisms and revival services. An example of a baptism at Peachtree Landing is seen in this image from the 1920s. (Courtesy of the Horry County Museum.)

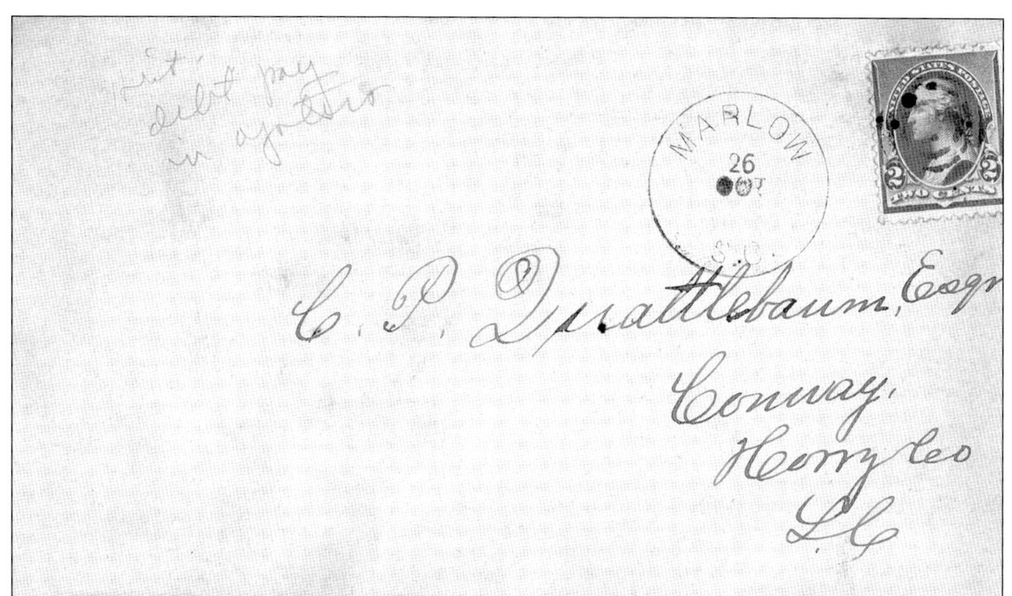

Settled in the late 1800s as a farming community, the present-day community of Burgess was once named Marlow. The community gained its original name from John Marlow, who served as the community's first postmaster from 1880 until 1881. The community's former name can be seen in this postal cancel mark from the 1890s.

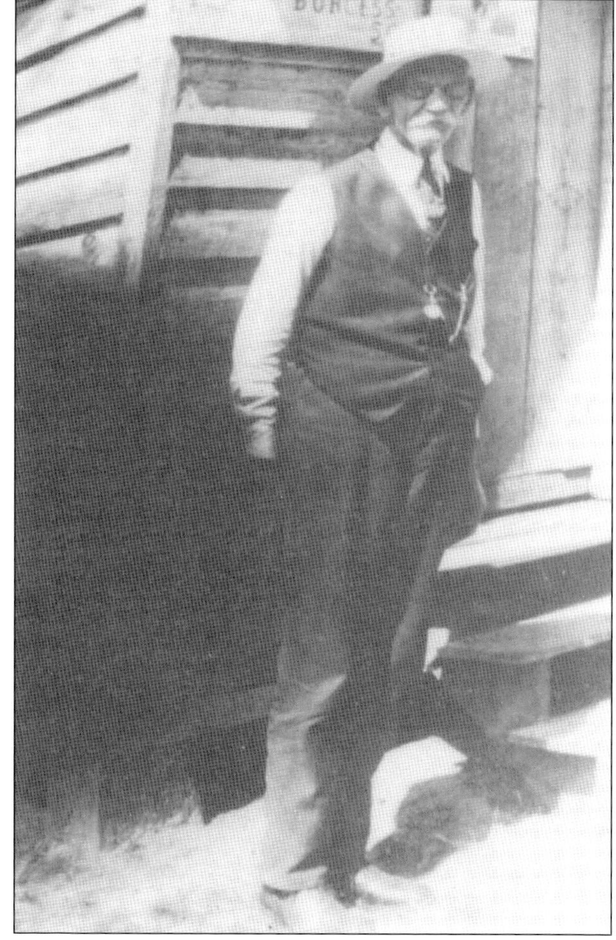

William Burgess, seen in this 1920s image, became Marlow's postmaster in 1887. He was the longest-serving postmaster in the community and, in 1906, helped change the community's name to Burgess. William Burgess remained the community's postmaster until he died in 1934. At this time, the Burgess community remains rather unchanged from its original state, with many of its residents continuing to work in the agriculture industry. (Courtesy of the Horry County Museum.)

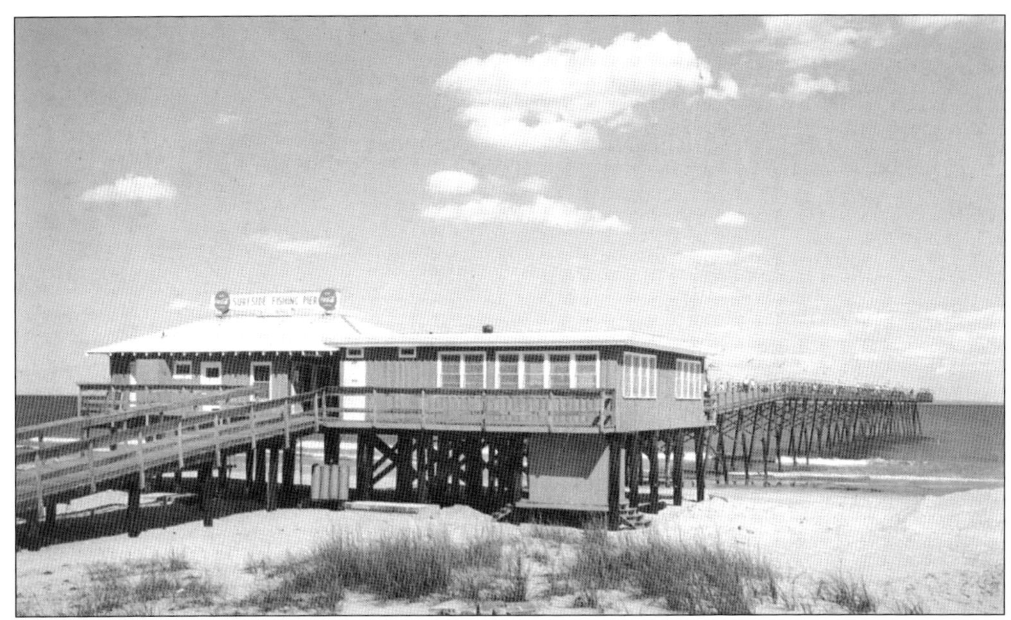

Surfside Beach sits on lands of the former Ark Plantation, which was parceled and liquidated after its last owner, John Tillman, died in 1865. Decades later, one of the coastal parcels was named Roach's Beach. This property was again sold to George J. Holliday, who renamed the area Floral Beach for his wife and daughter. In the 1920s, businessmen from Columbia, South Carolina, partially developed the property, and in 1952, it was again sold and renamed Surfside Beach. The Surfside Beach Fishing Pier is seen in the above image from the 1950s. Sparsely populated at this time, Surfside Beach's rural ambience is captured in the postal mark seen in the image below, which shows Surfside Beach maintained a rural station post office, once a satellite branch of the Myrtle Beach Post Office.

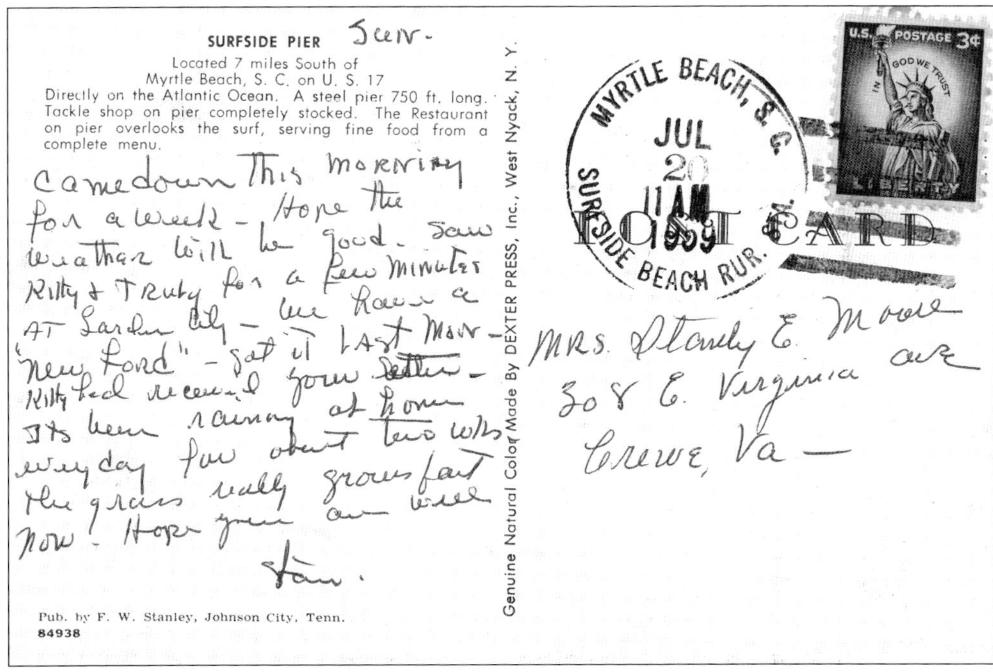

SURFSIDE PIER Sun.

Located 7 miles South of
Myrtle Beach, S. C. on U. S. 17
Directly on the Atlantic Ocean. A steel pier 750 ft. long. Tackle shop on pier completely stocked. The Restaurant on pier overlooks the surf, serving fine food from a complete menu.

Came down this morning for a week – Hope the weather will be good. Saw Kitty & Truby for a few minutes at Garden City – we have a "new Ford" – got it last Mon. – Kitty had received your letter – It's been raining at home every day for about two wks the grass really grows fast. Hope you are well now!

Stan.

Pub. by F. W. Stanley, Johnson City, Tenn.
84938

Genuine Natural Color Made By DEXTER PRESS, Inc., West Nyack, N. Y.

POST CARD

U.S. POSTAGE 3¢
IN GOD WE TRUST
LIBERTY

MYRTLE BEACH, S.C.
JUL 20 11 AM 1959
SURFSIDE BEACH RUR. STA.

Mrs. Stanley E. Moore
308 E. Virginia ave
Crewe, Va –

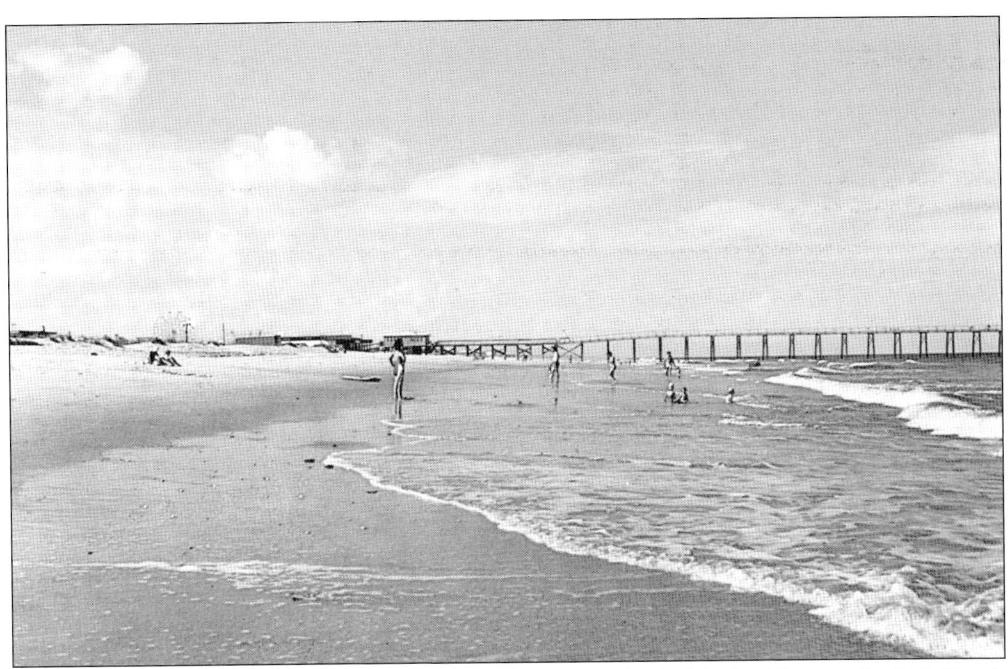

In the 1950s, though Hurricane Hazel destroyed almost one-third of the buildings in Surfside Beach and only six families permanently resided in the community, development nonetheless continued. By the early 1960s, Surfside Beach had drawn more transplants and numerous retirees and was becoming a popular tourist destination on its own accord. In the above image, one can see a 1950s view of the Surfside Beach Fishing Pier. As a result of the community's growth, Surfside Beach was incorporated as a town in 1964. Its first town hall, seen in the image below from 1983, served as the center of its municipal government and as a bank, jail, police department, fire station, and courthouse. It was eventually demolished in 2023.

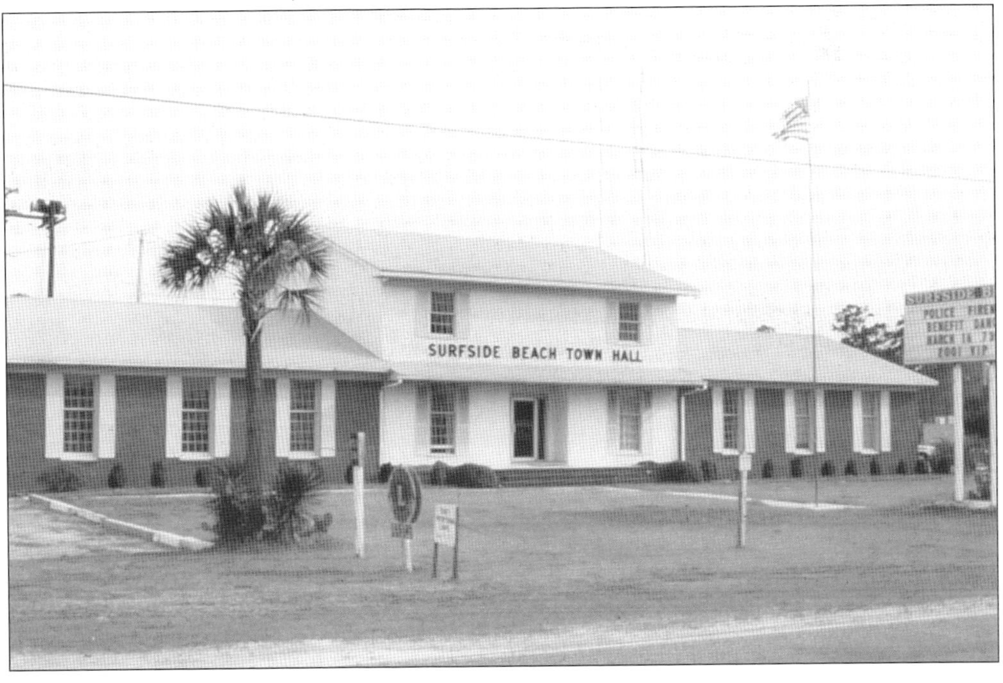

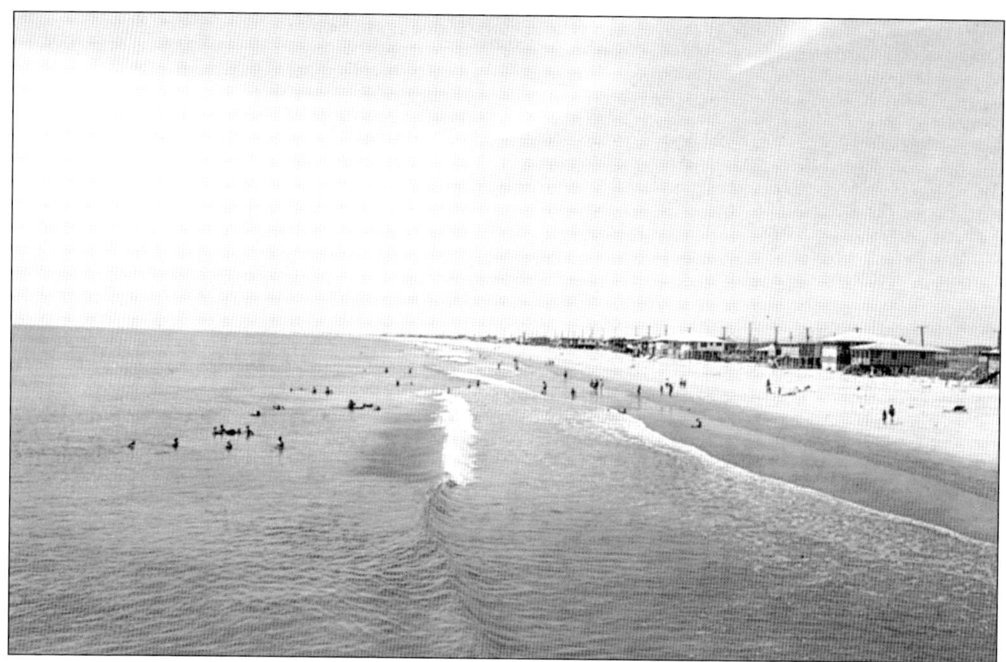

The community of Garden City also originated from lands once sitting on the former Ark Plantation. Largely devastated in 1954 by Hurricane Hazel, which left only two Garden City residences habitable, the community recovered, and development continued in the ensuing decades. However, Garden City's once-sparse nature can be captured in this early-1960s image, which shows only a few buildings along Garden City's shoreline.

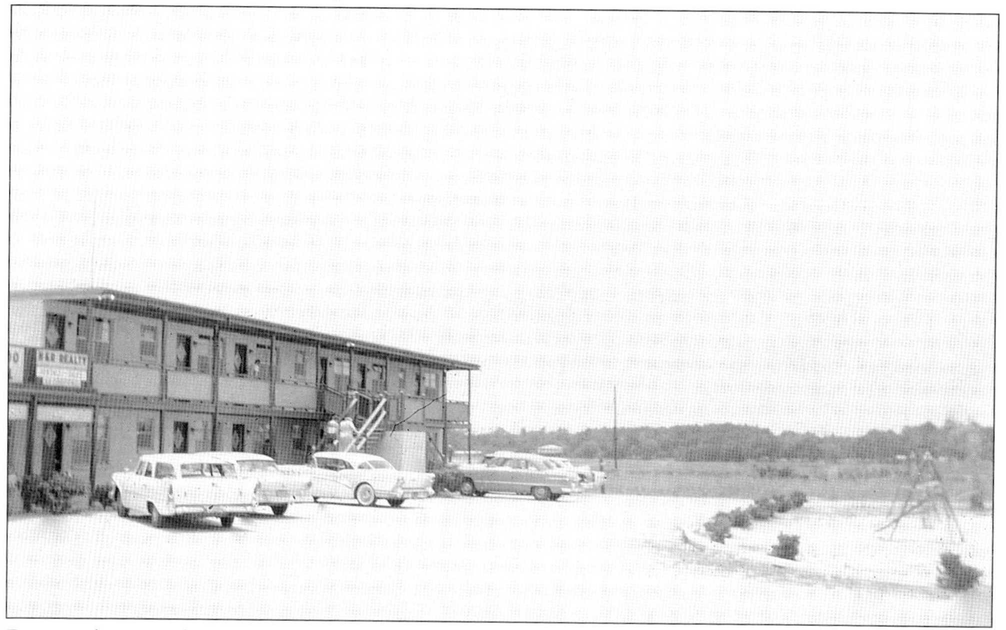

During the growth of Garden City's hospitality industry after Hurricane Hazel, several hotels and lodges were constructed, allowing Garden City to gain its own tourist clientele. In the above image from 1962, unidentified tourists are seen outside the Bamboo Motel. The Garden City Motor Inn is another example of the community's early hospitality enterprises.

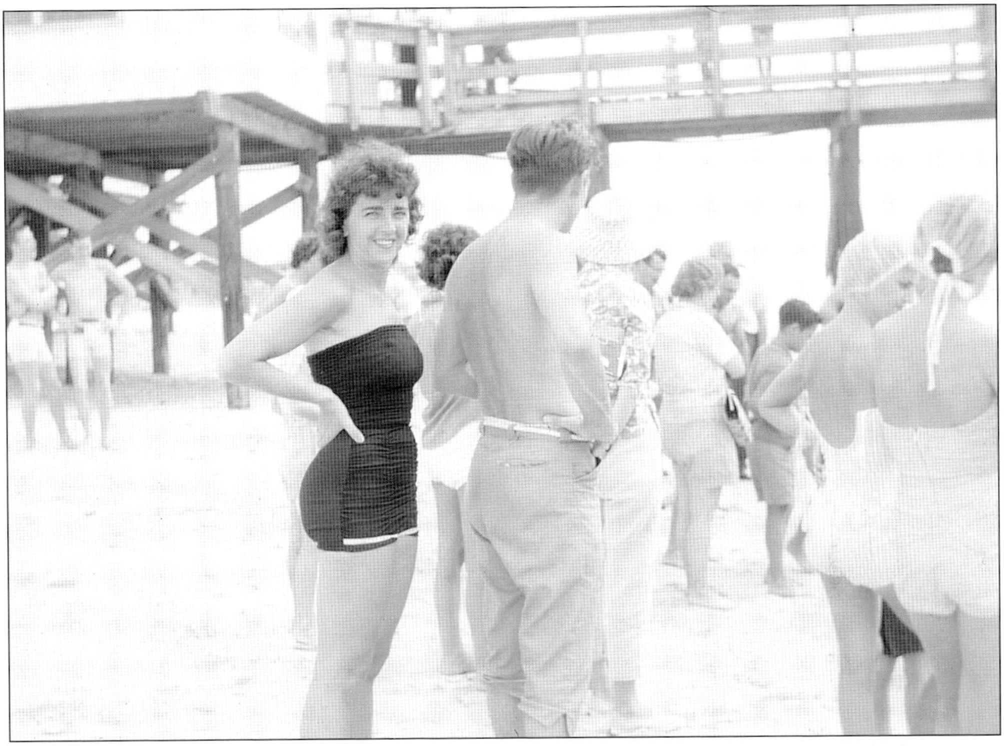

The Garden City Beach Fishing Pier, also known as the Kingfisher Pier, was built in the late 1950s following Hurricane Hazel's aftermath. The original pier, seen in these early-1960s images, was a popular community and tourist attraction. As Garden City was sparsely populated until the latter 20th century, the Kingfisher Pier is one attraction (like the Garden City Pavilion) that helped Garden City gain attention as its own reputable, family-friendly vacation destination. Well-loved by locals, fishermen, and tourists alike, the first Kingfisher Pier was destroyed in 1989 by Hurricane Hugo, which left 43 percent of Garden City's structures in ruin. After that disaster, the pier was rebuilt in 1992 to its current state and is now known as the Pier at Garden City.

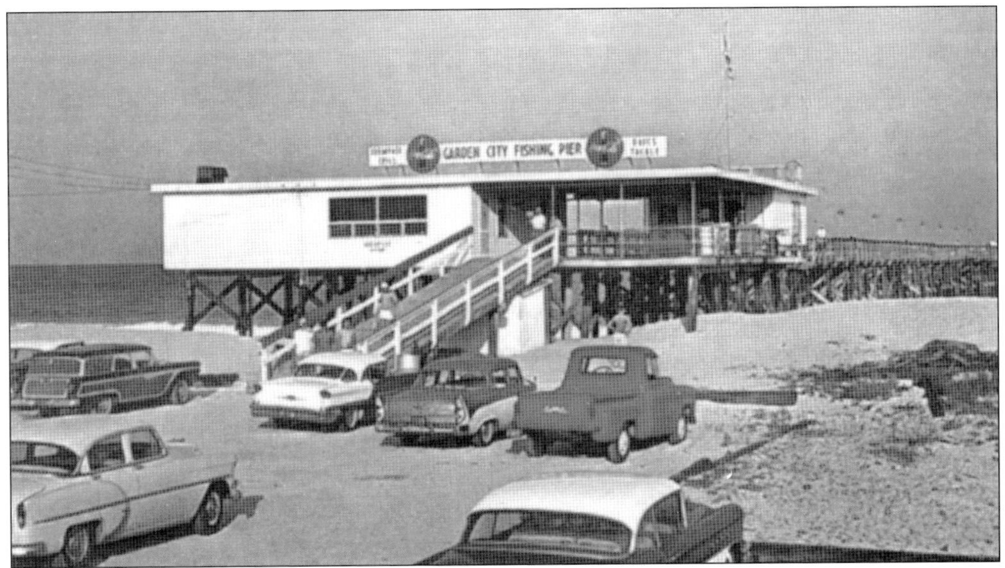

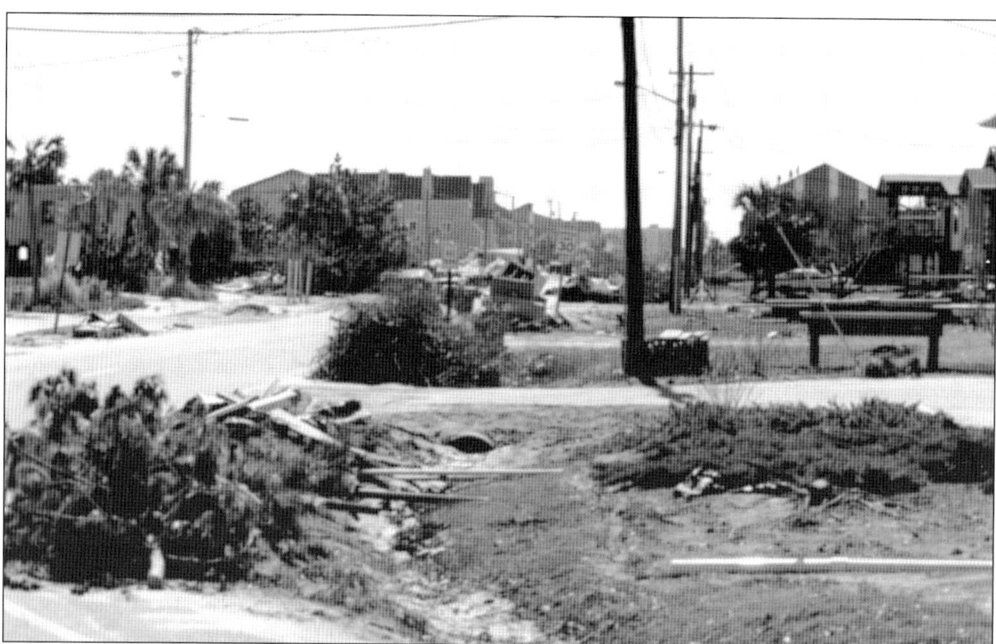

In terms of recorded pressure, Hurricane Hugo was the most intense Atlantic hurricane of the 1980s. Reaching Category 5 strength, Hurricane Hugo decimated several Caribbean islands during its first landfall. Its second landfall, with 140 mile-per-hour winds, occurred on September 22, 1989, at Sullivan's Island, South Carolina. This unleashed devastation along South Carolina's coast that drew parallels to Hurricane Hazel in 1954, and the Grand Strand faced widespread destruction. Damage from Hurricane Hugo in southern Horry County can be seen in the above image. Nevertheless, the region gathered after the crisis, and this sentiment is represented by the image below of a Myrtle Beach resident, Kathy Heaton, seen helping clear local storm damage during Hurricane Hugo's aftermath. (Below, courtesy of Angela Heaton McRae.)

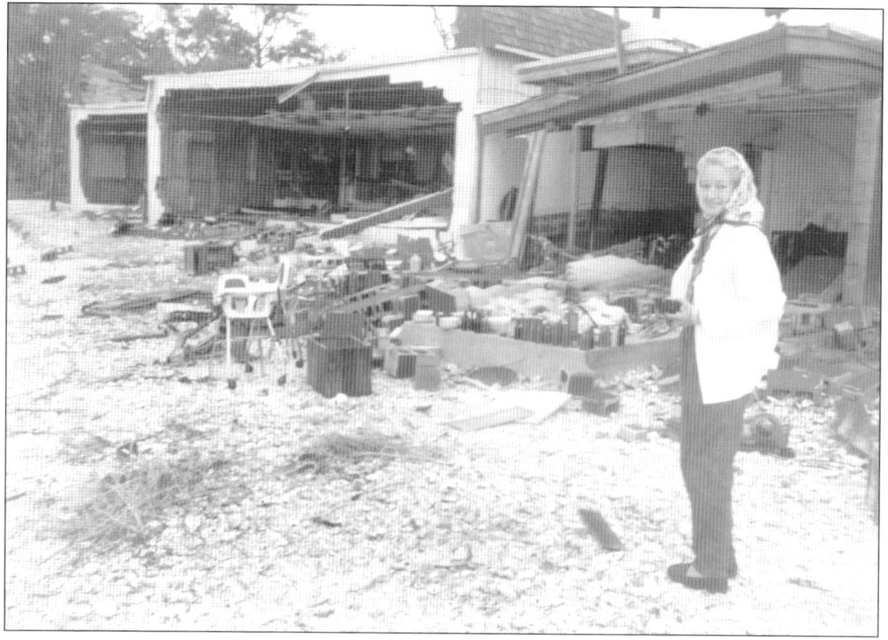

Four

From Maritime Scenes to Tobacco

Northern and Western Horry County

Though northern and western Horry County share similarities in the fact that both sections are historically rural, they also have their own features that make them unique. For example, northern Horry County holds Little River, a noted fishing haven believed to be Horry County's oldest settlement. This section of Horry County also held the small townships of Ocean Drive Beach, Crescent Beach, Cherry Grove Beach, and Windy Hill Beach, all of which were merged and consolidated into the city of North Myrtle Beach in 1968. A popular dance, the shag, is believed to have originated in the North Myrtle Beach area. Nearby is the historic town of Atlantic Beach, known as the "Black Pearl," which was once Horry County's sole beach for African Americans and was one of the East Coast's most popular Black-only resorts. Going farther into northern Horry County, one will find the city of Loris, once immensely popular for the production of turpentine and tobacco, as well as the communities of Green Sea, Longs, Floyds, Goretown, and Finklea, among others.

As of 2024, even with intense regional development, western Horry County has remained geographically similar to yesteryear. Still lined with farm fields and small communities, western Horry County holds Aynor; the community of Galivants Ferry; the present-day headquarters for the Waccamaw Indian People; and numerous unincorporated communities (including census-designated places). These communities include but are not limited to Jordanville, Poplar, Cool Spring, Red Hill (not to be confused with the other unincorporated community outside of Conway), Dog Bluff, Horry, Bakers Chapel, Gunters Island, and Ketchuptown. Though images of these communities are scarce, some are included in this chapter. Additionally, western Horry County has been known for its immense history within tobacco cultivation. Several communities in western Horry County stand out with history in the tobacco industry, especially Galivants Ferry. Galivants Ferry's tobacco production was noted nationally, especially due to the prominence of the Holliday family, and the community is still remembered for its immense contributions to Horry County's agricultural history and for the iconic Galivants Ferry Stump.

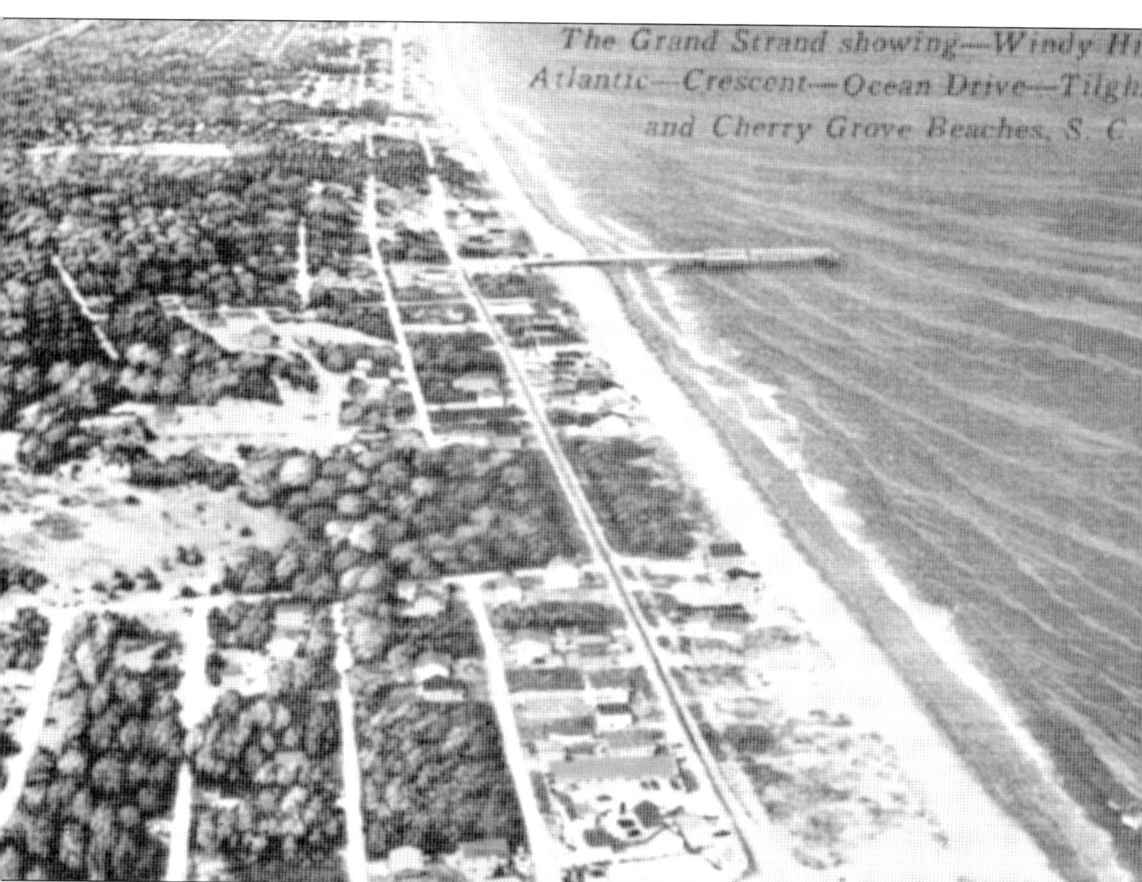

Incorporated as a city in 1968, North Myrtle Beach was formed from a consolidation of four townships: Ocean Drive Beach, Windy Hill Beach, Crescent Beach, and Cherry Grove Beach. Notably, North Myrtle Beach is quite younger than other communities in Horry County and not solely for its incorporation date. Though long frequented as a summer resort (even by Indigenous forebears of the Waccamaw and Winyah tribes), the land where North Myrtle Beach sits was largely owned by several families before tracts were sold off by the mid-20th century. By the 1940s and early 1950s, when most other communities in the region had been founded, tourists and inland Horry County residents had just begun establishing houses in what would become North Myrtle Beach, similar in style to what is seen in this 1940s postcard image. In 1954, Hurricane Hazel destroyed many buildings in the area, causing a redevelopment phase and subsequent growth surge by the time North Myrtle Beach incorporated in 1968.

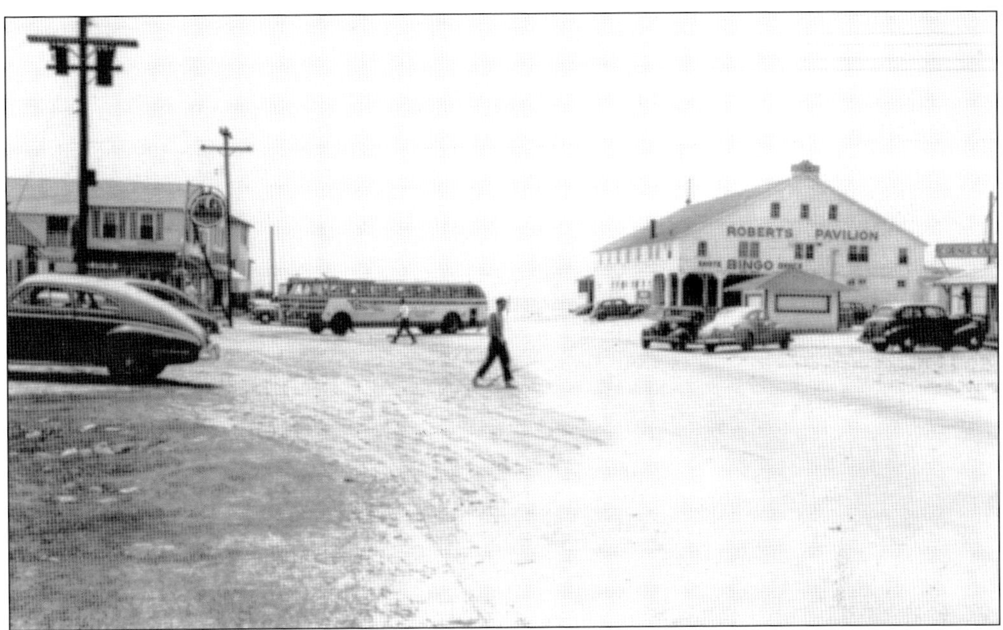

The largest of the four former townships merged to form North Myrtle Beach, Ocean Drive Beach was developed by investors from nearby Florence. Located in the township was the former Roberts Pavilion, seen in the 1947 image above, which was a popular attraction in the region before it was destroyed by Hurricane Hazel in 1954. The OD Pavilion subsequently opened on its site. Like most of coastal South Carolina and Horry County in general, Hurricane Hazel completely destroyed most of the buildings in Ocean Drive Beach, causing a redevelopment phase to ensue in the later 1950s. Growth of the community continued into the 1960s, when the image below was taken, at a time when the Grand Strand saw increasing popularity in its tourism industry. (Above, courtesy of the University of South Carolina.)

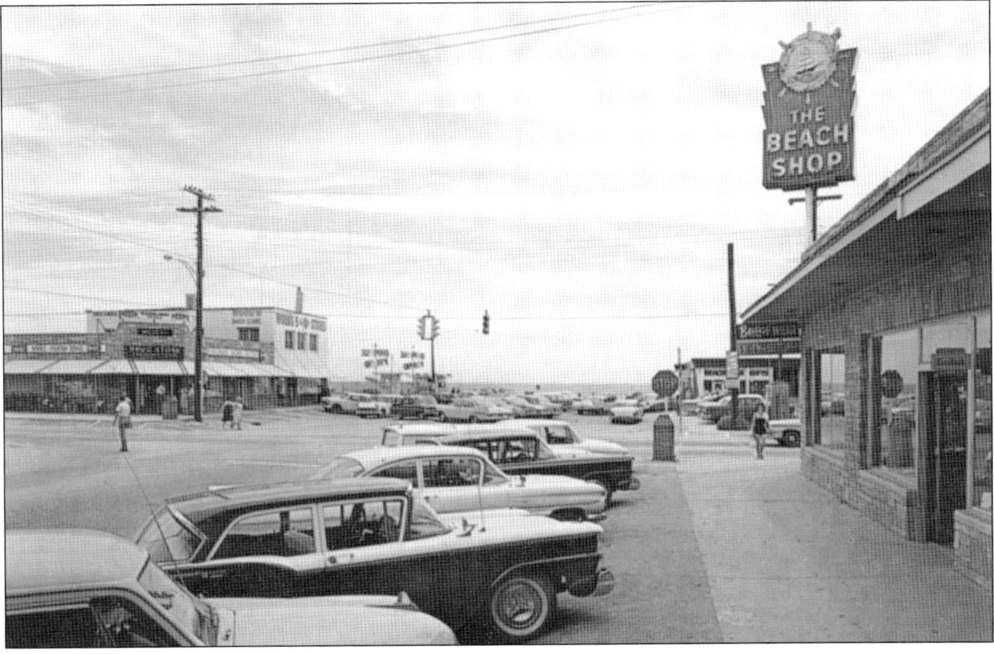

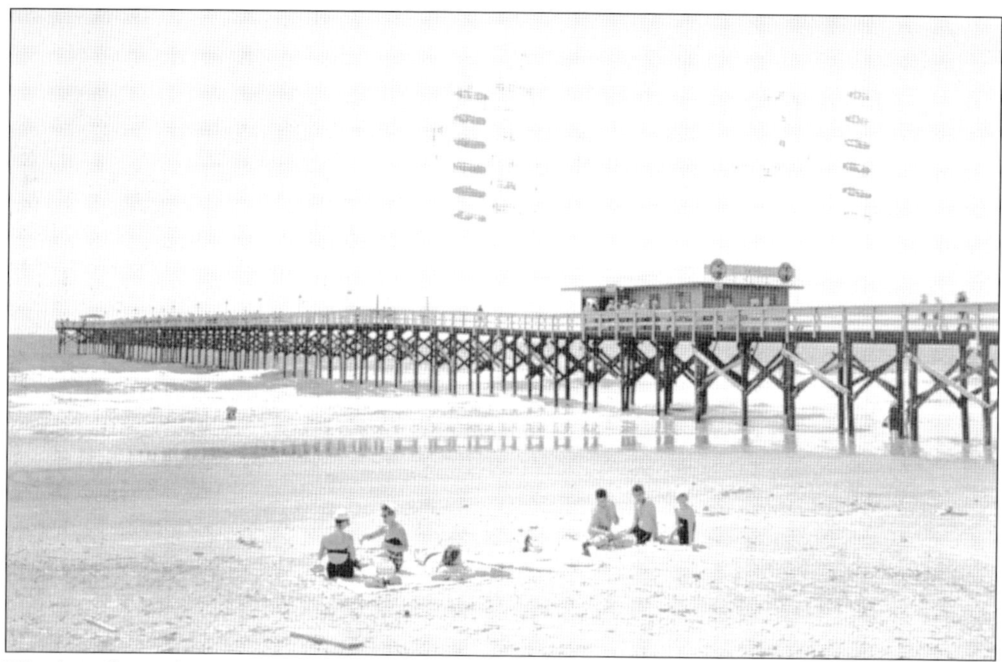

Windy Hill Beach traces its modern origins to the 1700s, when settler William Gause purchased much of the land in this vicinity for farming. Though the soils in the region were largely infertile and the timber industry took precedence, by the 1940s, when local roads were paved, this area began to be developed. In Windy Hill Beach's case, this community was developed by investors from Conway, who began planning the community following World War II. The Windy Hill Beach Pier is seen in the above image. The image below shows an early-1960s view of Crescent Beach, a community known for its wide shoreline. It was the smallest of the townships merged to form North Myrtle Beach in 1968.

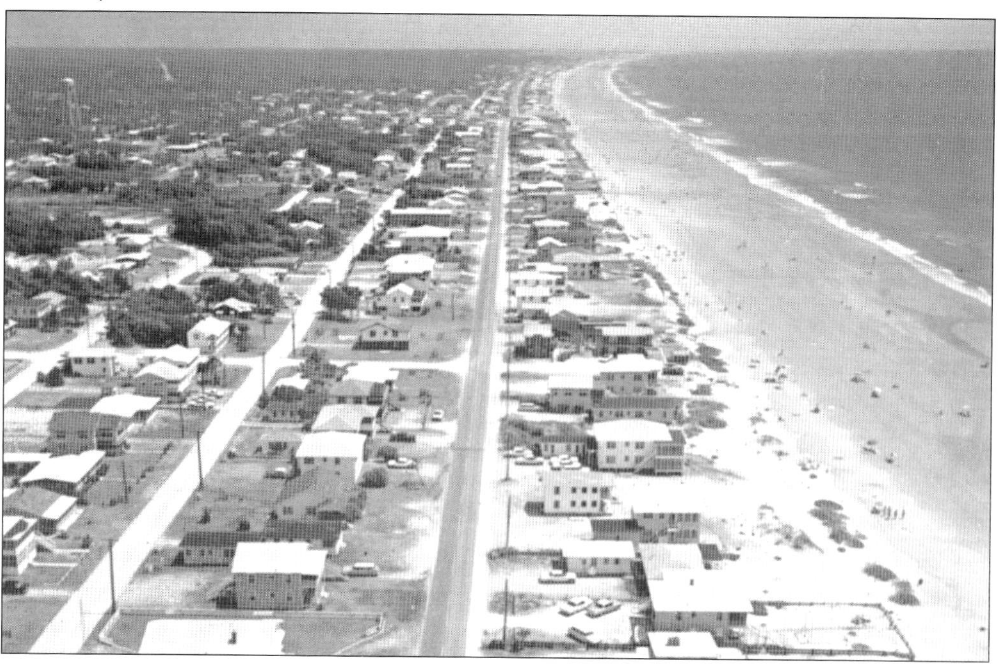

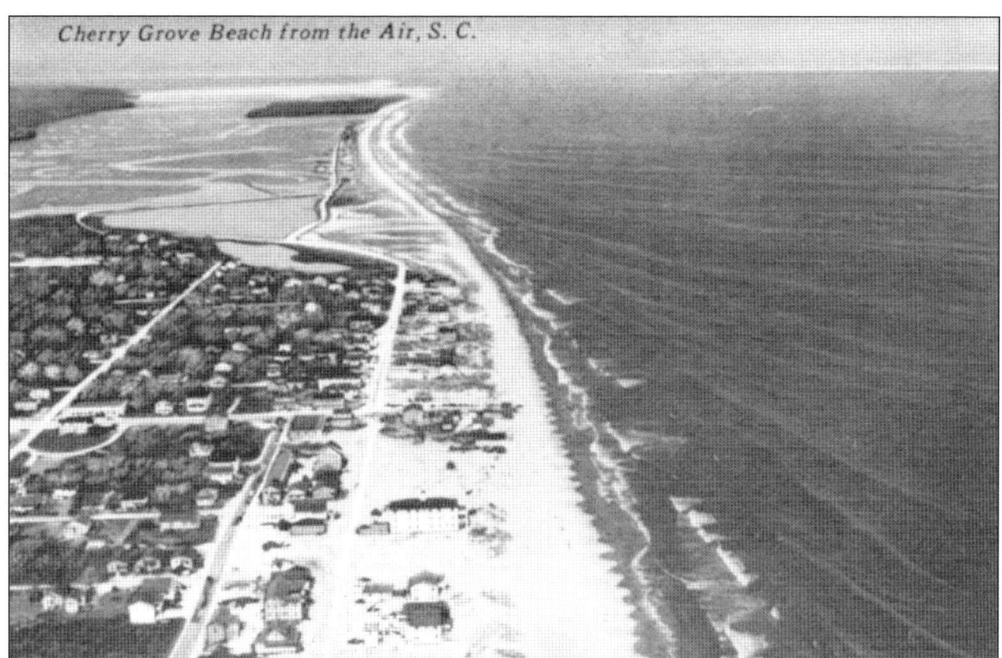

Cherry Grove Beach, seen above, sits on the former Cherry Grove Plantation, which derives its name from the wild cherry trees that once grew in the vicinity. Though the construction of the Atlantic Intracoastal Waterway destroyed many of these trees, the community retained its name, and growth continued. By 1950, the township of Cherry Grove Beach was officially founded from the consolidation of Futch Beach and another adjoining property.

Though several nearby locations claim to hold the origins of the shag, South Carolina's state dance, North Myrtle Beach is the shag's reputed birthplace. In the 1930s and 1940s, shag dancing was an integral feature of local nightclubs, and it would become a southeastern cultural phenomenon, especially upon the development of beach music. In this 1950s image, a young man is seen shag dancing at the Roberts Pavilion. (Courtesy of the Horry County Museum.)

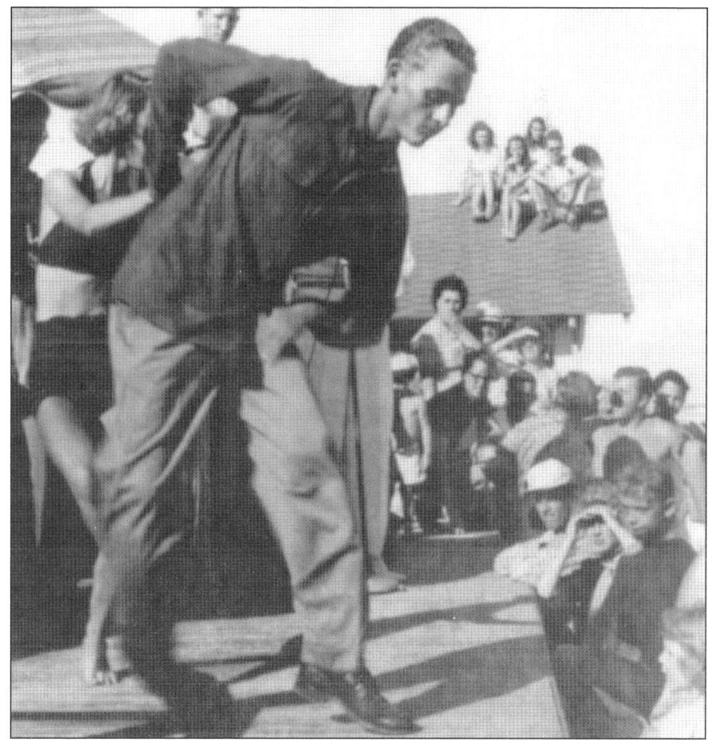

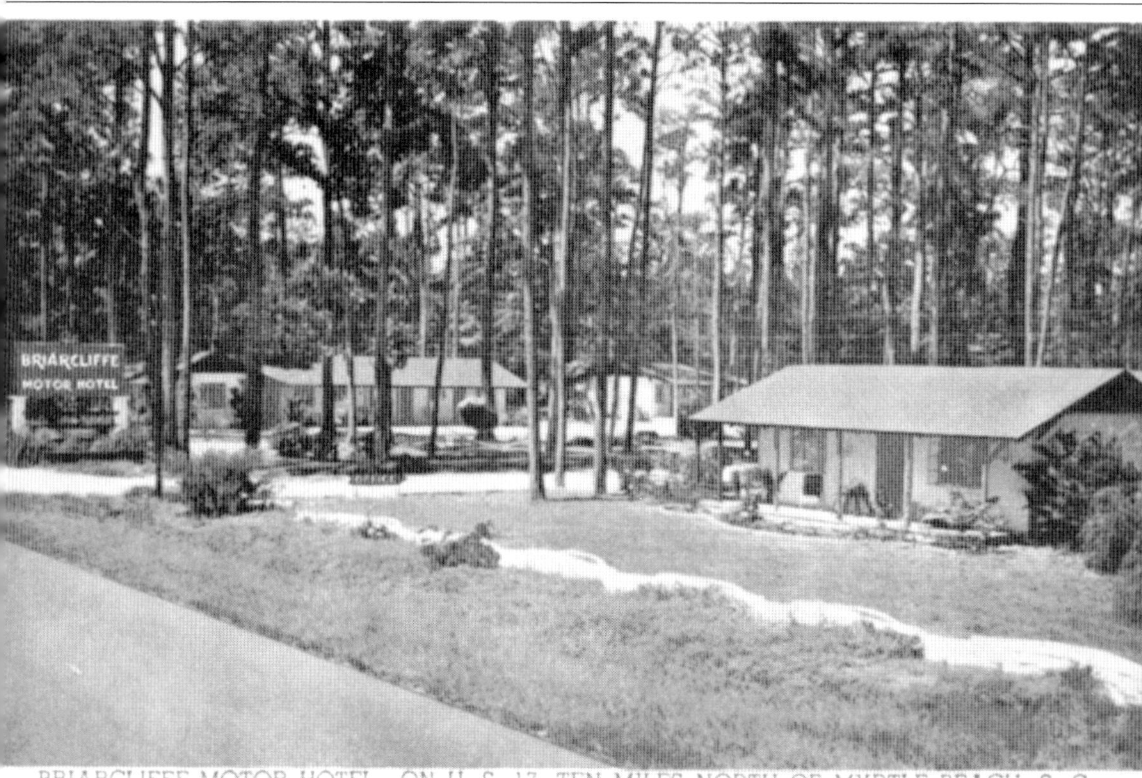

Briarcliffe Acres was founded in 1946 by Kenneth Ellsworth, the owner of Yaupon Acres (a local real estate company). Ellsworth purchased the 600 acres Briarcliffe Acres sits on for $150,000 and named it after his hometown of Briarcliff Manor, New York. Initially sparsely populated, Briarcliffe Acres only held a few families in the 1940s. Briarcliffe Acres suffered intense damage following Hurricane Hazel in 1954, but much of the community was rebuilt. Originally mainly a retirement community, once Myrtle Beach Air Force Base reopened in 1956, military officers began settling in the community along with families looking to find secure neighborhoods. One of the first planned communities in South Carolina, Briarcliffe Acres was gated by the late 1950s and incorporated as a town in 1976. A 1950s postcard of the Briarcliffe Motor Hotel is shown above.

Located on the border of Briarcliffe Acres and Myrtle Beach is the Meher Spiritual Center, named for Meher Baba, an Indian spiritual leader who is seen visiting the center in these images from 1952. Land was given for the center's creation by Simeon Chapin, whose daughter Elizabeth Patterson cofounded it in 1944 along with Norina Matchabelli. Patterson is seen with Meher Baba in the image at right. The location was chosen for its warm climate and features that would allow for a self-sustainable community. The Meher Spiritual Center also holds importance to followers of the Baha'i faith, which gained a slight following in South Carolina during the segregation years due to its messages of unity. (Both, courtesy of Meher Nazar Publications.)

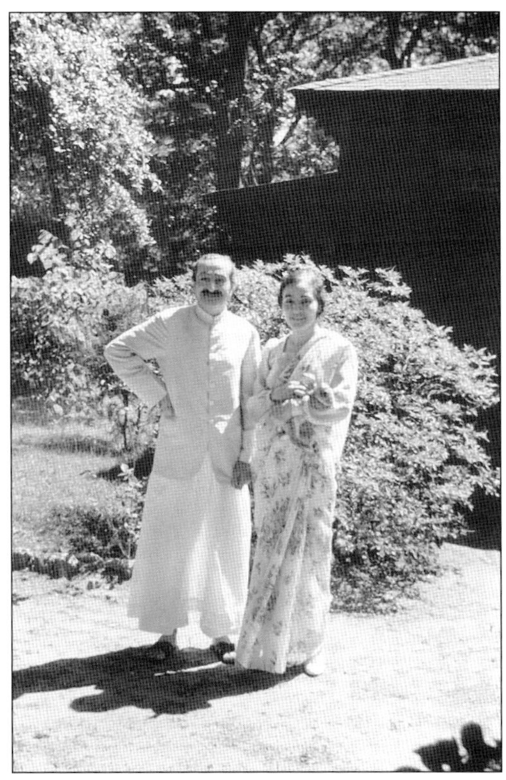

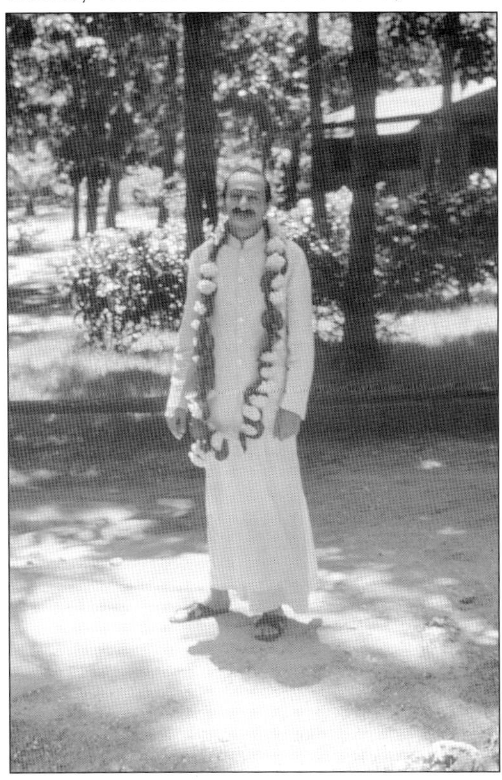

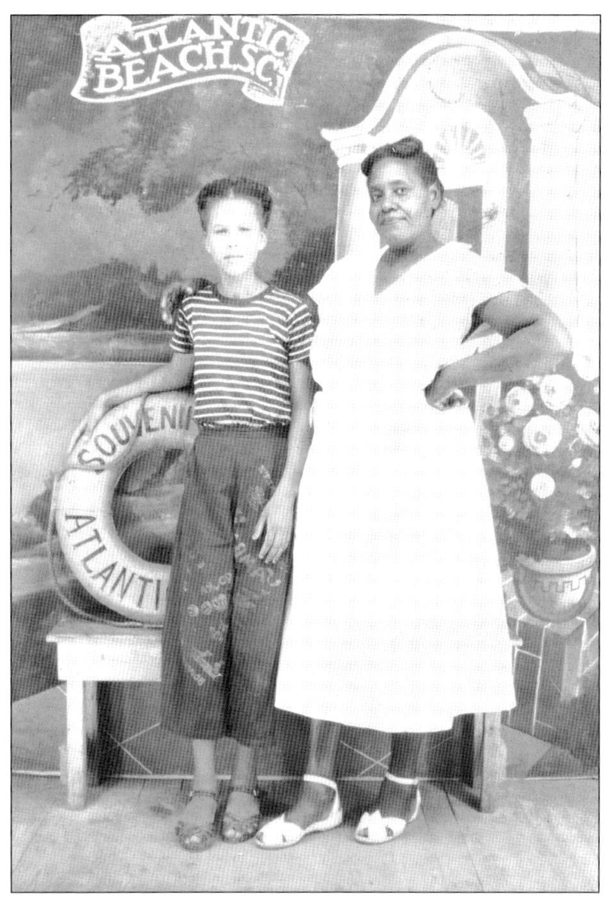

Before the 1960s, African Americans were barred from accessing Horry County beaches due to segregationist policies. As a result, African American entrepreneur George Tyson purchased 47 acres of land in northern Horry County in 1934, and Atlantic Beach's origins began. Atlantic Beach was soon established as a Black-only resort, allowing minority visitors to enjoy beachside attractions. In the image at left, two tourists, only identified as being from Burgaw, North Carolina, are seen posing in this 1940s souvenir photograph. In the ensuing years, a pier and more hotels were developed, while some families constructed homes to reside in the community full-time. Throughout the 1940s, Atlantic Beach continued to expand and became one of the Eastern Seaboard's most popular African American resorts; it is seen in the postcard below from approximately 1945.

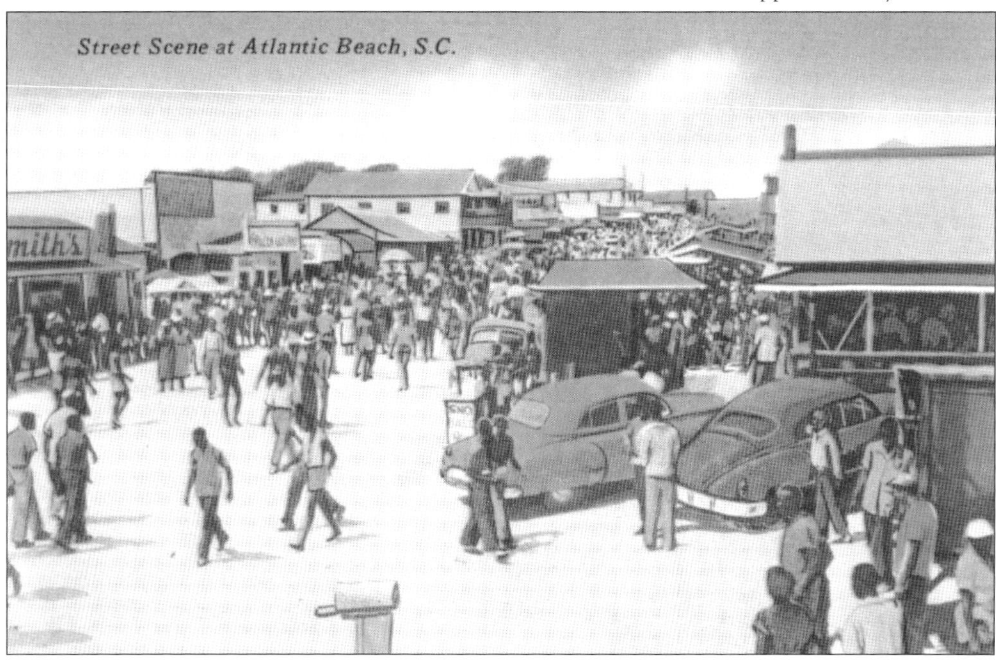

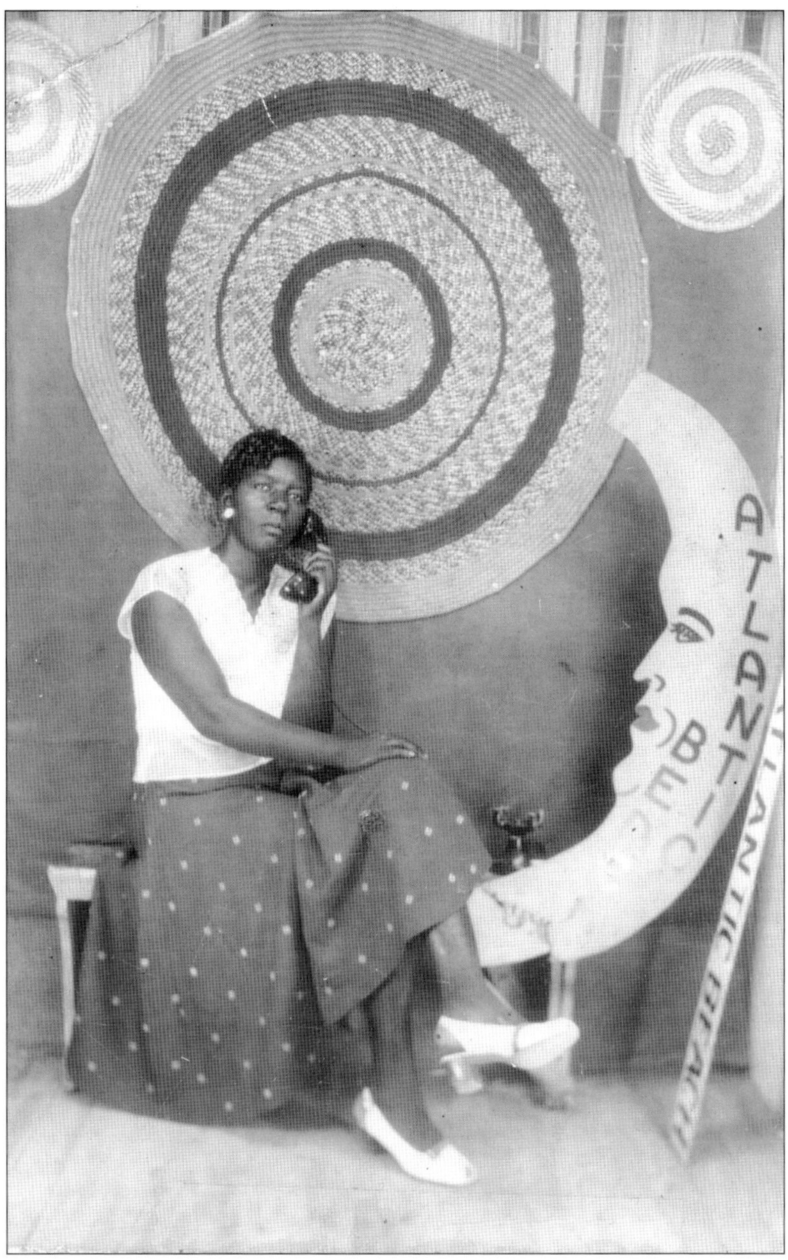

In 1941, George Tyson bought another tract of land from Viola Bell, this time measuring approximately 49 acres. It is said this tract of land was called Pearl Beach for Bell's daughter, who notarized the transaction. After this purchase, Atlantic Beach, nicknamed the "Black Pearl," now doubled in size and with further expansion, continued to attract more visitors like the woman seen in this image. In 1954, Hurricane Hazel destroyed the community's pier along with numerous buildings, but the 1960s saw a time of further development. As surrounding municipalities were planning to incorporate as North Myrtle Beach, Atlantic Beach instead chose to incorporate independently in 1966, during a period where public places were desegregating. Though a victory for civil rights, integration led to a loss of the community's identity, as many Black tourists chose to visit surrounding beaches instead, causing Atlantic Beach's tourism industry to decline in the 1970s.

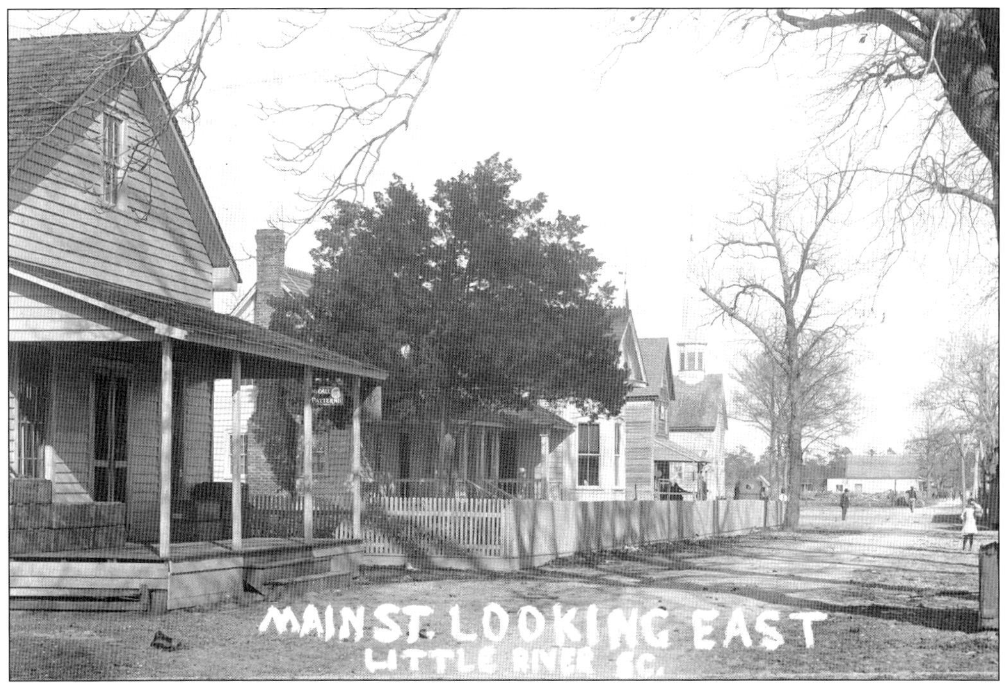

Little River, named for an inlet that forms at the North and South Carolina border, is said to have been called Mineola by Native Americans. Founded by 1700, Little River is believed to be Horry County's oldest continuous settlement and was also visited by George Washington in 1791. Once frequented by shipwreck victims and likely pirates who scourged the coastline, Little River has remained a rustic village for centuries, and the above image of Little River's Main Street, from roughly 1900, represents this concept. Fishing in Little River has been a generational industry essential to the community's survival. It was commonplace for many to enter the maritime industry at a young age or help their families who worked in the business. In the image below from the 1950s, Little River fishermen process their catch as a child carefully observes. (Above, courtesy of the Horry County Museum.)

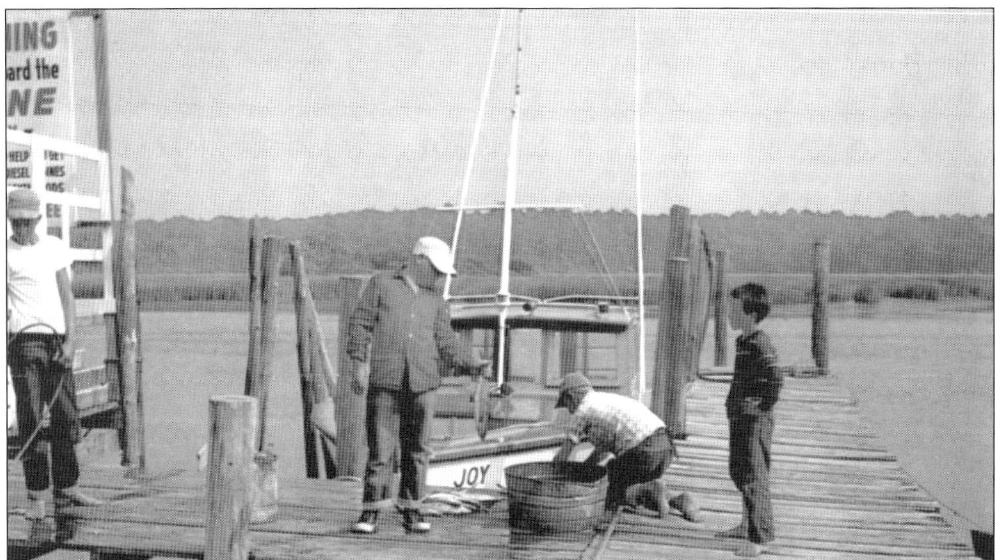

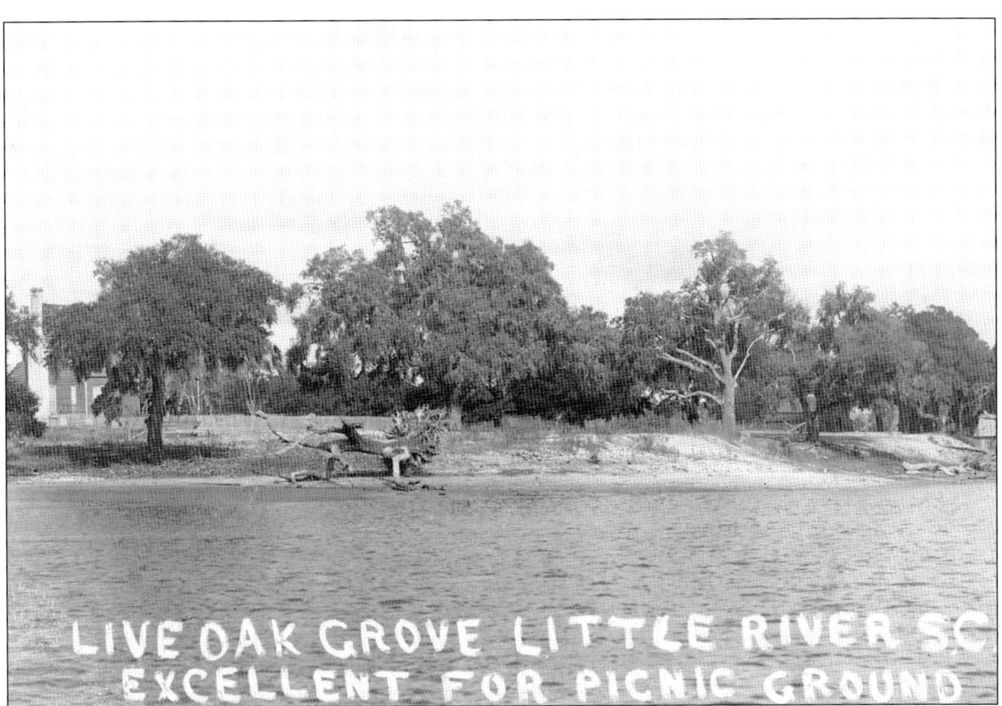

Little River has numerous southern live oaks, and in this image from the 1910s, an oak grove in the community is seen. Little River is also known for having an untouched barrier island, Waties Island, which holds prehistoric oyster beds, signs of Indigenous habitation, as well as Fort Randall, a Confederate fort that was built to protect Little River's port from Union forces and which was the site of a battle in 1863. (Courtesy of the Horry County Museum.)

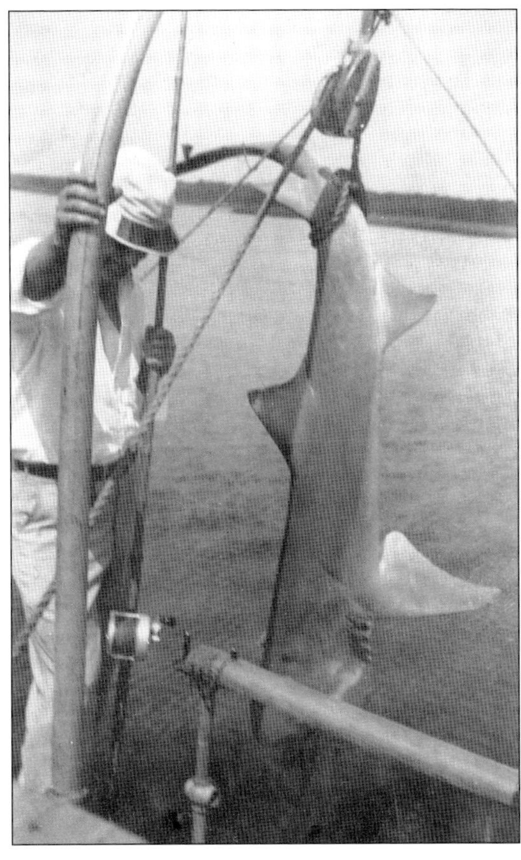

In further evidence of Little River's maritime heritage, though deep sea fishing normally yields numerous fish sent to market, it is not uncommon to catch sharks in the inlet, which is home to bull, spinner, tiger, dusky, and blacktip sharks as well as dogfish. In this 1935 image, an unidentified fisherman from Conway is seen with a shark caught during a voyage in Little River.

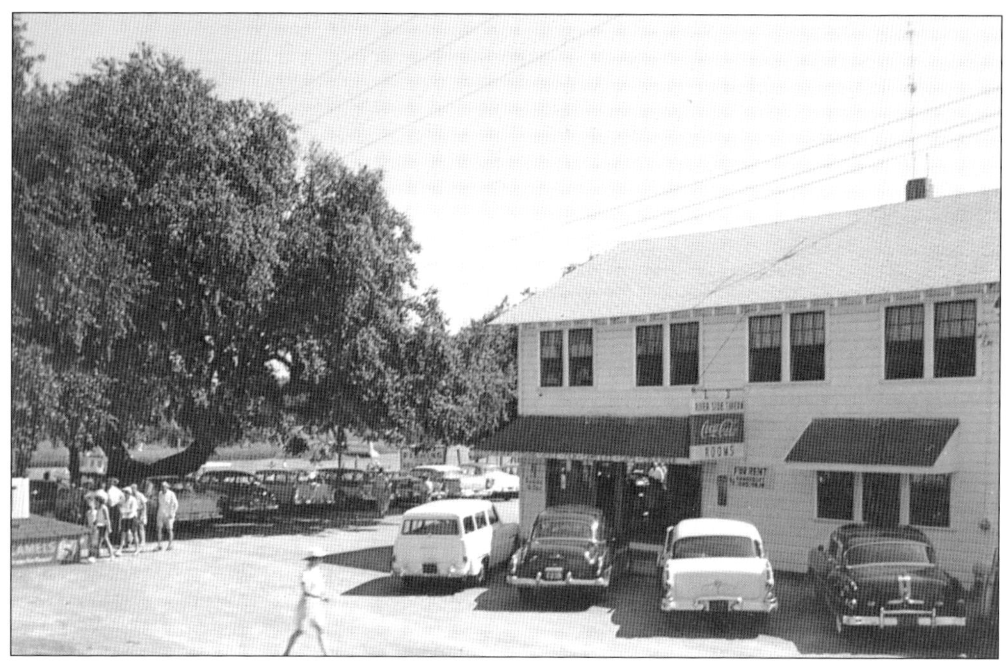

Little River has changed little since it was established, and its downtown area still holds numerous buildings reminiscent of yesteryear. In the above image, Mineola Avenue in Little River is seen in a 1950s postcard. Below, Little River's maritime ambience is caught in this 1957 image of Liar's Lodge, a former restaurant whose name is a reference to tall tales fishermen told of their voyages. One of numerous restaurants in the community, this image is symbolic of the popularity of Little River's seafood industry and maritime heritage.

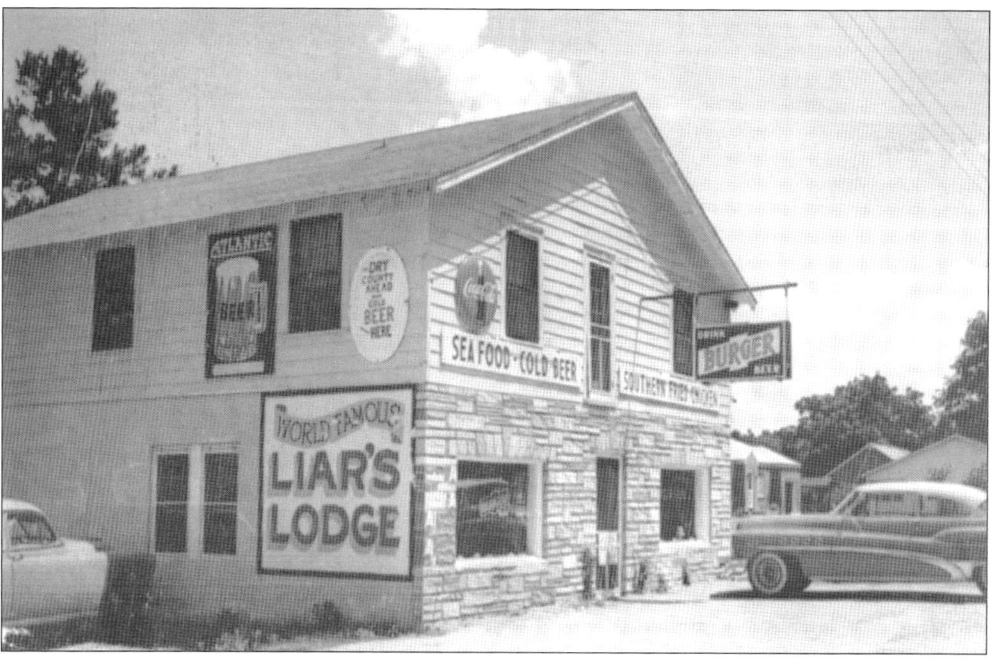

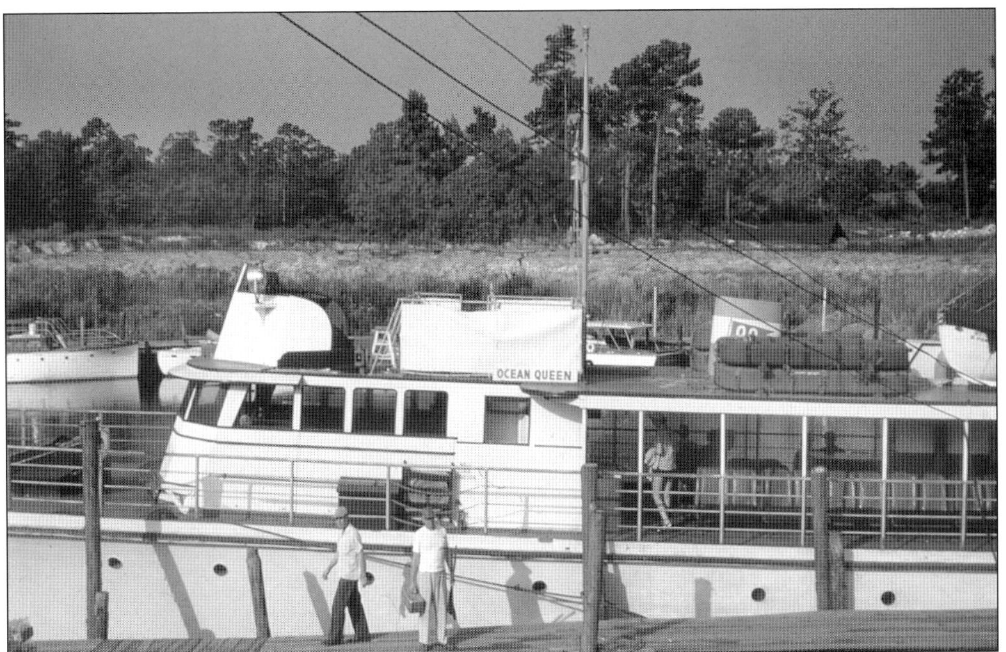

In addition to many local commercial fishing enterprises, cruising liners also operated out of Little River. One example of Little River's popular deep-sea cruising liners was *Ocean Queen*, owned by Sam Vereen. *Ocean Queen* offered cruises to various coastal locations and operated for two decades before sinking after a shipwreck in Charleston, South Carolina, in November 1965.

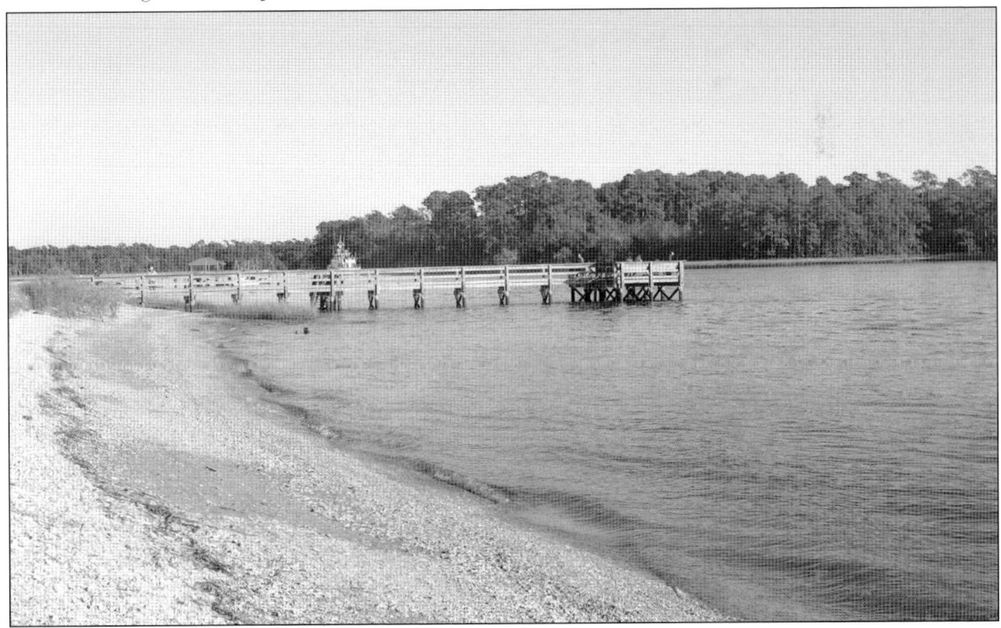

Vereen Memorial Gardens sits on the former Big Landing Plantation, founded by Jeremiah Vereen Jr. in 1797. The land was passed down through generations of the Vereen family until Jackson Vereen eventually deeded over 100 acres to the Horry County Historic Preservation Commission in 1971. Vereen Memorial Gardens was then born and features a plethora of natural scenery, including marshes similar to those shown here. (Courtesy of the University of South Carolina.)

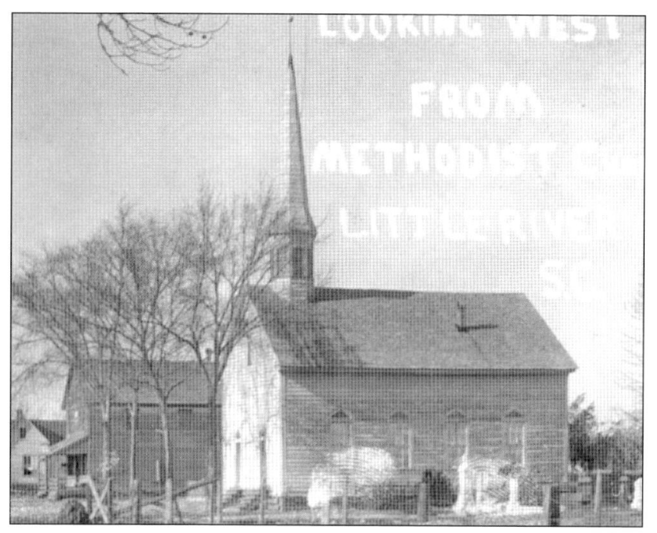

Little River Methodist Church, established in 1830, is one of the oldest church congregations in northern Horry County. Though now housed in a brick building, the original sanctuary, seen here in roughly 1915, was subsequently converted into a commercial enterprise. St. Paul African Methodist Episcopal Church is another local historic church and is especially important to the heritage of Little River's African American community. (Courtesy of the Horry County Museum.)

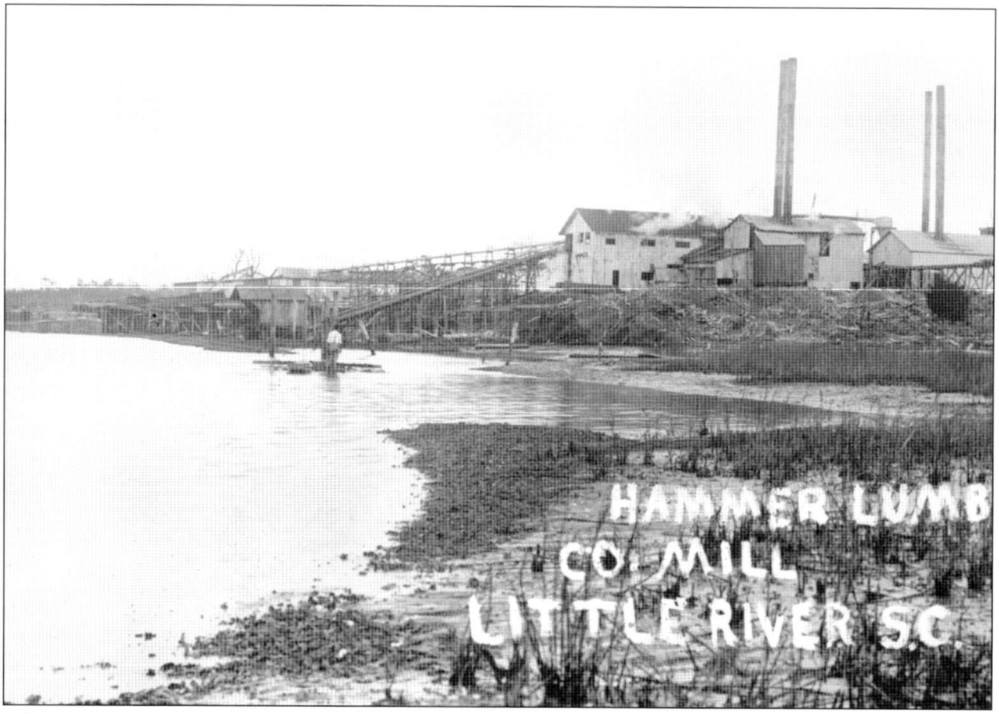

Like most of Horry County, Little River saw many of its residents find work within the lumber industry during the early 20th century due to the region's bountiful timber supply. Raw lumber harvested from Horry County forests was processed, sold, and used to make finished products. In this image, the Hammer Lumber Company, which operated in Little River, is seen in the 1910s. (Courtesy of the Horry County Museum.)

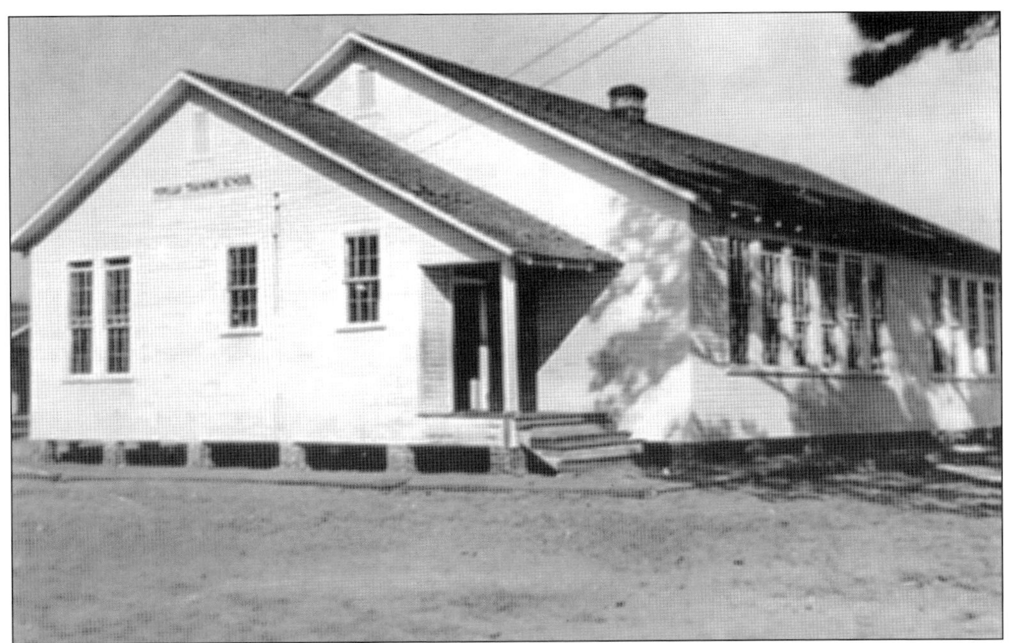

Though unknown for certain, Wampee is believed to have been founded around 1830. Its name is believed to be derived from the Indigenous word *wampee*, which means pickerelweed, a plant eaten by birds Native Americans hunted. Wampee historically held a significant African American population, many of whom were slaves and, in later generations, sharecroppers. Wampee maintained both White and Black public schools, neither of which currently stand. The Poplar Training School, seen above, is a Rosenwald school, which were schools built for African American children with funds from businessman Julius Rosenwald and philanthropist Booker T. Washington. The Wampee Post Office was opened in 1860 and stayed open during the Civil War under Confederate control. It operated until 1956. An 1884 postal cancel mark from Wampee is shown below. (Above, courtesy of the Horry County Museum.)

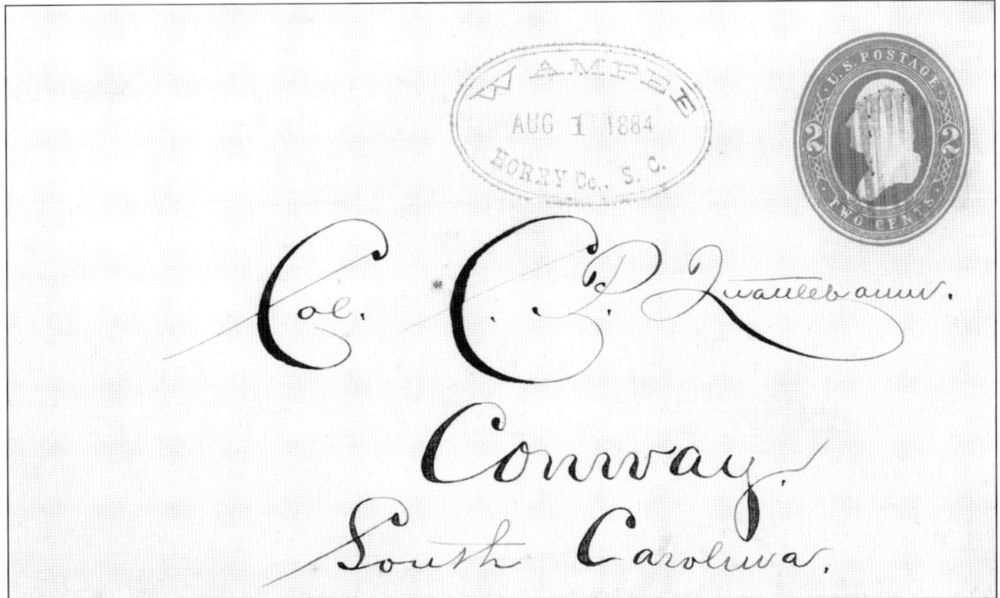

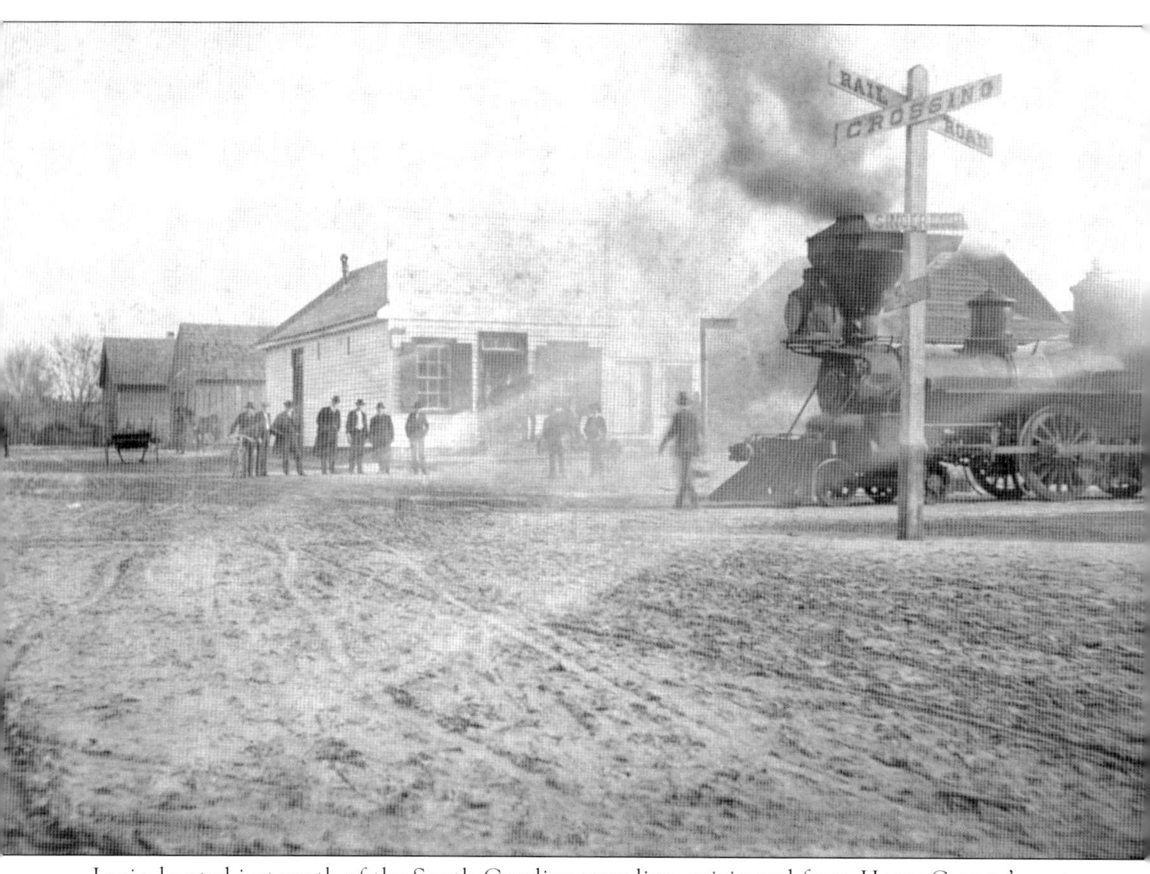

Loris, located just south of the South Carolina state line, originated from Horry County's roots in the turpentine and timber industries. In 1887, the Chadbourn Lumber Company opened rail lines into Horry County through the Wilmington, Chadbourn & Conway Railroad. More land was soon sold to Chadbourn associates, who then opened a depot. Loris, as it is now known, was created, and in the next five years, several stores would be established as the railroad brought an influx of new residents into the community. A railroad scene from roughly the time of Loris's inception can be seen in the above image. Loris's name is derived from unknown origins, but by 1902, the community was incorporated as a town, also gaining a nickname of the "Gate City" for its direct location under the North and South Carolina border. In the ensuing decades, once the turpentine industry ceased, agriculture became Loris's dominant industry, and numerous tobacco and cotton farms were established in Loris by the 1920s. (Courtesy of the Horry County Museum.)

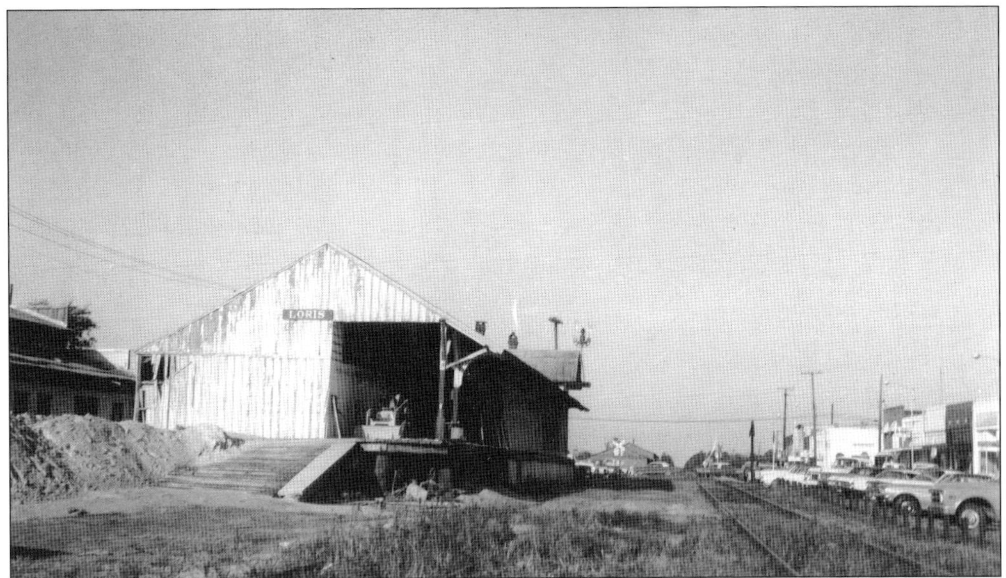

The first recorded brick building in Loris, the Bank of Loris, dates to approximately 1907, at a time when Loris was steadily growing as a result of the railroad and lumber industries. Other businesses in Loris that date to around this time period include the Prince Hotel, Loris Hardware and Furniture Company, A.W. Hodges and Sons Stables, and the Loris Drug Store. Seen here is the former Loris Train Depot, built in roughly 1911 to accommodate the growing town. It is no longer in existence. (Courtesy of the South Caroliniana Library.)

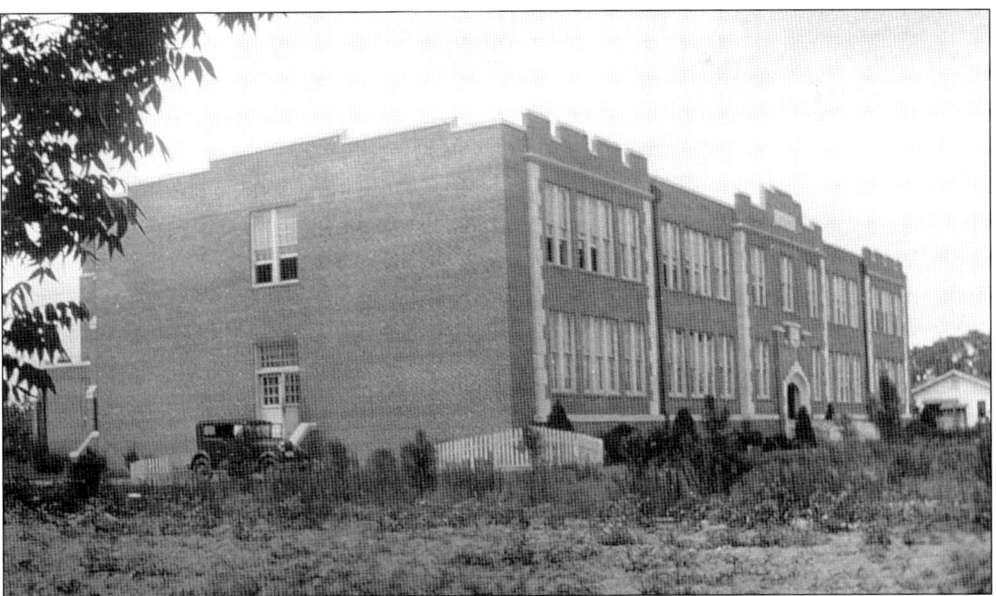

Opened in 1930, the original Loris High School is an ornate two-story brick building in downtown Loris. The high school was integrated in 1970 and closed in 1988, when a new high school was built. Soon converted to an elementary school, it closed permanently in 1996. It was then abandoned and fell into disrepair, but as of 2024, it is the focus of local preservation efforts. (Courtesy of the Horry County Museum.)

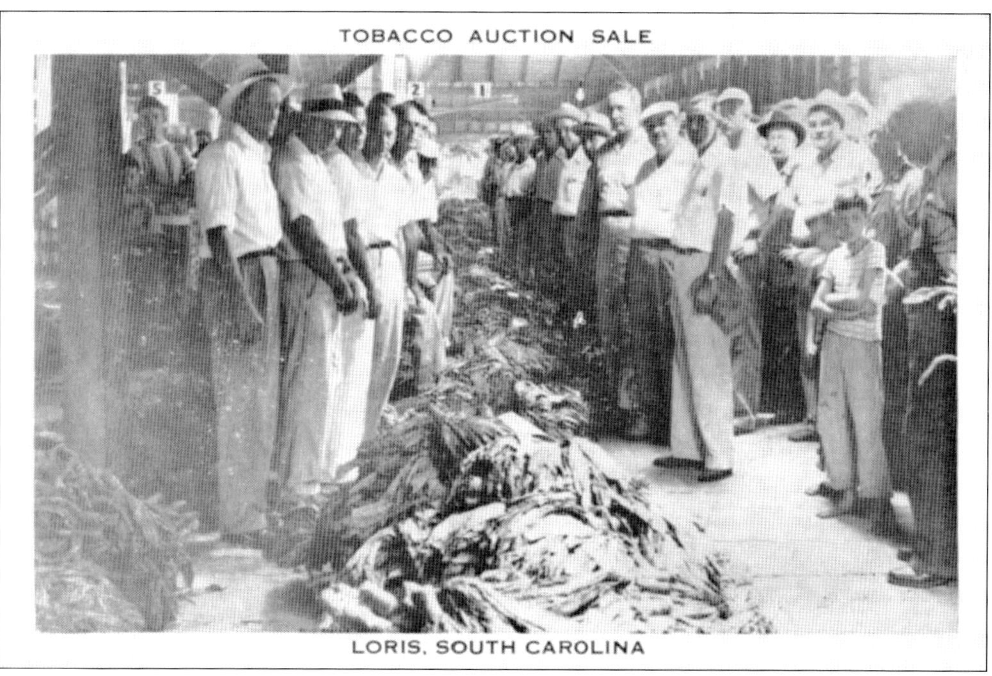

After the dissolution of the turpentine industry in Horry County, tobacco farming took precedence as a major industry for locals. Loris was a major producer of the crop and held numerous tobacco farms. Like Conway, tobacco was brought here to warehouses to be marketed, and the above image from the early 1950s represents a typical tobacco auction scene in Loris from that time. Though Loris has consistently been rather rural, the 1950s saw the beginning of increased development, and one can notice busy storefronts in the image below from roughly 1953. The 1960s brought Loris continued economic prosperity, saw the further expansion of its downtown, and brought the profitable textile mill industry to the community as well.

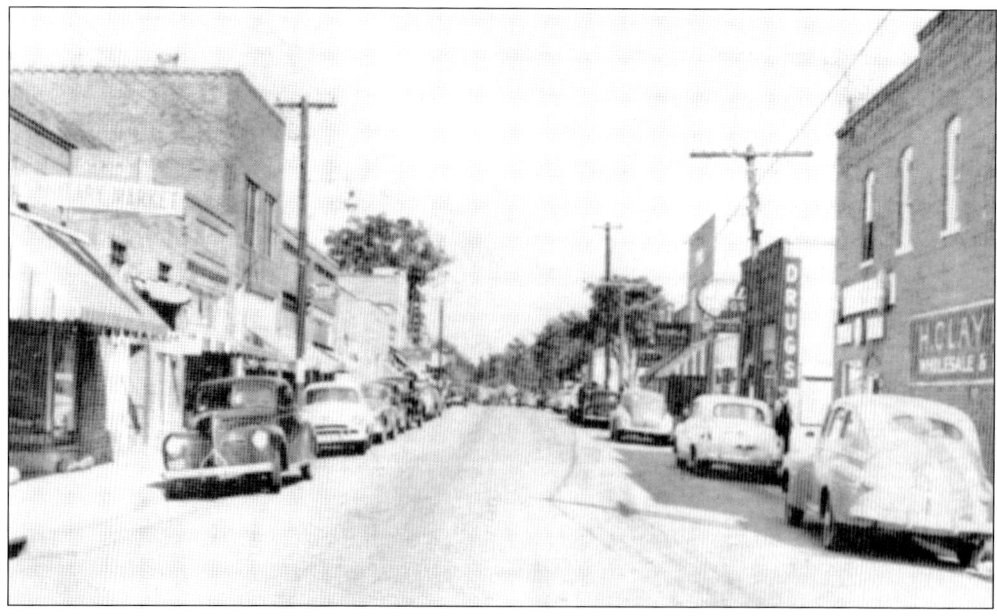

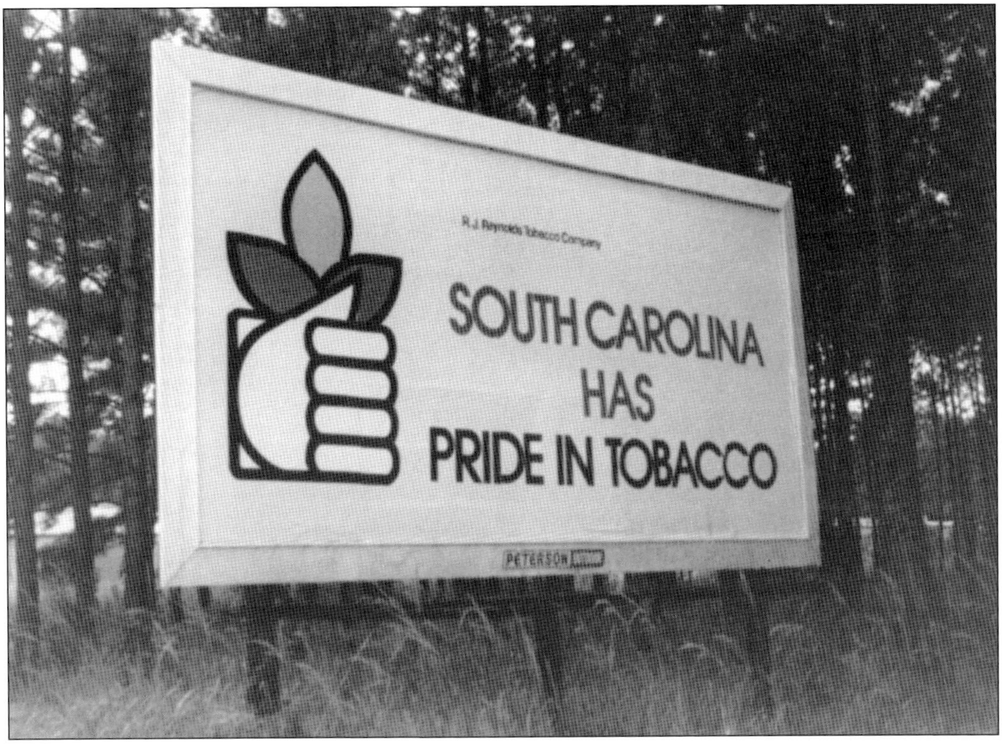

The 1970s marked a time when commerce was strong in Loris, leading to its incorporation as a city in 1976. Tobacco, though losing popularity, still maintained ties to community residents, which is portrayed in the above image of a Loris billboard proclaiming "South Carolina Has Pride in Tobacco." Though the 1970s were a blissful period in Loris's history, textile mills began closing in the 1980s, and the tobacco industry shuttered shortly thereafter. Even with its challenges, Loris has drawn new residents active in its preservation. For example, the Loris Bog-Off Festival is annually held in the community and celebrates chicken bog, a famous dish created in the 1920s and native to the region. A modern image of the community is seen below.

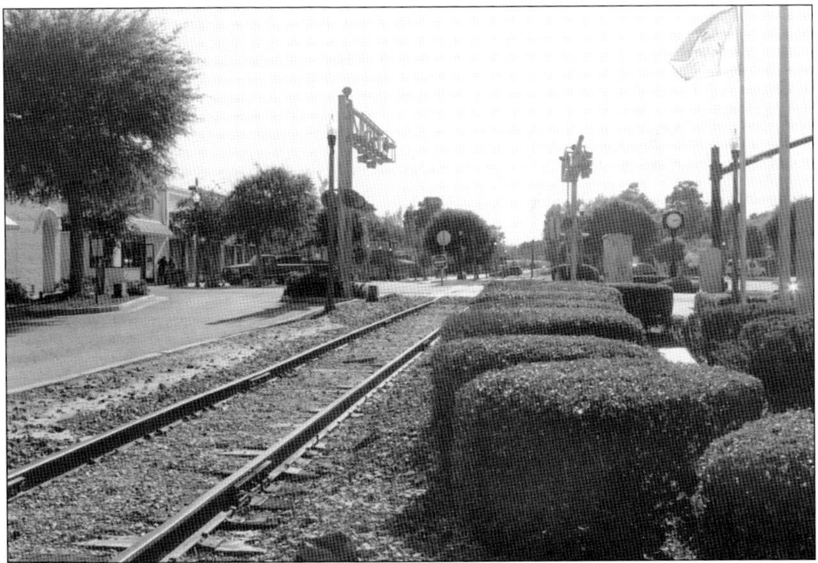

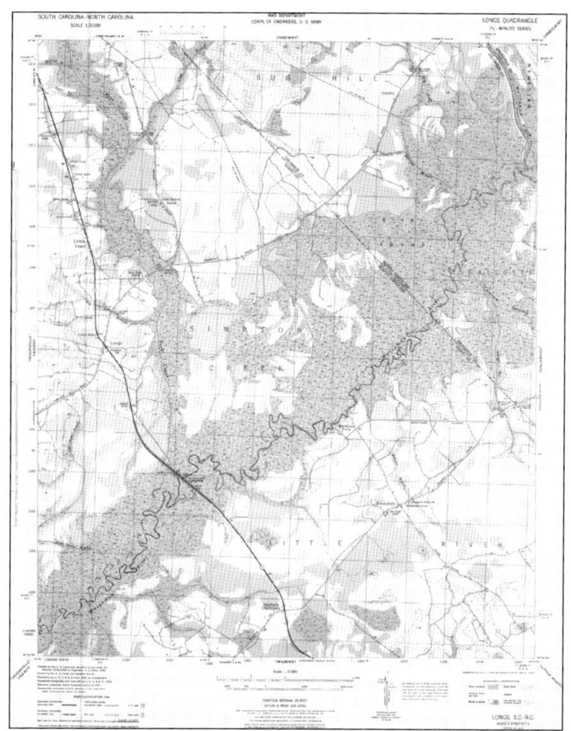

Like other small communities, religion played an important part in the customs of Longs, and churches in the community drew crowds from the immediate surrounding area to worship. Ebenezer United Methodist Church holds the oldest congregation in the community, established in 1801. Noted for its architecture, the current church building opened in roughly 1904, and the church also maintains a long-standing cemetery where many early Longs residents are interred. Seen here is a map showing Longs from the 1940s.

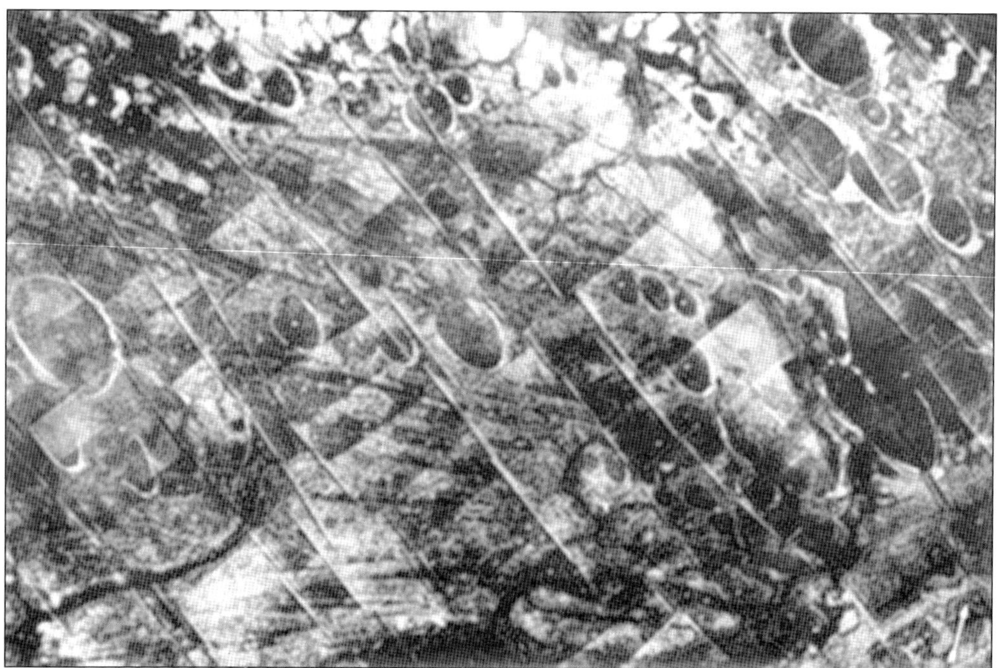

The Carolina Bays, approximately 10 million years old, are known for their swampy landscapes and importance within Indigenous culture. Thousands of bays (most likely formed from meteorite craters or prehistoric wave currents) exist across the eastern United States; four exist within Horry County. Discovered in 1930 by aerial photographers in Horry County, the Carolina Bays became a worldwide phenomenon when images of them were published during the Great Depression.

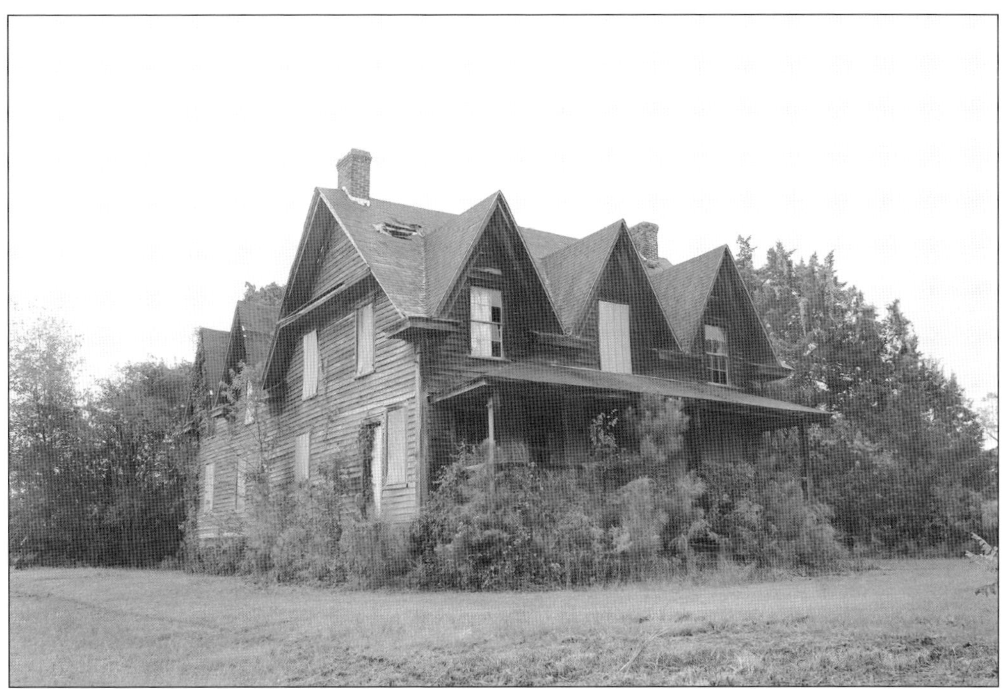

The "House of Eight Gables" was built between 1888 and 1890 by John Quincy Graham. The home was constructed using cypress wood and features eight gables, which gives the house its nickname. The property also held a barn built in the early 1900s by a later owner. Though in disrepair for many years, which can be seen in the above image from 2024, the house was relocated in 2025 in attempts to preserve it from further deterioration. It holds a reputation for being one of the area's most distinctively crafted homes and is located in the historic community of Finklea. Named for John Finklea, a local doctor, Finklea is a predominantly African American community historically populated by freed slaves. Their descendants, many of whom stayed, were farmers. The community once held the Finklea Colored School, seen below, in order to provide classes to its African American citizens. (Below, courtesy of the Horry County Museum.)

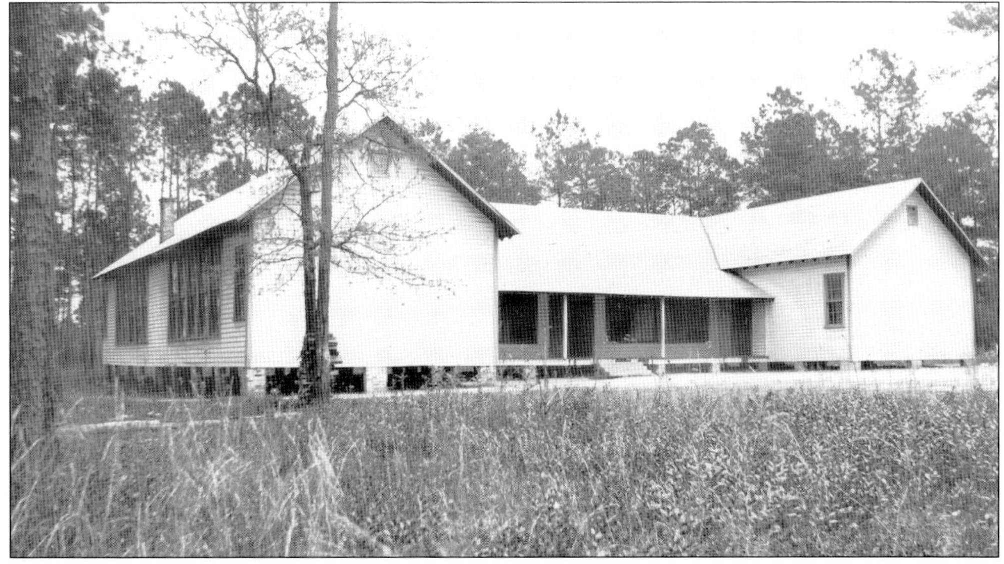

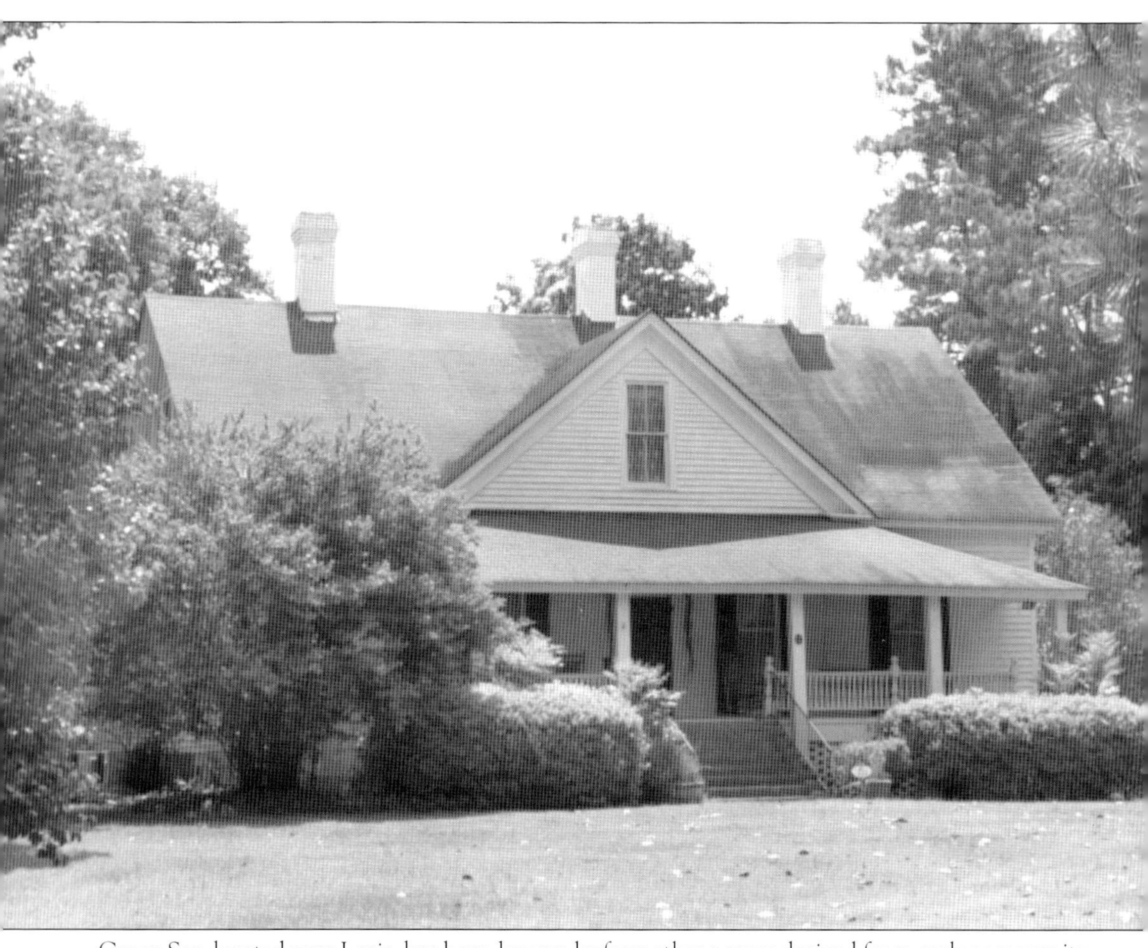

Green Sea, located near Loris, has been known by four other names derived from early community settlers, including Blanton's Crossroads and Blanton's X-Roads, both of which honor farmer Joshua Blanton; Norton's Mill, named for Richard Norton, a grain mill operator; and Powellville, named for Richard Powell, a longtime community postmaster. The community alternated these names, but Green Sea's long-standing name comes from the nearby Green Sea Swamp, though rumors have persisted about the origins of the community's moniker, including that it came from an early resident, John Derham. Though rumors of Derham's influence on the community's name are incorrect, his descendant, Joseph Derham, was another influential resident and South Carolina politician whose home is in the National Register of Historic Places. An image of the Joseph Derham House is seen above. Playcard Crossroads, established by 1905, is located near Green Sea. Stories vary, but the community is believed to be called "Playcard" because placard court notices were once posted at its crossroads. It is also known as the site of the Playcard Environmental Education Center, founded in 1987.

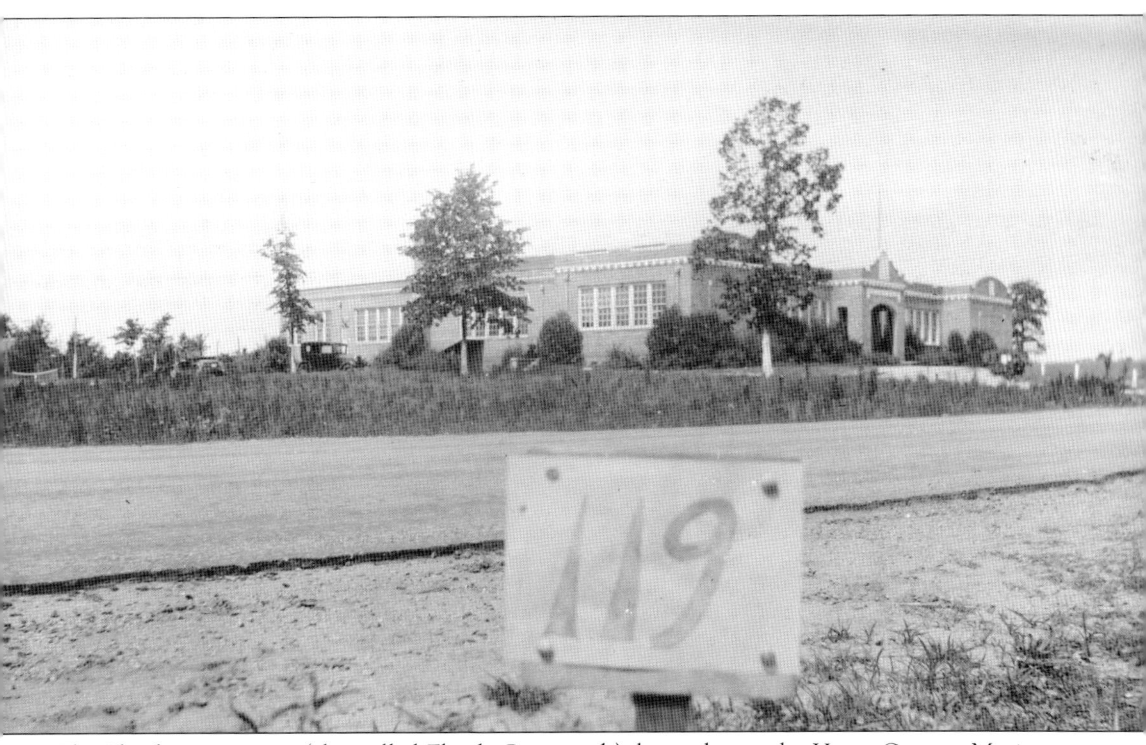

The Floyds community (also called Floyds Crossroads), located near the Horry County–Marion County border, has a rich heritage of its own largely relating to education. The Floyds School began operation as a private school in the 1890s and, in 1912, moved to a permanent building. The first Floyds School had been known for its rigorous programs but was noted for producing college attendees and graduates at a time when higher education was difficult to obtain. After this school closed in the early 1920s, students from Floyds briefly attended schools in Nichols before Floyds High School opened in 1928, replacing the original Floyds School. Floyds High School, seen here, offered classes to White students, and an elementary section was added to the property. Black children in Floyds attended nearby segregated schools. After calls grew from officials, Green Sea and Floyds schools were consolidated in 1976. Green Sea students were then relocated to Floyds High School, but the student body quickly outgrew this building (which was eventually abandoned), and Green Sea–Floyds High School opened in a new building in 1981. (Courtesy of the Horry County Museum.)

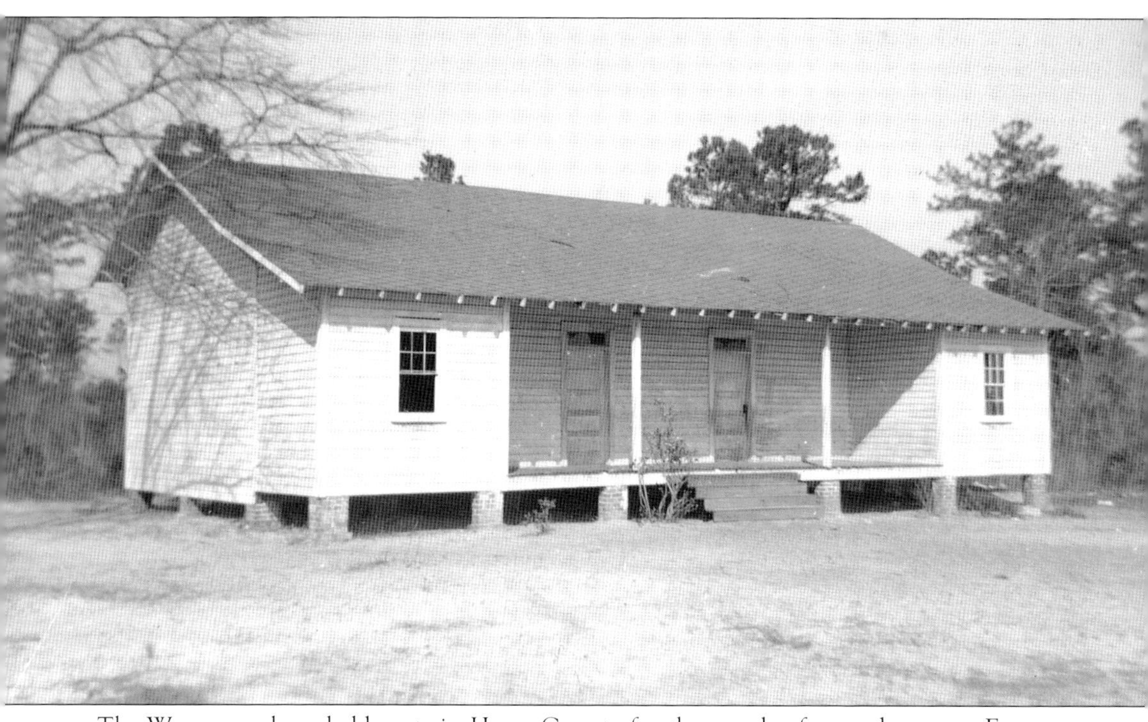

The Waccamaw have held roots in Horry County for thousands of years, but upon European colonization, many became enslaved and died in large numbers from disease or conflicts with Europeans. Many Native Americans who remained gathered in the Dimery settlement in western Horry County (now in the area of the former Dog Bluff Township). This settlement, founded by John and Elizabeth Dimery, held Indigenous and mixed-race residents classified as "mulatto" in records and who were designated as "free colored" people. Not characterized as White or Black, those in the Dimery settlement held their own school, shown here, and operated their own churches. Their descendants, who identify as the Waccamaw Indian People, have struggled for sovereign recognition and were known as the Waccamaw-Chicora people until the 1990s. Efforts to recognize the tribe on its own have gained momentum, and the Waccamaw obtained South Carolina state tribal recognition in 2005. With their tribal headquarters in Aynor since 2004, the Waccamaw Indian People still advocate for further recognition in the present day and continue to bring attention to their customs by educating community members of their heritage. (Courtesy of the South Carolina Department of Archives and History.)

Farming has been a prominent part of the lives of many western Horry County residents, especially those who relied on agriculture in order to survive and support their families, such as through sharecropping or tenant farming. Though cotton agriculture was historically popular in this region, in the early 20th century, tobacco became a cash crop and was soon essential to the survival of local families and farmers alike, such as those shown in these images. The growth of enterprises such as Holliday Farms, which only expanded the area's tobacco production, reinforced its significance to the local economy. Furthermore, given its local importance, these photographs showing people of different ages posing next to tobacco crops symbolizes the plant's impact on the lives of those across different generations. (Both, courtesy of the Horry County Museum.)

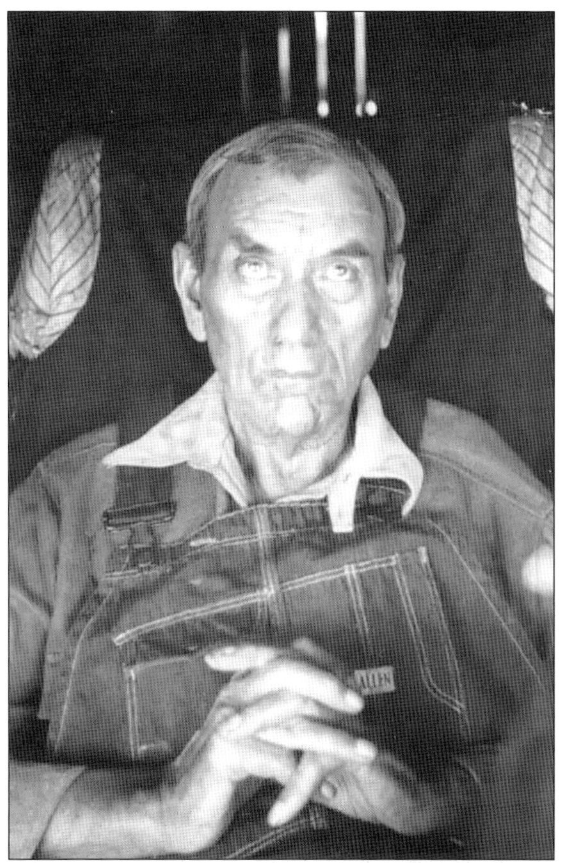

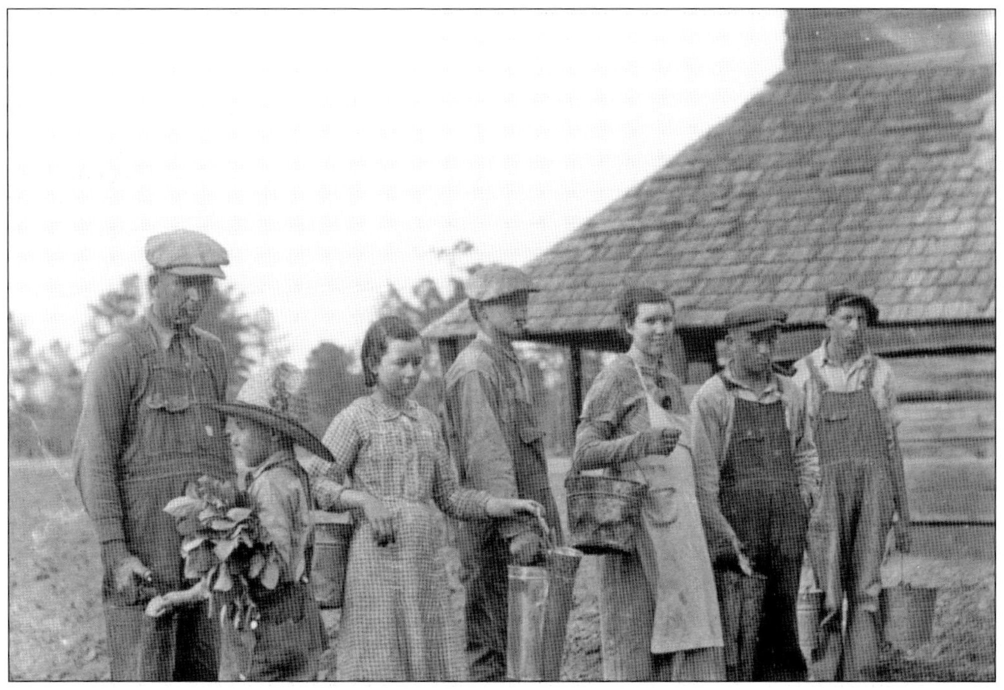

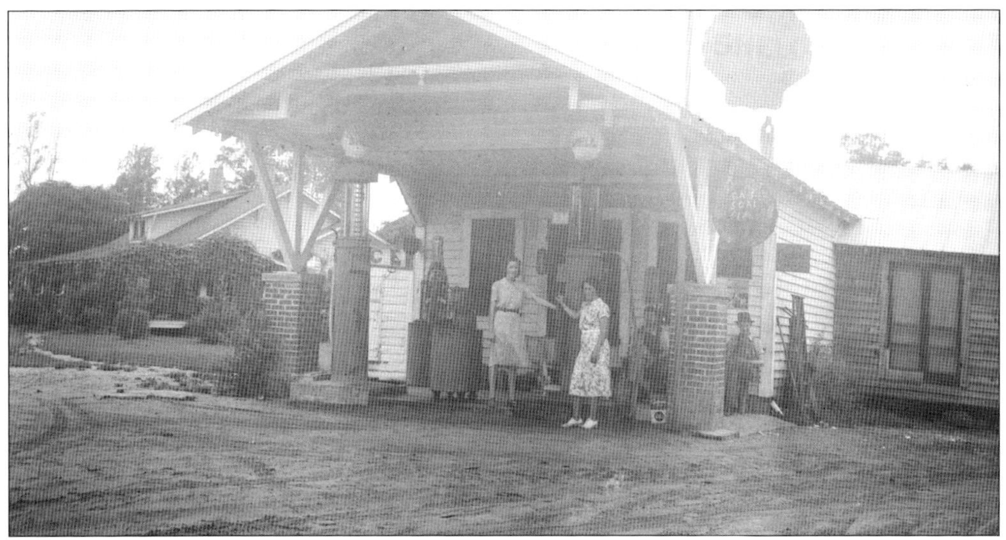

Ketchuptown is just one of this vicinity's numerous unincorporated communities. Settled in the late 1800s, this community was steeped in the agricultural industry, and prior to the popularity of the automobile, residents were isolated from nearby towns and stores they could frequent. Nonetheless, one store owned by Hubert Small, shown above in the 1930s, sold general goods for the residents of this rural community and proved to be a gathering place for area residents, who would say to each other that they would "catch up" on community news at the store. This led to the community being called Catch-up Town. However, Hubert Small's daughter is said to have misspelled Catchup Town as "Ketchuptown" on a homemade sign, and the well-liked spelling was kept. Eventually, Ketchuptown's population dissolved as residents relocated to nearby communities when roads were paved, marking the end of the community's peak. Below, a 2025 image of the building which held the Ketchuptown store is shown.

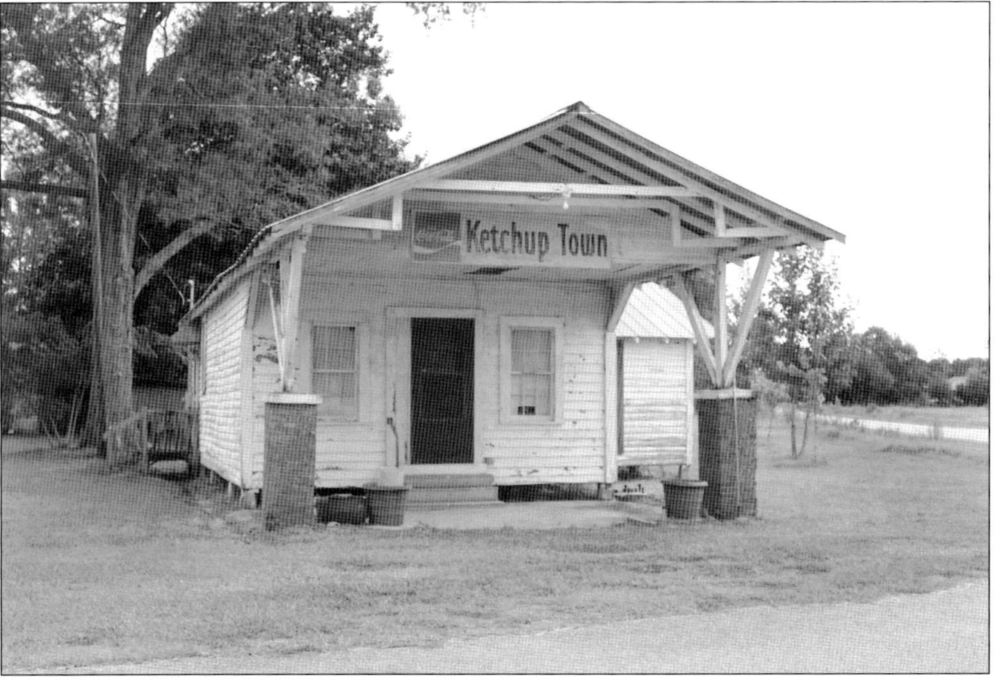

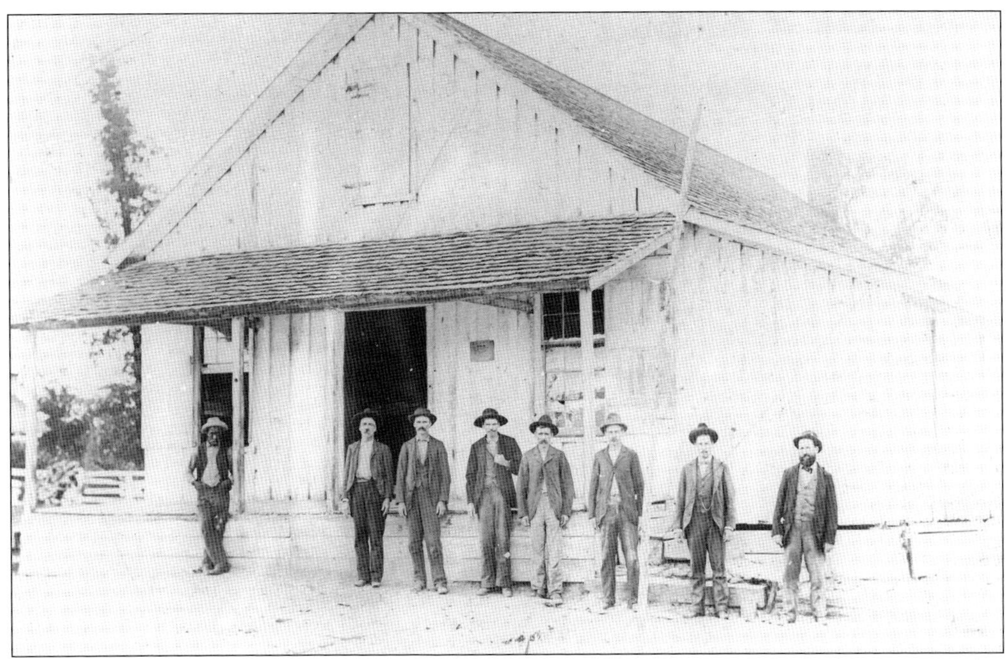

Cool Spring, located near Aynor, was named for a natural spring near Cool Spring Methodist Church, an early Methodist congregation. In the past, locals, especially from Conway, would occasionally visit the spring to escape the summer heat. Additionally, the Cool Spring community housed a turpentine operation, a general store (believed to be seen in this image), and schools for White and Black children. (Courtesy of the Horry County Museum.)

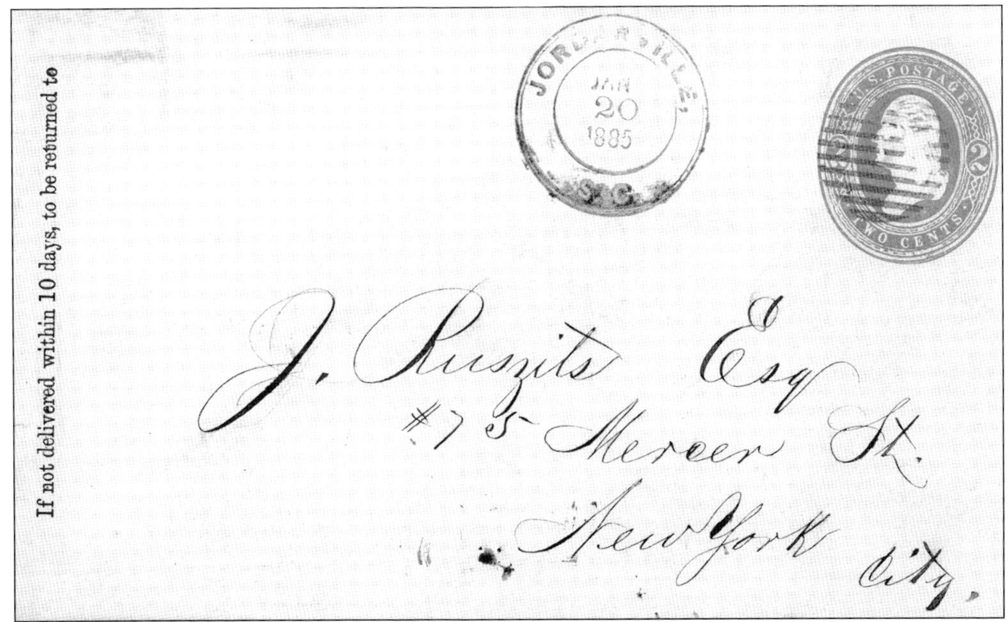

Jordanville, a crossroads farming community, was named for Richard Jordan, who began a store there by 1869. It also held a post office from 1881 until 1937; a postal cover from it is seen here. George Judson Holliday of Galivants Ferry bought the Jordanville store in 1910, and the area remained agriculturally dominant before eventually becoming largely abandoned by the late 20th century.

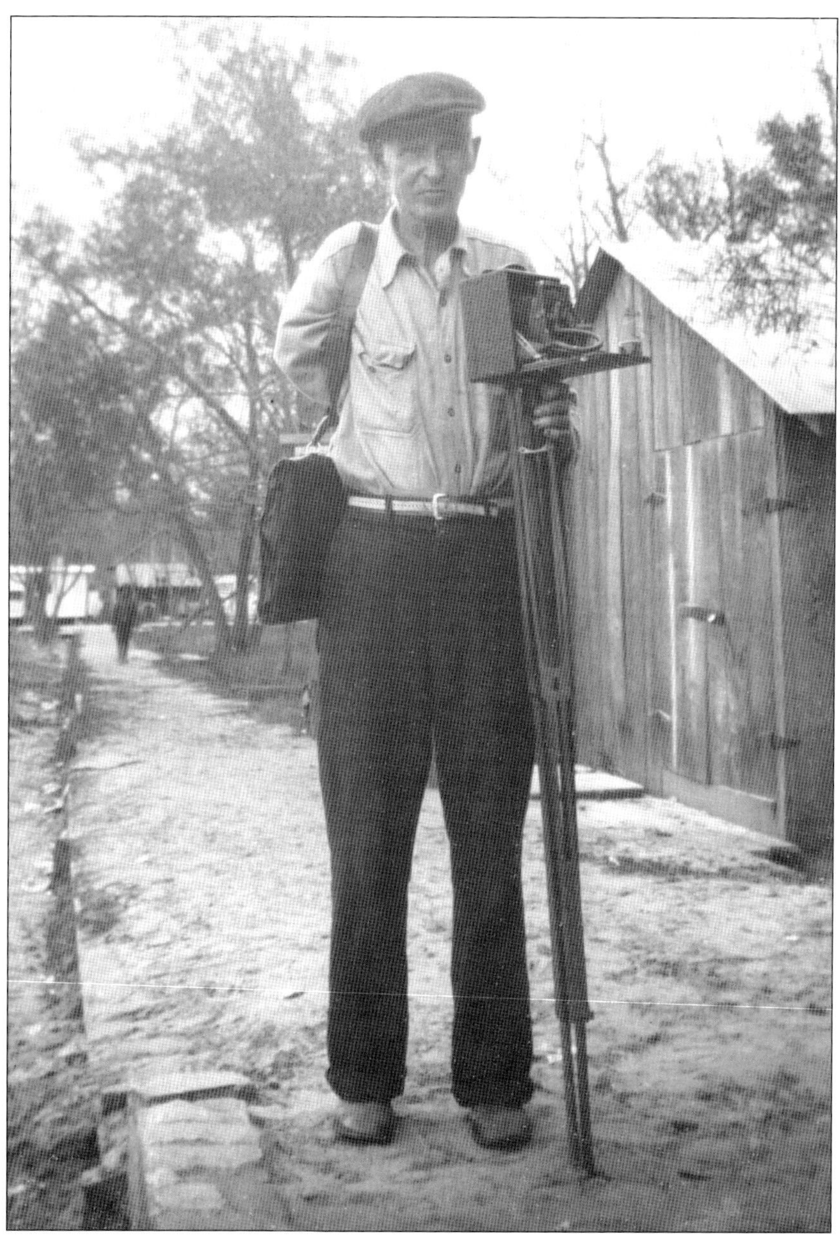

William Van Auken Greene, born in 1866, was a Minnesota native who spent his early years working in West Virginia coal mines, where his family claims he became locally known for his photographs of the Hatfield-McCoy feuds. It was here that one of his arms was amputated due to a mining injury. Later, in 1931 at the age of 65, he moved to Aynor and soon took up residence in a trailer, which he also used as a darkroom. He became well liked and well known in Aynor and took photographs of school classes, churches, funerals, families, and local sites. Greene, also a poet, died in 1952 and was buried in Aynor. Years after his death, during a demolition of a property he inhabited, his negatives were discovered, rescued, and eventually donated to the Horry County Museum. These negatives contain photographs that are historically invaluable, and Greene, seen here in the 1930s, is therefore credited with preserving much of the region's history through his photography. (Courtesy of the Horry County Museum.)

As many early photographs of Aynor are obscure, images of people from this time help one understand the ambience of the community during the Great Depression. For example, though South Carolina had financial and racial barriers to education, distance barriers also proved burdensome for many rural children, who, in western Horry County, once had to travel long distances to attend classes. In retrospect, the two people at right (believed to be school faculty members) played a significant role in the education of Aynor's youth by helping these children travel to attend classes they may not have not been able to go to otherwise. Below is the first Aynor High School, which educated generations of residents from the Aynor vicinity before it was demolished in 1976.

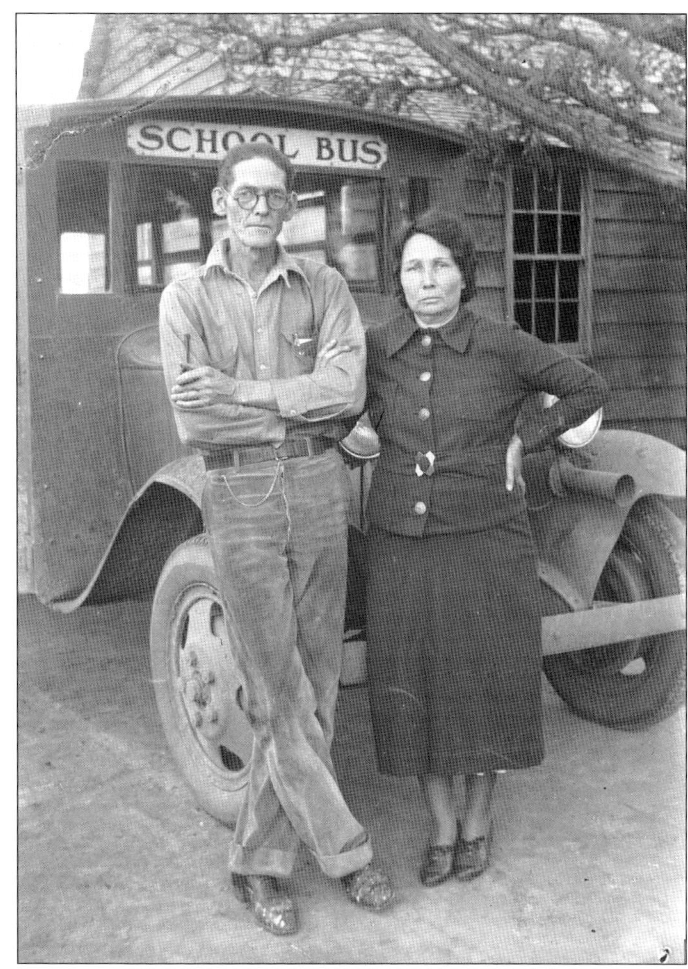

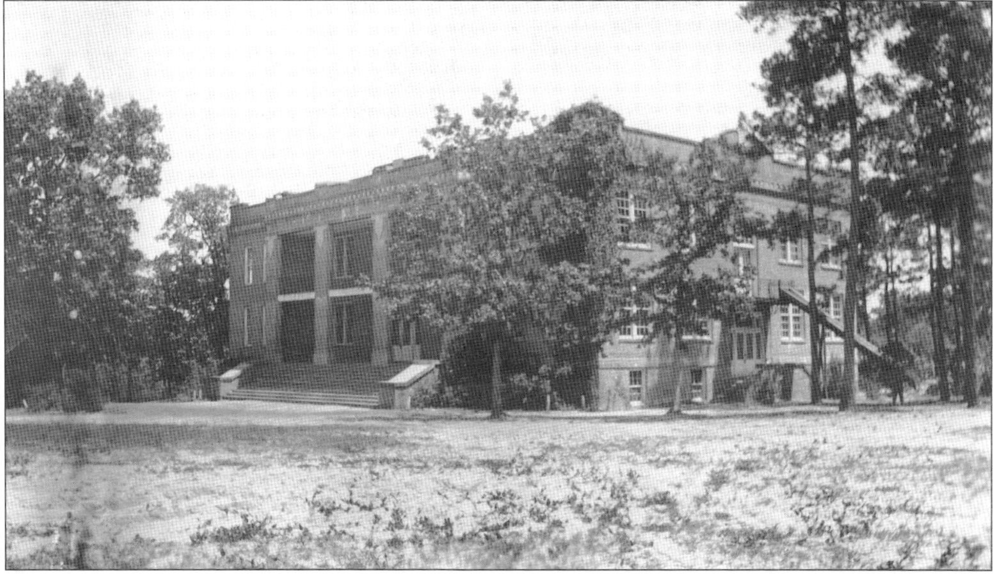

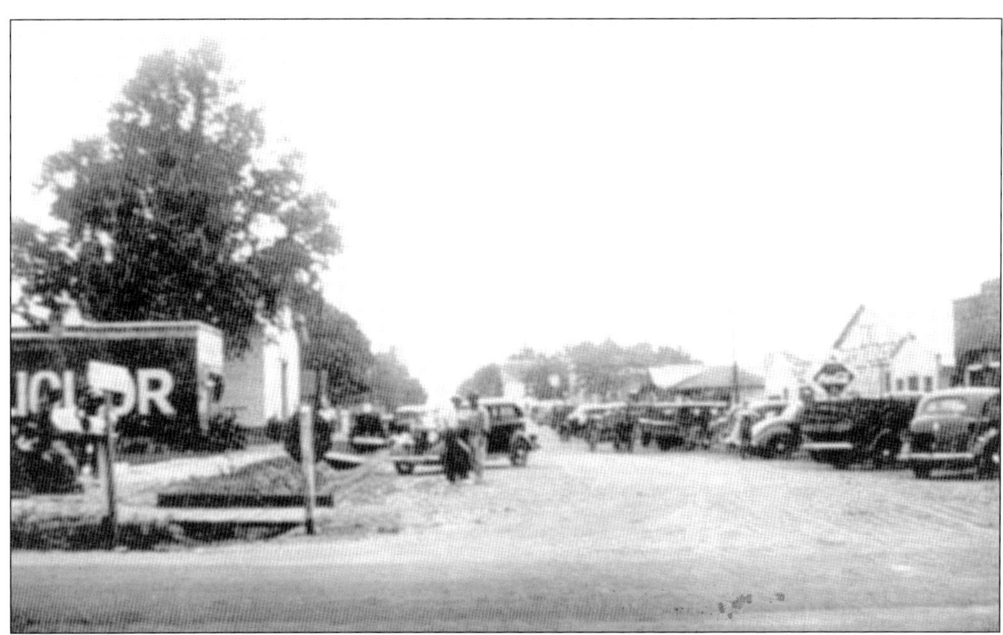

Though small, Aynor was the epicenter of western Horry County. By 1945, the community held three schools and a variety of residences, churches, and businesses, such as the Aynor Drug Store (seen in the image below). Nonetheless, the lumber and agricultural industries still dominated the vicinity's economy, especially for residents of communities outside of Aynor who worked on farms. As traveling was a difficult task at the time due to unpaved roads and the rural nature of the county, Aynor held vital services for many in the immediate rural area and allowed people to obtain necessities without having to travel to Conway or Mullins. (Above, courtesy of the Horry County Museum; below, courtesy of the Ambrose family.)

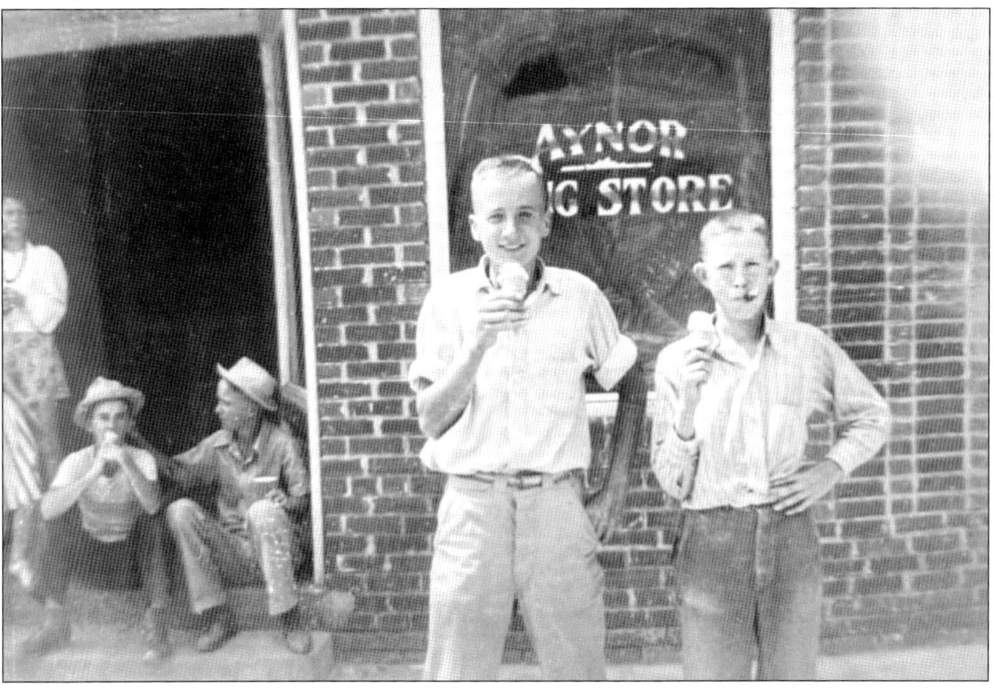

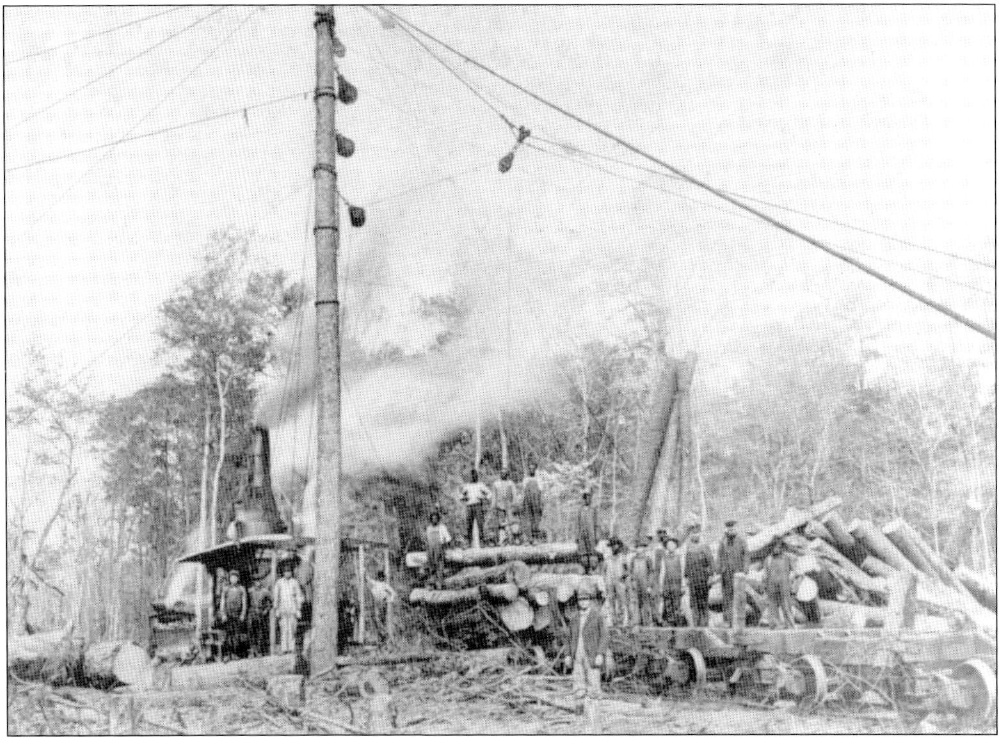

The lumber industry was an essential contributor to western Horry County's economy. Timbering was an especially popular occupation in Gunters Island, a small community near Aynor known for its relative isolation and unique, Archaic dialect among Native settlers. In the above image, a typical scene of a Gunters Island mill from the Great Depression is shown. Workers in Gunters Island were known to utilize train cars on the mill's railroad track as makeshift shelters; photographs exist in private family collections of this phenomenon but are of too poor quality for publication. Gunters Island was also known to have African American workers who often resided on-site due to "sundown" laws in the Jim Crow era, as the time it took to travel from these sites to their homes placed them in danger of violating these laws. Some descendants of earlier community residents also state that permission had to be granted for Black laborers to work on these projects due to segregationist laws. Seen here are African American workers at a Gunters Island sawmill. (Both, courtesy of the Ambrose family.)

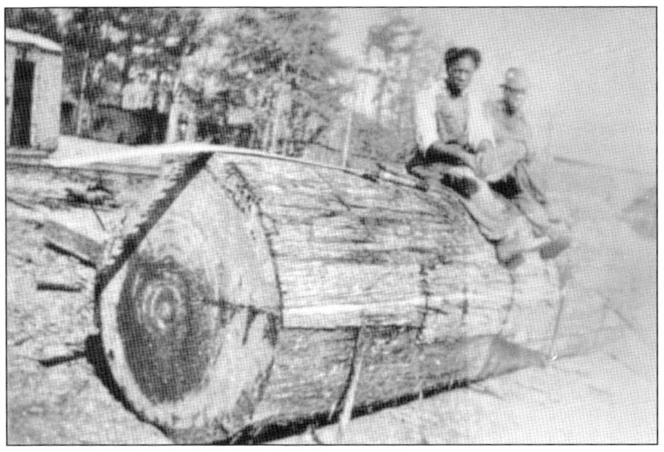

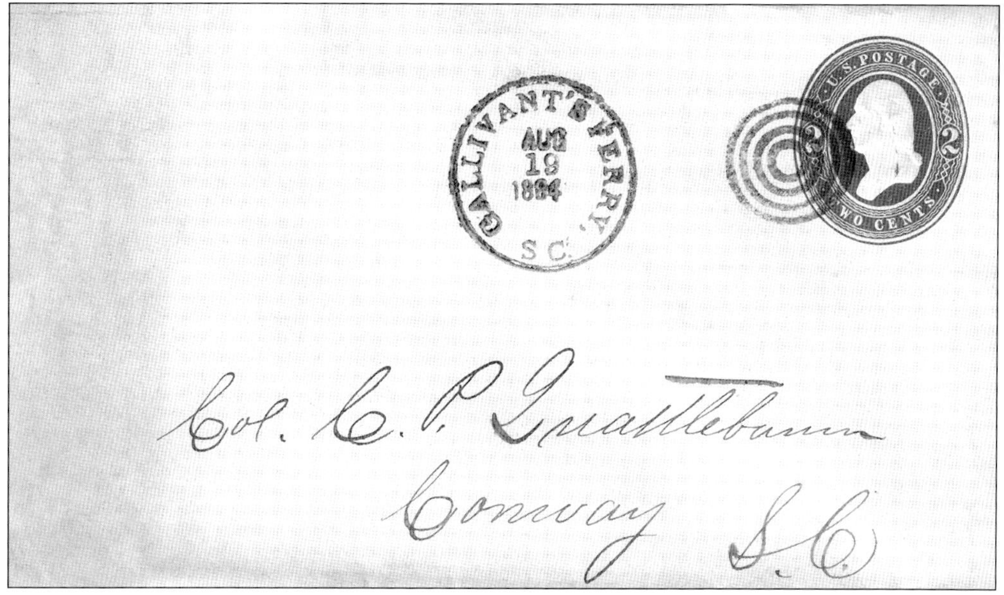

Named for Richard Gallevan, who operated a ferry there, Galivants Ferry was founded in the late 1700s and obtained its first post office in roughly 1817. Seen in the above image is an envelope addressed to Conway mayor C.P. Quattlebaum postmarked from Galivants Ferry; on its top right corner are spiral ink marks preventing illegal reuse of prepaid stamps. Galivants Ferry's history saw a turning point after 1865, when J.W. Holliday, a turpentine entrepreneur, settled there and open a farming enterprise. This would eventually blossom into the Holliday Brothers Tobacco Company (also called Pee Dee Farms Company), which would become nationally known for its flue-cured tobacco. Generations of the Holliday family continued the business, including John Monroe Johnson Holliday, seen in the image below from the 1960s.

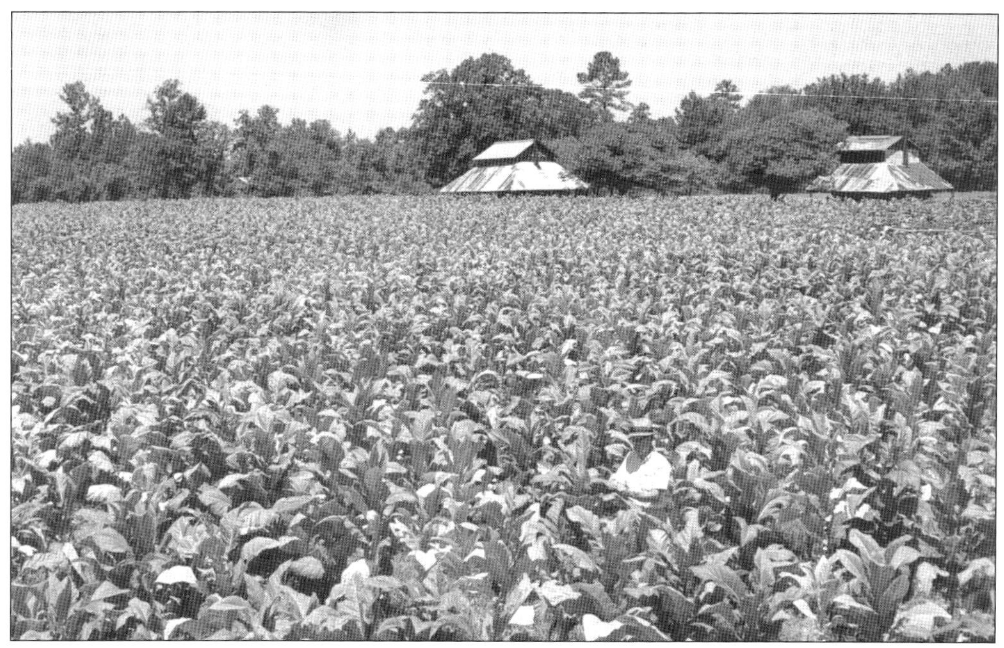

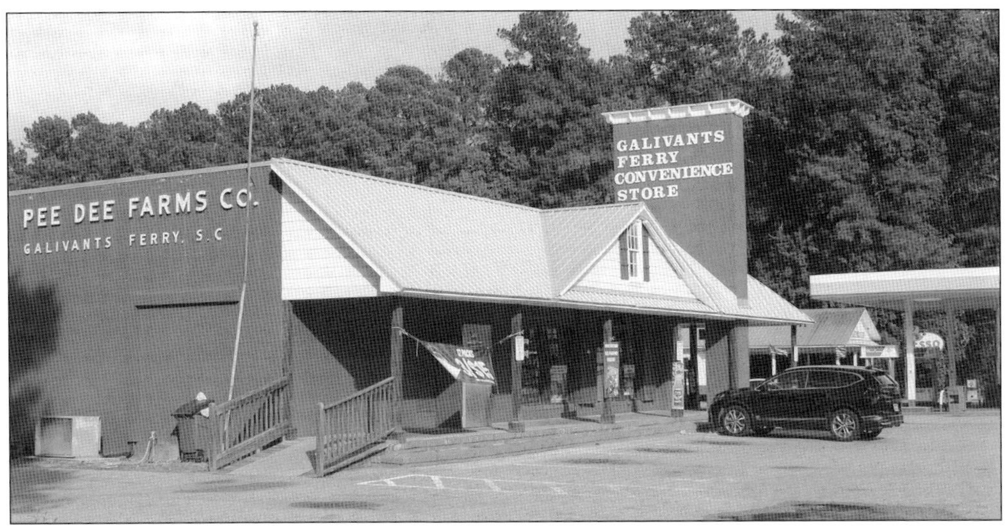

In 1869, Galivants Ferry's first general store was founded. The building of the present-day Galivants Ferry Convenience Store is the hosting site of the Galivants Ferry Stump, one of the most culturally and politically important events of Horry County, historically tied to Democratic Party politics. "The Stump," as it is commonly known, began in 1876, when South Carolina governor Wade Hampton III gave a stump speech in Galivants Ferry. "Stump speaking" is a term that comes from politicians standing on stumps to speak to crowds. Traditionally, a cypress stump is brought out for candidates to speak from at the event, which has been held for over 150 years. Additionally, located near this community's longtime store are more relics of its past. Another notable site in Galivants Ferry is Jack's Lookout Road, shown below. According to local lore, African American laborers who worked on farmlands here worshipped in a small church on this road led by a preacher named Jack, who kept the windows of the church open during worship to spot any members of the Ku Klux Klan who may have brought harm to the congregation. The road has since become recognized as another one of the community's historic places.

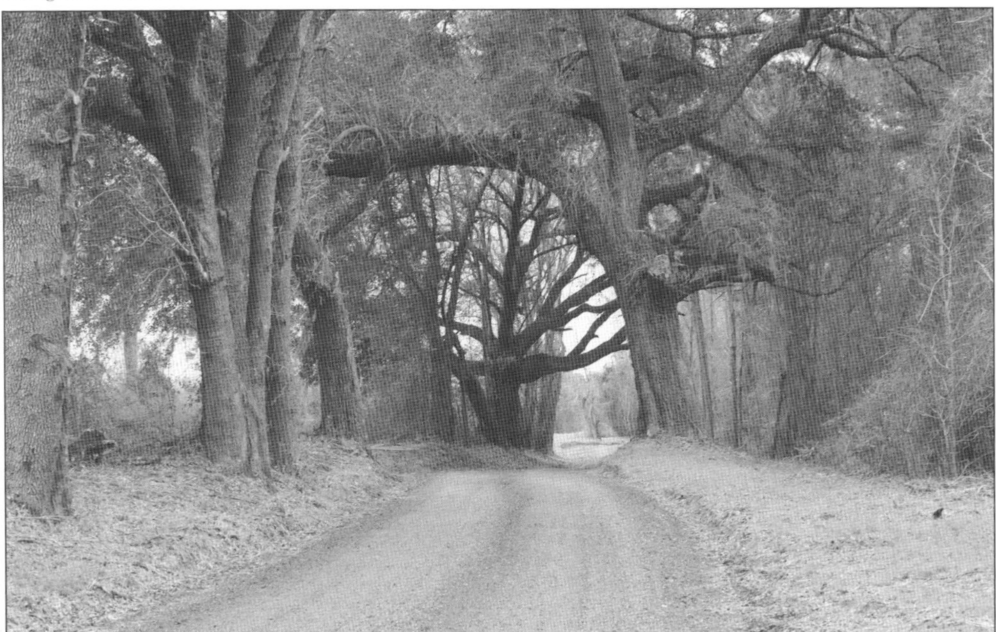

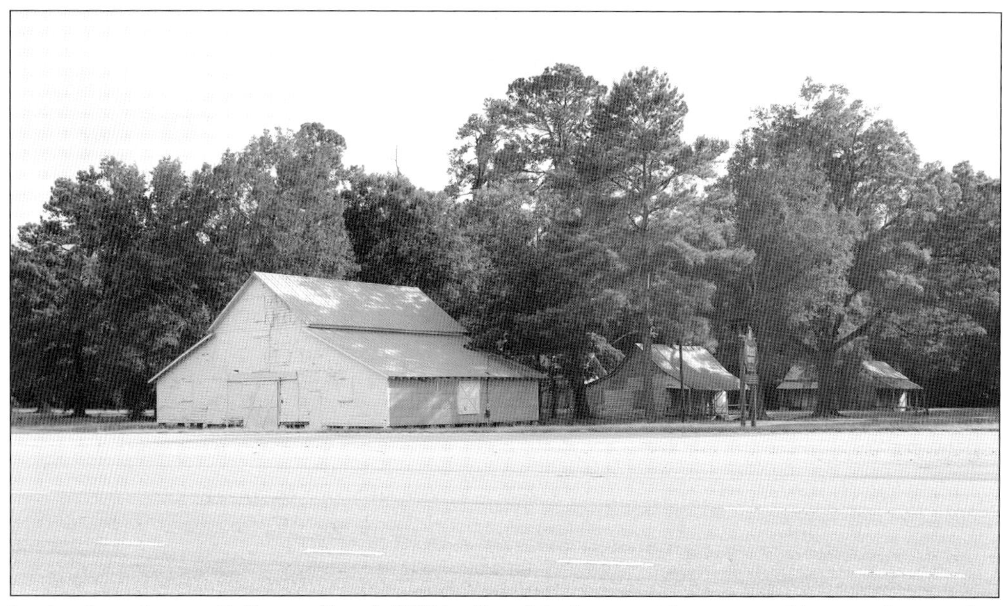

In the above image, Galivants Ferry's "White Barn" is shown with century-old tenant homes that housed sharecroppers. Galivants Ferry also holds an iconic three-story red and green barn that was once used for processing tobacco. The Little Pee Dee River, a 116-mile-long tributary of the Great Pee Dee River, which is named for the Pee Dee tribe, is shown in the image below at the Galivants Ferry Landing. At one time, a ferry was the only way to cross the Little Pee Dee River, which separates Horry County from inland locations. Wooden bridges were eventually built across the river, but a concrete bridge replaced them during the Great Depression. In the present day, two concrete bridges built in the 1970s are used for vehicular travel, and they mark Horry County's end and one's entrance into inland South Carolina.

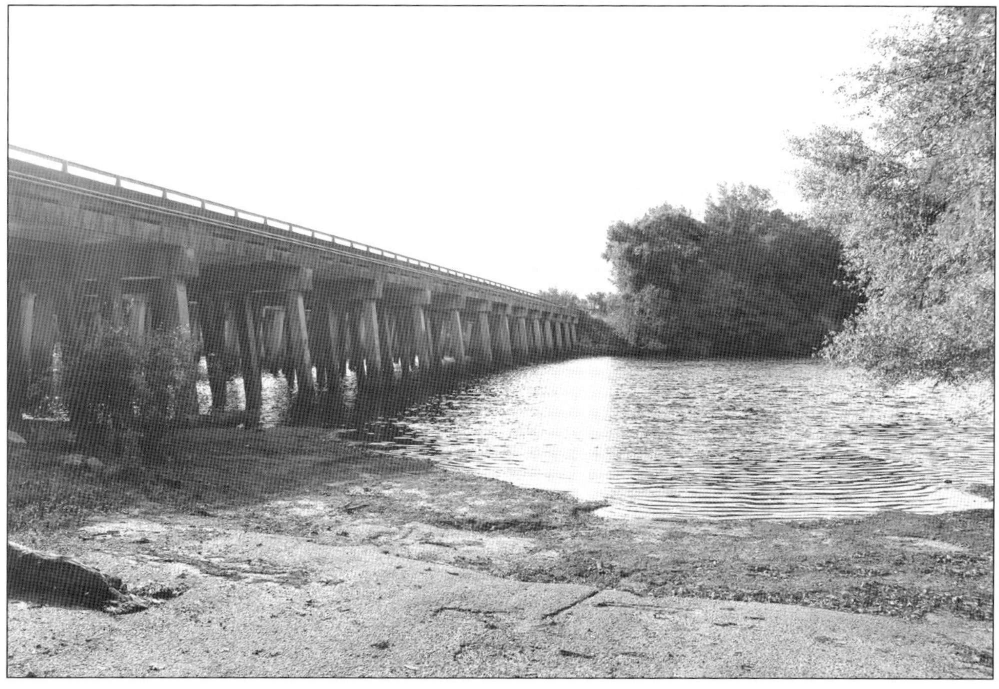

Bibliography

Coastal Carolina University. "History and Traditions." www.coastal.edu/aboutccu/history.

Edgar, Walter B. *South Carolina: A History*. Columbia: University of South Carolina Press, 2008.

Harvey, Bruce G. "Socastee Historic District." Columbia: South Carolina Department of Archives and History, June 14, 1999.

Independent Republic Quarterly 31, no. 1 (1997).

Independent Republic Quarterly 41, no. 1–4 (2007).

Lewis, Catherine Heniford. *Horry County, South Carolina, 1730–1993*. Columbia: University of South Carolina Press, 1998.

Loris Chamber of Commerce. "History of Loris." lorischamber.com/history-of-loris.

McMillan, Susan Hoffer. *Myrtle Beach and the Grand Strand*. Charleston, SC: Arcadia Publishing, 2004.

Surfside Beach. "History." www.surfsidebeach.org/207/History.